UNTOLD TALES OF OLD BRITISH COLUMBIA

DANIEL MARSHALL

UNTOLD TALES OF OLD BRITISH COLUMBIA

Ronsdale Press

UNTOLD TALES OF OLD BRITISH COLUMBIA
Copyright © 2024 Daniel Marshall

RONSDALE PRESS
125A – 1030 Denman Street, Vancouver, B.C. Canada V6G 2M6
www.ronsdalepress.com

Book Design: Derek von Essen
Cover Design: Dorian Danielsen
Cover Photo: City of Vancouver Archives, AM354-S4-2-: CVA 371-2345, Matthews, James Skitt, Major, photographer

Ronsdale Press wishes to thank the following for their support of its publishing program: the Canada Council for the Arts, the Government of Canada, the British Columbia Arts Council, and the Province of British Columbia through the British Columbia Book Publishing Tax Credit program.

LIBRARY AND ARCHIVES CANADA CATALOGUING IN PUBLICATION

Title: Untold tales of old British Columbia / Daniel Marshall.
Names: Marshall, Daniel Patrick, 1962- author.
Description: Includes bibliographical references and index.
Identifiers: Canadiana (print) 20240296273 | Canadiana (ebook) 20240296281 | ISBN 9781553807049
  (softcover) | ISBN 9781553807063 (PDF) | ISBN 9781553807056 (EPUB)
Subjects: LCSH: British Columbia‚ÄîHistory‚ÄîAnecdotes.
Classification: LCC FC3811 .M37 2024 | DDC 971.1‚Äîdc23

At Ronsdale Press we are committed to protecting the environment. To this end we are working with Canopy and printers to phase out our use of paper produced from ancient forests. This book is one step towards that goal.

Printed in Canada

CONTENTS

PREFACE: TRACKING DOWN HISTORY

On the occasion of the Canyon War anniversary, in search of the spots where B.C.'s future was made.

ON AUGUST 25, 2018, a group of colleagues and history aficionados launched our 160th Anniversary Raft Expedition from Boston Bar to Yale to commemorate the 1858 Fraser River gold rush and Fraser Canyon War.

Running the river through Hell's Gate and the Big Canyon was thrilling good fun and the chance to re-imagine the events leading to the Indigenous-newcomer conflict that began with the rapid influx of some thirty thousand-plus foreign gold seekers into the new El Dorado of the north.

Or, what would become British Columbia.

On August 16, 1858, thousands of gold seekers gathered in Yale, and elected officers to command miner-militias that would confront Indigenous populations blockading the Fraser River.

Remember, it was Indigenous peoples who were the discoverers of gold in B.C. and actively mined it before the gold rush commenced.

One such militia was commanded by Captain Henry Snyder, a well-known San Franciscan, whose plan was to make peace with First Nations. Snyder led the Pike Guards on a ten-day military-like campaign from Yale to Kumsheen (today's Lytton), but not before encountering an opposing militia at Spuzzum, led by Captain Graham of the Whatcom Guards;

Graham and his party were bent on exterminating all Indigenous peoples they might encounter.

In a letter to Governor James Douglas, Snyder reported, "They wished to proceed and kill every man, woman & child they saw that had Indian blood in them. To such an arrangement I could not consent to. My heart revolted at the idea of killing a helpless woman, or an innocent child was too horrible to think of."

Snyder demanded Graham stand down and let him broker a peace. If Snyder was successful, a white flag would be sent through the Big Canyon to let Graham know that Snyder's mission was successful.

Soon after Snyder left Spuzzum the Whatcom Guards were on the move again. Snyder sent runners back to plead with Graham once more to stay put; if he did not, Snyder would end his peace mission and head back to Yale immediately. Graham, once again, agreed to wait.

As Snyder and the Pike Guards climbed the steep, ancient Tikwalus Trail from the vicinity of Alexandra Lodge, the Whatcom Guards made camp "on a large shelving rock" opposite the vicinity of Chapman's Bar and placed sentries at either end for protection.

Snyder ultimately descended the Anderson River to Boston Bar, continuing to make treaties of peace with Indigenous villages along the way, and as promised sent a white flag down through the Big Canyon to Graham as evidence of his success.

Upon receiving the flag, Graham reportedly ordered it tossed aside, presumably upset that his campaign of extermination had been thwarted.

That night, pandemonium ensued.

Captain Graham and his first lieutenant were both shot dead, apparently by Indigenous peoples who had seen the treatment given to the white flag of peace.

Snyder reported, "Had he done as he promised to do, he would now be alive."

I had always wondered where exactly the leadership of the Whatcom Guards and their extermination campaign met their end that summer.

Sitting one day at a pull-off on the Trans-Canada Highway, I again looked down on the river corridor. I could clearly see Chapman's Bar on the left side of river — "bar" was California parlance for a sand and gravel bar — and could also see the "large shelving rock," a substantial rock point jutting into the river on the right.

Chapman's Bar, as seen from the Trans-Canada Highway.

It seemed to me that our raft expedition would be a grand opportunity to visit this site. Strategically, the rock point made sense for a military defence. When our expedition arrived there and stood atop this rock promontory, I immediately saw that it was the best place to post sentries, who could see clearly all the way up and down the river.

The Tikwalus Trail (on the left side of river), now restored as the Tikwalus Heritage Trail, is very steep for the first two kilometres. I imagined Snyder looking directly down and right across Chapman's Bar to the "large shelving rock" that fateful day. Below him were gold seekers clamouring for outright extermination of Indigenous peoples. Above him, in Lytton, waited the great Chief Spintlum (Cexpe'nthlEm) of the Nlaka'pamux Nation for their "grand council of war" in which, quite miraculously, peace was achieved.

I firmly believe that we were standing on the general location of the Whatcom Guards' camping ground.

Here, the worst aspect of the California mining frontier ("a good Indian is a dead Indian") was halted in its tracks, the leadership of the Whatcom Guards effectively decapitated, not unlike the headless bodies of foreign miners found drifting down the mighty Fraser River in the summer of 1858.

Here and at Lytton, a Californian and an Indigenous Chief chose peace — the great untold story of B.C.'s founding.

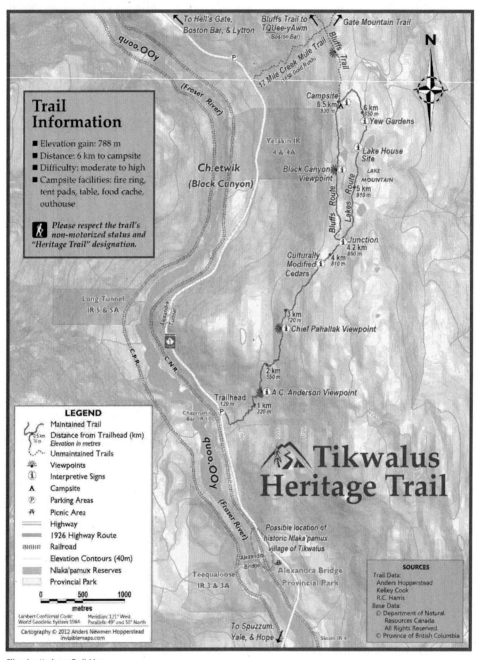

Tikwalus Heritage Trail Map.

INTRODUCTION

WELCOME TO THE HIDDEN WORLD of Old British Columbia. *Untold Tales* is not unlike a cabinet of curiosities. Take a look at any one of these untold stories and I invite you to gaze through the looking glass, a historical lens informed by my own family's history on the Pacific Slope region west of the continental divide and within the huge migration to the Fraser River gold rush of 1858 — the extraordinarily impactful and foundational event that led to the curious, at times calamitous, and in many ways quite wondrous creation of the place we call British Columbia.

Ever since my youth, I have sought the forgotten trails of our history, tracking down routes of early explorers, searching for "lost treasure," and more often than not, the increasing realization that British Columbia was part of a natural north-south world — the land west of the impenetrable Rocky Mountains, the vast Columbia Department of the Hudson's Bay Company, the new El Dorado of the north — before the slow and eventual realignment into the Canadian transcontinental dream of Sir John A. Macdonald, realized with the driving of the last spike at Craigellachie in 1885. Canada sought to arrest these natural north-south connections to the American states of Washington, Oregon and particularly California, by building a transcontinental railway, but the truth is that these links to the lands south of an "imaginary boundary" continued well into the twentieth century, the 49th parallel having more traction within the reorienting, shapeshifting, national narratives than the reality of a far distant Pacific province that remained isolated. The Trans-Canada highway, though proclaimed in 1962, was not fully realized until 1971 — or a century after British Columbia entered the Dominion of Canada.

Nations are themselves narrations. The national story aims to portray a unified and natural unfolding of a single all-encompassing sovereignty, but when we dig into the origins of British Columbia, we so often see competing narratives, the ones that lost (both Indigenous and non-Indigenous), and just how persuasive the evidence is for many of the opposing views. Old British Columbia does not easily fit the national stories of either Canada or the United States, the two countries tied in a race to reach the Pacific Ocean and then to quietly disregard the pre-existing, multicultural world that predated these rival, continent-wide expansions.

If you want to understand British Columbia you must necessarily look south of the border, and this is essential to fully grasp the principal reason for British Columbia's birth — Gold! Fraser River was the largest mass migration of gold seekers in history following that of California and Australia (and forty years before the Yukon), and the Colony of British Columbia was created because of it in 1858. You would think that an event this momentous would have a very big place in our national history, or that it would be taught in our schools (these days, some might even say university history departments). But the Fraser River gold rush is not prominent in our national history, and this belies the fact that there would be no Canada today, as we know it, but for British Columbia. Furthermore, it is rarely acknowledged that B.C. developed as a consequence of a comparatively immense insurgence of foreign gold seekers, and the early B.C. policies instituted with respect to people, land and the law were done in intense reaction to the surge of the ever-expanding American presence on the Pacific Slope. In my view, the mixed-race governor of colonial British Columbia, James Douglas, was a brilliant tactician, and kept this land — through the chaos of the 1858 gold rush — free of the reprehensible, racial discrimination and warfare then prevalent in the United States and safe from the threat of American annexation itself.

Originally written as history columns for *The Orca*, these untold tales garnered such a keen public response as to suggest the creation of this book. I enjoyed writing them immensely, hoping to provide some of our foundational history, along with more than a few curious and confounding tales to enliven the reader's journey. It is my hope that these untold tales will both delight and inform the reader, and encourage some greater awareness of the deep history of this extraordinary province.

If nothing else, after reading this book you will come away with a different view of British Columbia — indeed national history, too, that has neglected this pre-Confederation world on the shores of the Pacific, the traces or memory of which are increasingly forgotten. Since my youth, it is this insatiable curiosity that has driven my historical explorations, the need to see what might be found around the next corner — Curious to discover more? Then let the journey begin — have a look!

ONE:
MULTICULTURAL CANADA STARTS WITH THE FUR TRADE WORLD

The Colour-Blind Commonwealth

**Where did multicultural Canada get its start?
Right here.**

IN A WORLD THAT SEEMS increasingly divided by ethnic and racial tension, it's worth remembering those who sought asylum in Canada's southwest, before the international border was established in 1858, and when there was a period of joint British-American sovereignty on the Northwest Coast.

Imagine you are a Black American parent living in California. Your young daughter is assaulted by a white American. You have no legal recourse; Black testimony has become inadmissible in courts of law. Imagine how you'd feel as a high-ranking Hudson's Bay Company (HBC) official, partnered with an Indigenous woman, having your mixed-race children disenfranchised — their rights stripped — in their own home territory of southern "Old Oregon" (Washington, Oregon and Idaho). These grim imaginings actually happened — yet remain largely forgotten.

This is where — and when — Old Oregon was born, when American pioneers went west over the Oregon Trail to claim lands already occupied by the HBC, let alone by the Indigenous peoples of many nations and languages who had lived on these lands since time immemorial.

That same year, a substantial increase of American settlers forced the HBC to relocate its headquarters from Fort Vancouver on the Columbia River to Fort Victoria.

As U.S. historian John Jackson has noted, most of these early American pioneers "came from communities that feared and firmly repudiated racial intermarriage, believing it a threat to frontier survival." In 1845, they seized political control of Oregon's provisional legislature and made laws for their own benefit.

Governor James Douglas

James Douglas, the future governor of British Columbia, was himself of mixed race, Scottish–West Indian ancestry and had experienced, firsthand, the increasingly exclusionary policies adopted in Old Oregon, particularly after 1843.

Douglas's predecessor, Dr. John McLoughlin, wrote of the changing circumstances brought by these American squatters imbued with notions of manifest destiny, that is, it was God's will they expand to the Pacific coast and eventually all of North America. "It is reported that some of the immigrants last come have said that every man who has an Indian wife ought to be driven out of the country, and that the half-breeds should not be allowed to hold lands."

Policies of exclusion soon unfolded; Oregon's infamous "Lash Law" of 1844, though lasting less than a year, directed that Blacks, whether slave or free, be whipped twice a year "until he or she shall quit the territory."

By 1862, Oregon had adopted a law that required all Blacks, Chinese, Hawaiians and "mix-bloods" residing in the state pay an annual tax of five dollars. Black and white intermarriage was banned, and this prohibition was subsequently extended in 1866 to anyone who was one-quarter or more Chinese or Hawaiian and one-half or more Indigenous background.

Oregon became the model for California. Writing in the early 1860s, the historian John Hittell recorded similar exclusionary laws in the Golden State under the title "Inferiority of Colored Persons": "All white male citizens are equal before the law of California; but negroes, Indians and Chinamen are not permitted to vote or to testify in the courts against white men. In a criminal case, one-eighth negro blood and one-half of Indian blood, in civil cases one-half of either, disqualifies a witness for testifying against a white man."

By these provisions, if Governor Douglas had been implicated in a Californian criminal proceeding, he would have been precluded from

Lady Amelia Douglas

giving evidence. His wife, Amelia (whose mother, Miyo Nipiy, was of the Cree Nation), would also have faced such discrimination.

That much is still fairly well known. But mostly untold is that practically all HBC families after an extended period of partnership with Indigenous allies — a partnership that had built a shared and longstanding commerce — were now essentially pushed out to the British side of the new border.

The circumscribed fur trade society north of the forty-ninth parallel continued its unique relationship between British traders and Indigenous allies and partners. But the ethnic and racial diversity was actually more complex.

First, from a British perspective, there were the English, but also the Celtic peoples of the Scottish, Irish, Cornish, Welsh and Manx among others. So, too, there were the many Indigenous Nations along the West Coast, such as the Lekwammen, Quw'utsun, Nuu-chah-nulth and Kwakwaka'wakw to name but a few, and the Interior Indigenous peoples such as the Secwepemc, St'át'imc and Nlaka'pamux.

Add to this mix the French Canadians and Métis, along with the Cree, Kanien:keha'ka (Mohawk), Ojibwe, and Haudenosaunee (Iroquois), who came along with the fur trade.

Finally, significant numbers of Hawaiians were employed in the fur trade, and Mexican peoples were originally employed as muleteers for the HBC.

Clearly, the fur trade was synonymous with racial and ethnic diversity.

So while the American historian Susan Johnson notes the gold rushes were "among the most multiracial, multiethnic, multinational events that had yet occurred within the boundaries of the United States," the lands known prior to the 1846 partition and ascension of American settlers as Old Oregon had already experienced a much longer period of such diversity — but in a significantly more inclusive way.

North of the border, this shared world continued after 1846, immeasurably enlarged with the addition of gold seekers — who in many instances were also seeking asylum from persecution.

Many of these asylum seekers, including Victoria's first Black city councillor, Mifflin Gibbs, went on to make great contributions to British Columbia.

This is important context. It provides one of the key reasons British Columbia's gold rush unfolded much differently from the California gold rush experience, and in a comparatively much more inclusive way.

Without these early polices of inclusion, for example, it's doubtful whether the mixed-race politician Simon Fraser Tolmie — whose mother was part Spokane — could have become premier of British Columbia in 1928.

Today, it's interesting to reflect on B.C.'s early institution (against great odds) of true equality under the law — and that the fur trade is where modern Canada's multicultural roots may lie.

BRITISH COLUMBIA: REFUGE FOR POLITICAL EXILES?

Victoria honours Mifflin Gibbs, a trailblazer, civil rights activist — and its first Black city councillor (1866–69).

IN 2018, VICTORIA HONOURED the contributions of Mifflin Wistar Gibbs by naming a study room in its newest public library after the former city councillor. The city also proclaimed November 19 "Mifflin Wistar Gibbs Day" in honour of Gibbs becoming the first Black person elected to public office in British Columbia.

But there is far more to this story than a brief library announcement! The multicultural roots of our civic politics before British Columbia joined the Confederation in 1871 are extraordinary.

By 1858, the exclusionary policies and legislation of the California state legislature increasingly disenfranchised and discriminated against African American people. Meetings were held in San Francisco where the Black American population decided to leave and relocate for freedom's sake — either to Sonora, in Mexico, or to Vancouver Island.

A delegation was appointed to meet with Governor James Douglas (a Scottish West Indian married to an Irish Cree woman), who welcomed these persecuted peoples and extended to them full rights of citizenship and equality under the law.

Upon the delegation's return to San Francisco they passed a further resolution that favoured relocating north for freedom. A May 21, 1858 article in the *San Francisco Bulletin* titled "Another Meeting of the Colored People" reads in part:

> We are fully convinced that the continued aim of the spirit and policy of our mother country, is to oppress, degrade, and outrage us. We have, therefore, determined to seek asylum in the land of strangers, from oppression, prejudice and relentless persecution that have pursued us for more than two centuries in this our mother country.
>
> Therefore, a delegation having been sent to Vancouver's Island, a place which had unfolded to us in our darkest hour, the prospect of a bright future; to this place of British possession, the delegation ... have fulfilled and rendered the most flattering accounts.

With Governor Douglas's guarantee, these Black Californians moved north in 1858. Among them was the civil rights activist Mifflin Gibbs, who had commenced his equal rights advocacy in the eastern U.S. along with the famous abolitionist Frederick Douglass.

Gibbs recorded of his time in San Francisco that "they were ostracized, assaulted without redress, disenfranchised and denied their oath in a court of justice." By comparison, he viewed British Columbia as a land of freedom. In his autobiography, writing of their arrival in Victoria, Gibbs stated:

Judge Mifflin W. Gibbs

We received a warm welcome from the Governor [Douglas] and other officials of the colony, which was cheering. We had no complaint as to business patronage in the State of California, but there was ever present that spectre of oath denial and disenfranchisement; the disheartening consciousness that while our existence was tolerated, we were powerless to appeal to law for the protection of life or property when assailed.

British Columbia offered and gave protection to both, and equality of political privileges. I cannot describe with what joy we hailed the opportunity to enjoy that liberty under the "British Lion" denied us beneath the pinions of the American Eagle.

Three or four hundred colored men from California and other States, with their families, settled in Victoria, drawn thither by the two-fold inducement — gold discovery and the assurance of enjoying impartiality the benefits of constitutional liberty.

They built or bought homes and other property, and by industry and character vastly improved their condition and were the recipients of respect and esteem from the community.

The reception received by the Black Americans in 1858 was reminiscent of Gibb's mentor, Frederick Douglass's visit to Britain and Ireland the previous decade. Arriving in Ireland in 1845, Douglass was struck by the seeming racial colour-blindness he encountered:

I gaze around in vain for one who will question my equal humanity, claim me as his slave, or offer me an insult. I employ a cab — I am seated beside white people — I reach the hotel — I enter the same door — I am shown into the same parlour — I dine at the same table — and no one is offended . . . I find myself regarded and treated at every turn with kindness and deference paid to white people.

When I go to church, I am met by no upturned nose and scornful lip to tell me, "We don't allow n*****s in here!" (censored in the original)

The positive reception received by Douglass is seemingly comparable to that given Gibbs and other Black Americans in Victoria.

While in Britain in 1846, Douglass met Thomas Clarkson, one of the last living British abolitionists who assisted in persuading Parliament to abolish slavery in Great Britain and its colonies. Undoubtedly, the positive reception Douglass received in Britain would have been well known to Mifflin Gibbs and a further incentive to relocate to the new El Dorado of the north.

Frederick Douglass

While it must be acknowledged that there was racial prejudice in Victoria through the early gold rush period, much of this anti-Black sentiment left with American residents who returned to the U.S. at the commencement of the American Civil War.

As proof, Gibbs was subsequently elected in 1866 to Victoria's city council as the first Black councillor, representing James Bay — and served for a time as the acting mayor. He also was a delegate to the "Yale Convention" organized by Amor De Cosmos, a local newspaper publisher and politician, to discuss B.C.'s entry into the Canadian Confederation.

Having received early legal training in Victoria, Gibbs returned south of the border after the Civil War, and in Arkansas became the first African American judge in the United States.

James Douglas's final word regarding the Black people of California was made to Labouchere, the secretary of state for the colonies, on April 6, 1858 and it applies to other ethnic and racial minorities that also fled north to escape persecution. "I am glad that Her Majesty's Government ... generously grants, within the Colony of Vancouver's Island, a refuge for political exiles, provided they yield obedience to the Laws, and avoid public scandals, and lead quiet and honest lives."

Certainly, the attraction of British Columbia was gold, but for those outside full American citizenship, British Columbia represented much more than the potential for economic gain.

The new El Dorado also represented gains in political and social well-being, as opposed to the legislated policies of exclusion found south of the international divide.

The Forgotten Context of Canada's Oldest Chinatown

Victoria's Chinatown wasn't just a colonial outpost — it was a sanctuary.

DURING THE SUMMER OF 2019, while sitting at the bar of the Bent Mast Pub in Victoria, I met a recent arrival to our city who had relocated from California. What started as a casual conversation led me to comb my personal archives of historical notes and documents; this gentleman's relocation to Victoria was motivated solely by the memory of his mother, who had been born there. As we discussed his story further, I found out his ancestors — the Lee family — had come to Victoria at the height of the 1858 Fraser River gold rush and the founding of Canada's oldest Chinatown.

Serendipity had struck again. Here we were, two descendants of the gold rush — one of Chinese origin, the other Cornish — in a chance meeting!

In my opinion, current history writings have not sufficiently pursued the connection to San Francisco of these early Chinese who moved up the Pacific Slope. The Chinese peoples of California, like their Black and Hispanic counterparts, were increasingly discriminated against by the exclusionary legislation and practices of California gold rush society. As the California historian John Hittell wrote in the early 1860s of the "anti-Chinese mob": "The white miners have a great dislike to Chinamen, who

Chinese gold washers on the Fraser River. Painting by William Hind c. 1864.

are frequently driven away from their claims, and expelled from districts by mobs. In such cases the officers of the law do not ordinarily interfere, and no matter how much the unfortunate yellow men may be beaten or despoiled, the law does not attempt to restore them to their rights or avenge their wrongs."

Just three years before the B.C. gold rush, Chinese merchants based in San Francisco made an appeal to the American public, asking that their rights be respected. Recorded in the *Sacramento Daily Union* on September 12, 1855, "The Appeal of the Chinese Merchants" stated:

TO THE AMERICAN CITIZENS. — Americans: We, the undersigned, Chinese merchants, come before you to plead our cause, and that of our countrymen, residents of San Francisco, or diffused throughout California.

We come to ask for the moral and industrious of our race liberty to remain in this State, and to continue peaceably and without molestation in our various labors and pursuits ... Neither injustice nor severity has been spared us **... Instead of the equality and protection which seemed to be promised by the laws of a great nation to those who seek a shelter under its flag, an asylum upon its territory, we find only inequality and oppression.**

Frequently before the Courts of Justice, where our evidence is not even listened to — where, if it obtain a hearing, by favor, but rarely is any account made of it. Inequality before public opinion — which is so far, apparently, from considering us as men, that many of your countrymen feel no scruple in making our lives their sport, and in using us as the object of their cruel amusement. Oppression by the Law, which subjects us to exorbitant taxes imposed upon us exclusively — oppression without the pale of the law, which refuses us its protection, and leaves us a prey to vexations and humilities, which it seems to invoke upon our heads by placing us in an exceptional position.

Believe us, we have exaggerated nothing in this picture ... We see well that you appear to desire our departure ... [but] can they, at a given moment, provide themselves with the means of **quitting this country in a body, in order to seek elsewhere some less inhospitable land?**

PACIFIC CHIVALRY.
Encouragement to Chinese Immigration.

Anti-Chinese art from *Harpers Weekly*, August 1869.

UNTOLD TALES OF OLD BRITISH COLUMBIA

Berkeley law professor Charles McClain has stated that the 1855 session of the California legislature "was perhaps the high-water mark of anti-Chinese sentiment" for the whole of the 1850s, and a more than compelling reason to relocate to the new El Dorado of the north.

Hittell wrote of the California Chinese merchant class that "nearly all of them are members of five great companies, called the Yung-Wo, the Sze-yap, the Sam-yap, the Yan-wo, and Ning-yeung companies" and that in San Francisco "the merchants are usually in partnerships, with not less than three nor more than ten partners; all of whom live in the store, and deal chiefly in Chinese silks, teas, rice, and dried fish."

Two of the many Chinese companies that were apparent signatories to this 1855 petition were Sam Wo and Hop Kee. Just three years later, in 1858, Hop Kee and Company had contracted Allan, Lowe and Company (Governor James Douglas's favoured merchant house in San Francisco) to transport three hundred Chinese people to Victoria — the original copy of this document exists in the B.C. Archives collections. These early Chinese pioneers to British Columbia were likely labourers working under contract. As Hittell noted:

> The common laborers are brought to the state under contract to work for several years at a low rate of wages (from four to eight dollars) per month; and they usually keep these contracts faithfully. The employers in these cases are either the companies or associations of Chinese capitalists. The Chinamen generally are very industrious; indeed they are the most industrious class of our population, and also the most humble, quiet, and peaceful. The merchants are considered to be very faithful to their promises, and in San Francisco they can get credit among their acquaintances quite as readily as other men in similar branches of business.

As historian John Adams has noted, it is likely that just as "Captain Jeremiah Nagle of the SS *Commodore* had discussed the plight of the blacks in California with James Douglas during the early spring of 1858 when discrimination there was at a peak" (resulting in Douglas's invitation to Black people "to settle under the freedom of the British flag"), a similar invitation would have been extended to the persecuted Chinese peoples of California.

This is not surprising, considering that Douglas was himself a mixed-race Scottish West Indian who had experienced firsthand the growing racist, exclusionary policies adopted in Old Oregon.

Chinese in California were particularly hard hit by the institution of the foreign miners head tax, in addition to being routinely driven from their claims. For example, in 1858, Euro-American miners in Mariposa, California, ordered Chinese immigrants to leave their community within 48 hours.

Clearly, many did so. The *San Francisco Bulletin* reported on May 21, 1858, that three of the leading "aristocratic" businessmen left on the *Panama* for the Fraser River mines to prospect the country and make further preparations for those who would follow, the newspaper suggesting "that nearly the entire Chinese population ... will leave for the British Possessions."

Before B.C.'s Confederation with Canada, Chinese miners — like all other gold seekers regardless of race — were not forced to pay a foreign "head tax" but, rather, had to participate in a universally applied Crown licensing system. Crown privilege (as instituted in B.C.) appears in marked contrast to some of the more notorious "individual rights" practiced in California.

In this sense, Oregon was very much like California. Hittell, again writing in the early 1860s, recorded the similar exclusionary laws under the title of the "Inferiority of Colored Persons" that stated that only white males were equal before the law and in a criminal case men who had distinct proportions of Black or Indian blood could not testify against a white man.

It's worth pointing out that Chief Justice Matthew Baillie Begbie certainly insisted on the admissibility of Chinese testimony in local courts of law, unlike south of the border — making B.C. a comparative land of both mercantile and individual freedom.

To my mind, when placed in this context, Douglas's offer of equality under the law for all — which had become imperial policy — becomes more than understandable, and a unique welcome for the times extended to Chinese people, too.

As a consequence, starting in 1858, members of the Chinese merchant class of San Francisco took the necessary steps to purchase the first of twenty town lots in Victoria that formed the nucleus of what is still the oldest Chinatown in Canada.

Who were some of these Chinese pioneers?

While it is well known that Kwong Lee and Company were established in Victoria in 1858, surprisingly little research has been undertaken to establish their historic connection to other Chinese merchant companies operating in California prior to the Fraser River gold rush.

From my research in the B.C. Archives dating to 1858, it appears that Kwong Lee and Company were working as the northern agents for Hop Kee and Company of San Francisco, and the archival trail provides a fascinating collection of documents (financial papers, receipts and so forth) that confirm this. More importantly, the names of individuals noted on these documents, in effect, link our 1858 Chinese gold seekers to one of the most prominent and highly regarded members of the early nineteenth-century Chinese transpacific trade.

Envelope addressed to Kwong Lee & Co.

The B.C. Land Titles and Survey Branch holds the original town lot register for Victoria commencing in 1858. It highlights the frenzied rush for real estate that occurred at this time. The *Sacramento Daily Union* reported on June 24, 1858, that "Sam Wo & Co., and Hop Kee & Co., the Chinese merchants, have purchased an entire square for Chinese purposes. No more lots are now sold by the Government; the rush on the land office was so great that it was thought proper to close it."

It's easy to locate the identity of the Chinese representatives from San Francisco in the original Victoria town lot register for 1858. Both Chang Tsoo and Chaok Fan purchased some twenty separate lots, and there seems to be evidence that the Hudson's Bay Company (HBC) provided ongoing financing.

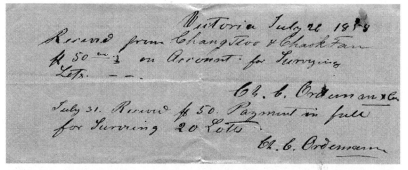

Receipt issued to Chang Tsoo and Chaok Fan for payment of surveying twenty Victoria town lots in 1858.

In particular, Chang Tsoo is directly associated with Hop Kee and Company of California. Not only was this company protesting discriminatory policies in California, but also was the leading mercantile house that established Canada's oldest Chinatown in Victoria. In my personal conversations with the historian Lily Chow, we are convinced that Kwong Lee was, in fact, a branch of Hop Kee. (For instance, Loo Gee Wing purchased Kwong Lee in 1887; before becoming one of the richest Chinese Vancouverites, Loo had worked for Hop Kee).

Chaok Fan remained in British Columbia well into the 1860s, as evidenced by his ownership of company stock in the Grouse Creek Flume Company. But it is a third name found on invoicing notes written from Victoria to San Francisco in 1858 that is particularly intriguing: Tong K. Achick.

Along with his two brothers, Tong Achick had been educated at the Morrison Education Society School in Hong Kong in the 1840s. The three Tong brothers, states historian Carl Smith, "may be considered to be representative of a new class of commercial bourgeoisie that emerged in the China coast cities at the end of the Ch'ing dynasty."

Smith continues. "This new class within the Chinese social system was composed of entrepreneurs, business men, financiers, and industrialists.

They were the key figures in the industrial and commercial modernization of China following the impact of the west on traditional China."

The home of the Tong brothers was the village of Tong-ka in the Heung Shan (modern-day Zhongshan) District of Guangdong Province. In 1839, the oldest of the three brothers, Tong Mow-chee, enrolled in the Morrison School under the name of Achick — becoming one of its very first students.

In the aftermath of the Treaty of Nanking, the British required interpreters for their new consular activities in port cities such as Shanghai. Achick was quickly drafted into the public service; few Chinese people were fluent in English at the time.

By 1847, Achick was appointed interpreter in the Magistrate's Court of Hong Kong, before travelling with his uncle to the California gold rush in 1852. As Smith notes: "The years spent by Tong Mow-chee (A-Chick) in California provided the first opportunity for the Tong brothers to serve the special interests of their countrymen. Although only 24 years of age, A-chick soon became an important leader and spokesman for the Chinese community in California. His English-language education and intimate knowledge of Western ways qualified him for this position."

Achick continued his interpreter's role while in California and quickly became a leader of the Chinese community who made direct representations to the governor of California. Smith quotes the missionary Speer: "This is the individual whose efforts last Spring (1852) in behalf of his countrymen, were the chief means in turning the tide of public opinion in their favour, when those unfriendly to them made the attempt to expel them from the country. And if he remains here, there is no man whose influence will be more felt among the large bodies of emigrants of his own race already in the State, or coming in the spring."

Apparently, sometime after 1857 Tong Achick returned to Hong Kong and joined the Chinese customs service — but documents in the B.C. Archives suggest that he came to Victoria in 1858.

The first document, written in Victoria and dated June 16, 1858, is an instruction to Hop Kee and Company of San Francisco by Tong K. Achick. Surely, this is one of the "aristocratic" Chinese men noted by the San Francisco press as travelling north to the Fraser River.

The second document was written by Chang Tsoo (one of the purchasers of the twenty town lots) while in Victoria, directed to Hop Kee

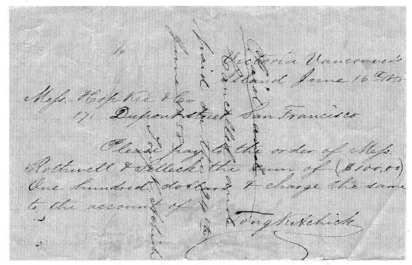

Instruction from Tong K. Achick to Hop Kee and Co., 16 June 1858.

and Company of San Francisco and subsequently signed off in cross-writing by Achick on June 24, 1858. This suggests that Achick had now returned from Victoria to California.

Along with these documents there is also a purchase order, dated August 1858, directed to Tong Achick from merchants Selleck and Rothwell who were newly and briefly established in Vancouver Island with large real estate holdings purchased in Esquimalt.

There is a clear connection shown here between Tong Achick, Chang Tsoo, Hop Kee and Company and the Fraser River gold rush of 1858 that demands further research.

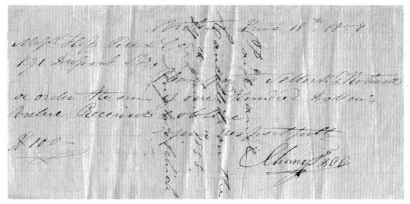

Document dated 18 June 1858, written by Chang Tsoo, signed in cross-writing by Achick, 24 June 1858.

Clearly, these early Chinese pioneers of the Pacific Slope came not only for gold but also, in the case of British Columbia, a better home.

In many ways, the founding of Victoria's Chinatown by the California Chinese merchant class — and seemingly led by their key spokesperson, Tong Achick — is very similar to the establishment of Fort Victoria by the HBC in advance of American expansion. Both are examples of early business partnerships that sought to work outside the discriminatory practices of the U.S. — it's no coincidence that the two largest landowners in early Victoria were first and foremost the HBC followed by Chinese. For the British, Vancouver Island was the Gibraltar-like fortress of the North Pacific; for the Chinese in 1858, the Island was possibly a new Hong Kong.

After James Douglas retired, the new governor, Arthur Kennedy, received an address from Victoria's Chinese merchants that speaks directly to the kind of persecution they escaped from. Reported in the *British Colonist* on April 5, 1864, it stated:

> Chinese Address to Gov. Kennedy
>
> In the reign of Tong Chee, 3rd year 2nd month, 26th day.
>
> Vancouver Island, 1864 year, 4th month 2d day.
>
> Us Chinese men greeting Thee Excellency in first degree Arthur Edward Kennedy . . . All us here be dwellers at Victoria, this Island, and British Columbia, much wish to shew mind of dutiful loyalty to this Kingdom Mother Queen Victoria, for much square and equal Kingdom rule of us.
>
> Just now most humbly offer much joined minds of compliments to Thee Excellency Governor Kennedy, on stepping to this land of Vancouver, that thee be no longer in danger of Typhoon, us much delighted. Us be here from 1858, and count over two thousand Chinese.
>
> Chinese countrymen much like that so few of us have been chastised for breaking Kingdom rule.

This Kingdom rule very different from China. Chinese mind feel much devoted to Victoria Queen, for the protection and distributive rule of him Excellency old Governor Sir James Douglas, so reverse California ruling when applied to us Chinese country men. Us believe success will come in obeying rulers, not breaking links, holding on to what is right and true.

In trading hope is good and look out large; big prospects for time to come.

Us like this no charge place, see it will grow higher to highest; can see a Canton will be in Victoria of this Pacific.

The maritime enterprises will add up wonderfully and come quick. China has silks, tea, rice, sugar, &c. Here is lumber, coal, and minerals, in return, and fish an exhaustless supply, which no other land can surpass.

In ending, us confident in gracious hope in thee, first degree and first rank, and first link, and trust our Californian neighbors may not exercise prejudice to our grief.

Us merchants in Chinese goods in Victoria mark our names in behalf of us and Chinese countrymen. Wishing good luck and prosperity to all ranks, and will continue to be faithful and true.

Us Chinese men much pleased Excellency continue to give us favor always. Us remember to thee.

Signed
Tai Soong & Co., by Tong Kee Yan,
Woo Sang & Co., by Chang Tsoo
Kwong Lee & Co., by Lee Chang, Tong Fat.

Upon receiving this address, Mr. Hall, who served as its translator, subsequently introduced the Chinese delegation to Governor Kennedy (later, Governor of Hong Kong, 1872–77). As reported in the *Colonist*, the governor's reply to the address went through Lee Chang, who interpreted the governor's words:

[T]hat he was very happy to receive their address. It was the desire of her Gracious Majesty the Queen and the Imperial Government to render equal justice to people of every nationality in her dominions, and he assured them that the Chinese population in this colony would be protected in their lives and property as well as any other of her subjects. His Excellency said he thought very highly of the sentiments expressed in their address, and said they showed a great knowledge of trade and commercial principles. He hoped they would also show the community that they would not be wanting in obedience to the laws, and they might depend on always receiving the protection of the laws.

His Excellency then asked several questions in regard to the Chinese population of this and the neighboring colony, which were intelligently answered by Lee Chang, who stated that there were about 2,000 Chinamen in the two colonies, of whom some 300 or 400 were in Vancouver Island. Those in British Columbia were chiefly employed in mining.

His Excellency remarked that he had always found the Chinese an orderly and industrious people, and he hoped they would keep up the same good reputation in this colony. He then courteously dismissed the deputation.

So, here we see quite plainly that James Douglas had "reversed" the California policies of prejudice and intolerance and this fits well with the governor's own views on the matter. Seen from this contextual perspective, I believe the words of Douglas written in 1858 to Labouchere, secretary of state for the colonies, must be given substantially greater credence. He declared that the government granted, within Vancouver Island, protection for political exiles as long as they obeyed the law and led quiet and honest lives.

The attraction of British Columbia was gold, but for those outside full American citizenship, B.C. represented much more than the potential for economic gain. In the case of the Chinese, it was a rush not only for gold but freedom itself.

TWO:
EARLY
TREATY-MAKING
ON THE
NORTHWEST COAST

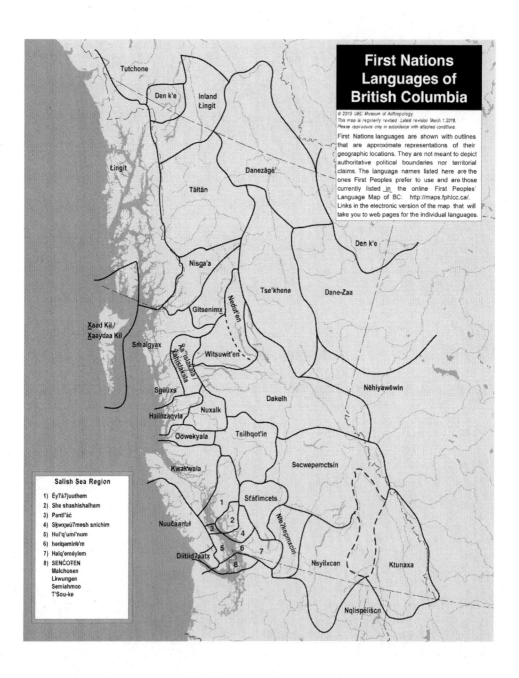

First Nations Languages of British Columbia

© 2018 UBC Museum of Anthropology
This map is regularly revised. Latest revision March 1.2018.
Please reproduce only in accordance with attached conditions.

First Nations languages are shown with outlines that are approximate representations of their geographic locations. They are not meant to depict authoritative political boundaries nor territorial claims. The language names listed here are the ones First Peoples prefer to use and are those currently listed _in_ the online First Peoples' Language Map of BC: http://maps.fphicc.ca/. Links in the electronic version of the map that will take you to web pages for the individual languages.

Tutchone

Den k'e

Inland Łingít

Łingít

Danezāgé'

Táłtān

Den k'e

Nisga'a

Tse'khene

Dane-Zaa

Gitsenimx̱

Nedut'en

Xaad Kil / Xaaydaa Kil

Smalgyax

Xa'islak'ala / Xa̱ʼislakala

Witsuwit'en

Nēhiyawēwin

Sgüüx̱s

Dakelh

Hailhzaqvla

Nuxalk

Oowekyala

Tsilhqot'in

Kwakwala

Secwepemctsín

Salish Sea Region

1) Éy7á7juuthem
2) She shashishalhem
3) Pəntl'ác̓
4) Sḵwx̱wú7mesh snichim
5) Hul'q'umi'num
6) hən̓q̓əmin̓ə̓m
7) Halq'eméylem
8) SENĆOŦEN
   Malchosen
   Lkwungen
   Semiahmoo
   T'Sou-ke

Sťáťimcets

Nłeʔkepmxcín

Nuučaan̓uł

Diitiidʔaatx̣

Nsyilxcən

Ktunaxa

Nqlispélišcn

LOST IN TRANSLATION?

How HBC linguists brokered early relations with First Nations during the fur trade era.

I WORK WITH FOUR Quw'utsun (Cowichan) Elders, assisting them with the translation of their stories — including their earliest foundation stories of a people whose ancestors, it is said, fell from the sky — from the Hul'qumi'num language (the dialect of Halkomelem, Coast Salish, on Vancouver Island) to English.

What a privilege it has been to meet with them a few times per month, fuelled by cups of tea and the occasional "culture break" — code for a smoke ... yes, I still smoke, darn it.

There is a sense of urgency; these Indigenous Elders are some of the few remaining speakers of their traditional language, and yet at times there is simply no English equivalent that conveys the subtleties of certain words in their language.

The place we now call British Columbia is considered one of the most culturally diverse regions of the Americas (second only to California) — and here I am talking primarily about the multitude of Indigenous languages due to the fact that B.C. is on the ancient highway that peopled the Americas.

"Is there a word for that in English?" I quite routinely ask, at times rather sheepishly. After all this time together they more often than not respond with bemused silence. Once we've had a good laugh, we get down to searching for some close equivalent that might capture the essence of the Hul'qumi'num word being discussed.

And so, as a historian, this got me thinking about what it must have been like trying to communicate with Indigenous Nations and allies during the fur trade era — these first Indigenous-newcomer encounters — and wondering just how much got lost in translation.

The use of linguistic interpreters has a very long history in Canada, especially by the Hudson's Bay Company (HBC) when it was established in 1670. To further early trade relationships, the HBC worked within the myriad of Indigenous languages found west and east of the Rocky Mountains. Clear conversation was paramount to establish forts within Indigenous territories, hire Indigenous labour, conduct trade and strengthen relationships through intermarriage.

Let's remember that there would not have been any fur trade without the key participation and consent of Indigenous peoples. As fur trade historian Richard Mackie asserts, HBC's success came from grafting company operations onto extensive, pre-existing Indigenous trade networks. In the early years, before the colonies of Vancouver Island and British Columbia were founded, the fur trade corporation also seemingly worked within pre-existing systems of Indigenous law.

In B.C., improving Indigenous language skills and collecting Indigenous vocabularies was a common practice for HBC personnel, and of utter necessity. The diary entries of Dr. William Fraser Tolmie, written from the HBC fur trading post Fort McLoughlin on Campbell Island, B.C., contain multiple instances of recording Indigenous languages. Here are some to consider:

Date	Diary Entry
Friday, February 21 [1834]	Visited by several parties of Indians ... Rec[eived] from one several Bilbilla [Bella Bella] words. Have tonight been arranging & putting in a portable form a vocabulary given me by Mr. Dunn & purpose making additions to it tomorrow.
Saturday, February 22 [1834]	... made considerable additions to vocabulary.
Sunday, May 11 [1834]	A party of Billichool [Bella Coola] arrived & from the Chief Nooshimald I obtained a brief vocabulary of their language, it resembles at

	most word for word that of the tribe [Alexander] Mackenzie met with on this coast & they are probably identical.
Sunday, July 20 [1834]	I entered an office of Indian Trader & procured a vocabulary of the language of this tribe — the Chimmesyan [Tsimshian].
Friday, July 25 [1834]	Busy trading cedar bark during forenoon, assisted in communicating with the natives by an Indian who understands the Milbank or Haeeltzuk [Heiltsuk] language of which I acquired a slight knowledge at Fort McLoughlin.
Monday, December 29 [1834]	The dialect of the Kitamats [Haisla] does neither resemble the Chimmesyan nor that of the Haeeltsuk — in pronunciation it approaches more to the former, but in the form of the words to the latter, indeed it is similar in many words.
Wednesday, January 7 [1835]	I have to . . . arrange in a tabular form the different Indian languages of which I have got vocabularies.
Tuesday, April 21 [1835]	Yesterday & today occupied in making a vocabulary in a tabular form of the different Indian languages of which I have collected words — they are the following — Nusqually, Noosclalom, Haeeltzuk [Heiltsuk], Billichoola, Gueetilla or Nass, Haida or Queen Charlotte's Island & Tumgass or Kittichunnish. Have had a Nucelowes & Milbank Indian giving me the words of their proper languages.

Clearly, more was being spoken than simply Chinook Jargon (the composite trade language of the eighteenth- and early nineteenth-century maritime fur trade) in these early cross-cultural encounters. HBC employees such as Tolmie were effectively responsible for perfecting such communications through ongoing studies of Indigenous languages.

The HBC was well aware of the need for good interpreters. On the rare occasion an interpreter was unavailable, the results were deemed incredibly disadvantageous to HBC operations. For example, Archibald McDonald, writing from Fort Colvile to Chief Factor John McLoughlin on August 8, 1842, stressed the importance of company-employed linguists. Attacked by Indigenous peoples through some misunderstanding, he blamed the company's recent cutbacks in interpreters as the main cause:

> It was an ugly affair as it was, but had very nearly gone the length of something more disastrous in the helpless condition we were in with our property exposed along the rapids, & worse still with not a man of the party able to speak two words of the language to bring us to a better understanding. I mention this last circumstance seeing so little is made of the young linguists brought up in the district, all now I understand ordered away as a useless burden on the Establishment. Let the maxim never be lost sight of among Indians that much mischief can be prevented by a timely & proper understanding of exist- ing difficulties, which in the absence of such simple explanations it might take years of main strength to cor- rect, & then after all in nine cases out of ten we only come off second best. Interpreters are a necessary evil.

Hopefully the Elders I work with do not see me as a necessary evil!

A quick check of existing fur trade literature shows, time and again, that interpreters were employed as salaried staff formally appointed pri- marily for their linguistic abilities. Historian Bruce McIntyre Watson has compiled a massive biographical dictionary of fur traders, *Lives Lived West of the Divide*, from which the following quotes are drawn. HBC employee Joseph McKay recalled that "Most of the intercourse with the Indians was carried on through the interpreters, who were under the control of the clerks or other officers who might have charge of the trade department for the time being, each officer having his special charge, for the good conduct of which he was responsible to the Chief Factor."

Michel Laframboise, a member of James McMillan's 1824 reconnais- sance expedition to the Fraser River, which led to the establishment of Fort Langley in 1827, was one of many interpreters employed on the Northwest Coast in the early 1800s. (See the appendix for a brief list of just some of the better-known interpreters employed on the Northwest

Coast.) Laframboise also accompanied the Clallam Expedition to avenge the murder of the Alexander McKenzie party in January 1828. That year, Chief Factor John McLoughlin ("The Father of Oregon") wrote to HBC's Governor Simpson stating that he "could sooner dispense with a gentleman than him [Laframboise]. People only know the value of an interpreter when they have none." This was certainly the case during John McLeod's 1824 Nahanni Expedition whereby "the trader's inability to get sound geographic information [was] for want of an interpreter."

Fort Vancouver, Washington Territory, c. 1845, by Lieutenant Henry Warre.

One of the principal interpreters employed at Fort Victoria during the negotiations of the Douglas Treaties (a.k.a. Fort Victoria Treaties) was an individual referred to as "Thomas." In a letter written by Joseph McKay to Dr. John S. Helmcken in 1888, McKay — charged with conducting the treaty councils in southern Vancouver Island — recalled, "Mr. Douglas was very cautious in all his proceedings. The day before the meeting with the Indians, He sent for me and handed me the [treaty-related] document above referred to telling me to study it carefully and to commit as much of it to memory as possible in order that I might check the Interpreter Thomas should he fail to explain properly to the Indians the substance of Mr. Douglas' address to them."

If McKay's words are correct, then it would seem that James Douglas had taken added precautions to ensure that Indigenous representatives assembled at these treaty councils fully understood the meaning of the treaty negotiations. The "Thomas" referred to here is none other than Thomas Quamtany, one of Douglas's most favoured interpreters, employed in this role at Fort Victoria through the critical years between 1843 and 1851. Watson's biographical dictionary of the fur trade states this important linguist "spent the majority of his career at Fort Victoria acting as interpreter ... Because of Ouamtany's [*sic*] ability with languages, he was often called upon when a reliable competent interpreter was needed."

Quamtany's facility with languages was the likely basis for his work with a series of expeditions to explore Vancouver Island. He joined not only Adam Horne's 1856 expedition from Qualicum to Alberni but also Joseph D. Pemberton's 1857 crossing of the Island from Cowichan to Nitinat. Captain Thomas Sherlock Gooch, who accompanied Pemberton in 1857, stated of the interpreter, "By birth an Indian of Lower Canada [Haudenosaunee (Iroquois was the anglicized name)], he spoke the French dialect of that province well, and also English, and many Indian languages . . . a valuable addition to any pioneering expedition in North America."

Quamtany joined Robert Brown's Vancouver Island exploring expedition of 1864. Brown, whose writings were compiled by University of Victoria professor John Hayman, gives his testimonial of this interpreter's linguistic talents: "He was at one [time] high in favour with Governor Douglas whose constant factotum he was on every expedition. He served for some time in the H B Company in several capacities, as guide, hunter, and interpreter in all of which capacities he stands unrivalled ... Tomo [Thomas is pronounced Toma or Tomon in French] spoke English without an accent, besides understanding nearly every Indian language on the Island."

These "unrivalled" language skills suggest to me that the Douglas Treaties negotiated in and about Fort Victoria would have been conducted in the languages of the local Indigenous peoples.

Joseph McKay, the principal negotiator of the treaty councils on behalf of Douglas and the HBC, was also known to speak languages other than English, French and the Chinook Jargon. In 1932, Saanich Chiefs presented legal documents to the provincial government stating that they did not recognize the treaty and had not sold their land, and the agreement was actually a peace pact. But in the documents quoted in archaeologist

Grant Keddie's history of the Songhees People, they also stated they fully understood the treaty negotiations; it had been communicated in their own language. "The Indians fully understood what was said as it was interpreted by Mr. McKay, who spoke the Saanich language very well."

McKay's response to Helmcken in 1888 that Douglas "was very cautious in all his proceedings" and instructed McKay "to check the Interpreter Thomas" and, perhaps more importantly, "to explain properly to the Indians the substance of Mr. Douglas' address" are important to reconsider in light of the HBC's concerted efforts to learn Indigenous languages.

But at the same time one must necessarily ask: What was lost in translation?

THE FORGOTTEN TREATY-MAKING OF CHIEF MAQUINNA

Or, how British Columbia avoided becoming American Columbia or even Spanish Columbia.

IT'S EASY TO TAKE FOR GRANTED TODAY, but the "British" part of British Columbia's history was never a foregone conclusion.

Spain, the United States and even Russia had equally viable claims — and were it not for a remarkable Indigenous leader and the way he dealt with the first Europeans and Americans to his shores, history may well have unfolded differently.

For centuries, Spain treated the Pacific Ocean as a Spanish lake. Only the occasional British freebooter — such as Sir Francis Drake — challenged their otherwise unrivalled supremacy. In 1778, this changed with the arrival of Captain James Cook, launching the maritime fur trade in sea otter pelts and the great rush — from a European perspective — to the last unmapped coastline in the world.

Landing at Nootka Sound, on the west coast of Vancouver Island, Cook recorded one of the earliest European views of Indigenous conceptions of property rights. Cook instructed his crew to obtain a variety of resources and quickly found that the Mowachaht people demanded fair payment. With respect to his men cutting grass in particular, Cook stated, "I had not the least imagination that the natives could make any objections to our furnishing ourselves with what seemed to be of no use to them, but was necessary for us. However, I was mistaken; for the moment our men began to cut, some of the inhabitants interposed and would not permit them to proceed, saying they must makook; that is, must first buy it."

Captain Cook's observation is important. He had entered an Indigenous world that had yet to experience, or be altered by, the intense trading practices of the maritime fur trade that would shortly ensue. Cook continued,

> Here I must observe that I have nowhere, in my several voyages, met with any uncivilized nation, or tribe, who had such strict notions of their having a right to the exclusive property of everything that their country produces, as the inhabitants of this Sound.
>
> At first, they wanted our people to pay for the wood and water that they carried on board; and had I been upon the spot, when these demands were made, I should certainly have complied with them. Our workmen, in my absence, thought differently; for they took but little notice of such claims and the natives, when they found that we were determined to pay nothing, at last ceased to apply. But they made a merit of necessity; and frequently afterward took occasion to remind us that they had given us wood and water out of friendship.

As Cook wrote in his journal, his instructions were "with the consent of the natives, to take possession in the name of the King of Great Britain of convenient situations in such countries as you may discover"; nevertheless, he made no attempt to formally claim sovereignty at Yuquot (what Cook called "Friendly Cove") on Nootka Island. In fact, he concluded that the Mowachaht "considered the place as entirely their property, without fearing any superiority."

In short order, the maritime fur trade commenced, primarily by British and American commercial enterprises.

Spain quickly reacted. The Spanish fort of San Miguel was immediately established, then abandoned — but not before two British ships were confiscated and their captain, James Colnett, incarcerated in San Blas, Mexico.

This led the British government to demand restitution and press a competing claim of sovereignty.

Restitution would also demand recognition of land purchased by English explorer John Meares at Yuquot for the establishment of a fort, apparently conveyed by Chief Maquinna — though the Chief later denied it.

The tension between Spain and Britain — the "Nootka Crisis" — coincided with the fall of the Bastille in July 1789 and the beginning of the revolution in France. Without Spain's old ally, Britain realized Spain was substantially weakened — and seized the moment.

Seizure of Captain Colnett during the "Nootka Crisis." Engraving c. 1791.

Britain asserted that Spain's claim of prior rights of discovery were insufficient for exclusive ownership and instead argued (with the threat of military force) that rights of discovery could only be maintained through continuous occupation.

Spain acceded and relinquished its claim of territorial rights over the Northwest Coast. The Nootka Crisis proved to be a decisive turning point not only in the decline of the Spanish Empire but also, ultimately, in the extension of Canadian sovereignty to the Pacific some eighty years later.

The story doesn't end there. Mostly forgotten today, there were other competing non-Indigenous sovereignties on the Northwest Coast during the Nootka Crisis.

In 1791, Chief Maquinna and five other Chiefs sold land in Nootka Sound to John Kendrick, an American captain. Ten muskets were apparently traded for the purchase, and the Chiefs put their *X*'s to a formal deed of sale.

Like Meares's claim, which was used by England to argue that continuous use and occupation were required from the point of discovery onward, Kendrick's purchase was viewed as a possible basis for American

Chief Maquinna

sovereignty in the region — particularly by President Thomas Jefferson. The Kendrick Treaty, discovered in an archival search by historian Warren L. Cook, reads as follows:

> To all persons to whom these presents shall come: I, Macquinnah, the chief, and with my other chiefs, do send greeting:
>
> Know ye that I, Macquinnah, of Nootka sound, on the north-west coast of America, for and in consideration of ten muskets, do grant and sell unto John Kendrick, of Boston, commonwealth of Massachusetts, in North America, a certain harbor in said Nootka sound, called Chastacktoos, in which the brigantine Lady Washington lay at anchor on the twentieth day of July, 1791, with all the land, rivers, creeks, harbors, islands, &c, within nine miles north, east, west and south of said harbor, with all the produce of both sea and land appertaining thereto; only the said John Kendrick does grant and allow the said Macquinnah to live and fish on the said territory as usual.

And by these presents does grant and sell to the said John Kendrick, his heirs, executors and administrators, all the above mentioned territory, known by the Indian name Chastacktoos, but now by the name of the Safe Retreat harbor; and also do grant and sell to the said John Kendrick, his heirs, executors and administrators, a free passage through all the rivers and passages, with all the outlets which lead to and from the said Nootka sound, of which, by the signing these presents, I have delivered unto the said John Kendrick.

Signed with my own hand and the other chiefs', and bearing even date, to have and to hold the said premises, &c., to him, the said John Kendrick, his heirs, executors, and administrators, from henceforth and forever, as his property absolutely, without any other consideration whatever.

In witness whereof I have hereunto set my hand and the hands of my other chiefs, this twentieth day of July, one thousand seven hundred and ninety-one.

Largely forgotten to history, the Kendrick Treaties are extraordinary for their time. The land purchase was confirmed the following year by both Spanish and British authorities through interviews with Chief Maquinna himself. As historian Warren L. Cook stated, "A year later the Spanish would endeavor to secure a deed of purchase from Ma-Kwee-na. Loyal to his agreement with Kendrick, in the new sale the old chief expressly exempted the land conveyed to his American friend. Although not then at Nootka, Kendrick heard about this; conceiving that his deeds possessed diplomatic importance, he registered them with the American consul in Canton and remitted duplicates to the American government."

The American claim to what is today British Columbia was substantial, especially having subsequently inherited Spain's prior rights of discovery to the Northwest Coast in 1821 with ratification of the Adams-Onís Treaty, which divided U.S. and Spanish territorial claims in North America. It wasn't until the Oregon boundary settlement of 1846 (which extended the border along the forty-ninth parallel from the Rocky Mountains to the Strait of Georgia in the Pacific) could Britain claim "undivided sovereignty" of what is today Canadian territory.

That's why 1846 is considered the critical year for confirming preexisting Indigenous sovereignties within British Columbian and Canadian courts today. By then, land transactions between Indigenous peoples and colonial authorities were based on the principle that continuous use and occupation determined rights and title.

For Indigenous Peoples in coastal British Columbia, the historic record of the maritime fur trade provides substantial evidence of continuous use and occupation of traditional territories prior to 1846 — the kind of evidence demanded by courts.

For inland Indigenous Nations, the written historic record prior to 1846 may be slim at best, thus making it difficult to provide "proof" according to the seemingly self-justifying European rules of the game.

The Nootka Crisis not only defined how rights and title would be defined in British Columbia but also set a different course for B.C., which could otherwise just as easily ended up part of Mexico, the United States, or possibly even Russia.

That, also, is something to reflect upon these days.

FORT RUPERT AND THE FORGOTTEN COALFIELDS OF SUQUASH

B.C.'s first labour stoppage happened before B.C. was B.C.

WHEN THE HUDSON'S BAY COMPANY (HBC) expanded its land-based fur trade operations west of the Rockies to include coastal sailing craft, they introduced the first steamship to the West Coast.

As the SS *Beaver* was a coal-fired ship, the company became increasingly interested in finding coal resources on the Northwest Coast to replace cost-prohibitive imports from Britain.

The discovery of local coal became the impetus for an expanding coal trade to external markets, the establishment of the Colony of Vancouver Island and B.C.'s first labour strike asserted by Indigenous people.

The *Beaver*'s inaugural tour, in 1836, of the upper Northwest Coast visited the coal-bearing grounds at Suquash, south of present-day Fort Rupert, near Port McNeil on the northeast coast of Vancouver Island. John Dunn, an HBC explorer, trader and interpreter, verified the earlier Indigenous reports:

> The cause of the discovery was as curious as the discovery itself was important. Several of the natives at Fort McLoughlin having, on coming to the fort for traffic,

observed coal burning in the furnace of the blacksmiths; and in their natural spirit of curiosity made several enquiries about it; they were told it was the best kind of fuel; and that it was brought over the great salt lake — month's journey. They looked surprised... The Indians explained, saying, that they had changed, in a great measure, their opinions of the white men, whom they thought endowed by the Great Spirit with the power of effecting great and unusual objects; as it was evident they were not then influenced by his wisdom, in bringing such a vast distance and at so much cost that black soft stone, which was in such abundance in their country.

The SS *Beaver*, first steamship on the West Coast of North America.

Dunn further stated that the Kwakwaka'wakw peoples subsequently delivered coal to the *Beaver* and "were anxious that we should employ them to work the coal; to this we consented, and agreed to give them a certain sum for every box. The natives being so numerous, and labour so cheap, for us to attempt to work the coal would have been madness."

Duncan Finlayson, who accompanied Dunn, confirmed in a letter to John McLoughlin on September 29, 1836, the strong proprietorial stance of the Kwakwaka'wakw. "They informed us that they would not permit us to work the coals as they were valuable to them, but that they would labour in the mine themselves and sell to us the produce of their exertions."

Soon, considerations of building a fort or "purchasing the mine" were discussed at both local and larger HBC corporate levels.

By October 14, 1839, James Douglas, then an HBC chief trader, reported that about one hundred tons of coal had been purchased from the Kwakwaka'wakw.

Through the 1840s, the HBC continued to discuss the possibility of establishing a fort, especially considering that other parties, particularly the Royal Navy, had become interested in the coal deposits.

In later years, Vancouver Island coal was considered some of the very best in the British Empire. It was this coal that ultimately provided the additional incentive to colonize Vancouver Island.

By the spring of 1848, even private interests took notice. Samuel Cunard, of the well-known steamship lines, urged the British government to reserve the coalfields for the Crown, perhaps not realizing that the Oregon boundary settlement had secured Vancouver Island for the Crown: "Individuals in the Oregon territory will be alive to the advantages resulting from the possession of this valuable article, and will endeavour to obtain the best situations, or acquire any right the natives may have, or suppose they have." Immediate steps should be taken to "prevent the natives or others from acquiring or ceding rights to these mines."

This information was subsequently forwarded to Lord Grey, secretary of state for the colonies. As a result, later that year, in July, Captain George W.C. Courtenay wrote to Douglas (now an HBC chief factor) with orders from Rear Admiral Geoffrey Hornby, commander-in-chief of British naval forces in the Pacific, to obtain further intelligence.

In a separate letter to Douglas that July, Courtenay enclosed a copy of the Cunard letter and "strongly recommend[ed] the Officers of the Honorable Company of Hudson's Bay to keep a vigilant look out thereon in the event of any persons settling near the Coal Mines or attempting to work them, either to cause their removal or serve them with notice to depart."

Moreover, "it would be desirable to take possession of that district for Her Majesty," stated Courtenay, and "I am informed that the practice in these parts on taking possession of Land is to build a Hut thereon."

In the Admiralty's view, this was a means to assert occupation.

The Hudson's Bay Company Archives holds Courtenay's letters, along with the inscription he prepared on August 17, 1848, to be attached to the "Hut":

> These and the adjacent Lands together with the Coal and Minerals contained therein are taken possession of through the agency of the Honble. Hudson's Bay Company by me George Courtenay, Esq. Captain of Her Britannic Majesty's Ship Constance, acting on behalf of Rear Admiral Hornby, CB, Commander in Chief of Her Majesty's Squadron in the Pacific, For Her Majesty Victoria Queen of Great Britain and Ireland, Her Heirs and Successors.
>
> All persons are therefore warned not to settle thereon, or to visit these the said Lands for the purpose of working the Coal or other Mines.
>
> God Save the Queen
>
> Given onboard the Constance in Port Esquimalt the 17th August 1848.
>
> The twelfth year of Her Majesty's Reign
>
> Signed G.W.C. Courtenay

For his part, James Douglas was just returning from the Hawaiian Islands. Upon arrival he conveyed his impression of the Admiralty's steps to assert sovereignty in a letter to the HBC governor and committee dated December 5, 1848 (reprinted in a Hudson's Bay Record Society volume compiled by historian and archivist Hartwell Bowsfield): "Captain Courtenay ... has taken possession of the Coal mines of Vancouver's Island, in behalf of the Crown, a measure recommended in a letter, bearing the signature of 'S. Cunard', to the Lords Commissioners of the Admiralty, to prevent the encroachments of American citizens, an alarm which appears groundless, as since the late Treaty no American Citizen can, by settlement, acquire any legal rights to the lands within the limits of British Oregon."

Douglas was right. But with the imperial government and Admiralty so interested in the Island's coal resources, the HBC, through Douglas, began to take the long-awaited steps of building the fort.

The imperial government was increasingly determined to formally colonize Vancouver Island as the best means to control these strategic coal reserves.

There was one problem: there was no safe harbour in close proximity to these mines. Larger ships had to anchor upwards of two miles from Suquash to receive the coal-ladened canoes of the Kwak'wala-speaking peoples.

In 1849, the HBC decided upon Beaver Harbour, with its deeper waters, as a more practical port to locate the new fort named Fort Rupert.

The imperial gaze was about to bring the most far-flung of HBC operations into the bold light of colonial power. Not coincidentally, both the fort and the Colony of Vancouver Island were established in the same year, 1849.

As the HBC entered Beaver Harbour to build the fort, HBC clerk George Blenkinsop entered into the HBC post–diary that the "Indians appear friendly and well pleased at our coming to establish amongst them, and have so far done all in their power to assist us." Blenkinsop also noted "it is but justice to say they [the Kwakwaka'wakw] work uncommonly well and appear uncommonly friendly."

The construction of Fort Rupert was an incredibly multicultural project, with many employees relocated from HBC operations at Fort Stikine, in Alaska. In addition to the usual Scottish, French Canadian and Métis employees, there were also Hawaiians, Russians and Tlingit wives, including four Nations of Kwak'wala speakers numbering upwards of twelve hundred workers.

While these HBC employees concerned themselves primarily with the fort's construction, the Kwakwaka'wakw continued to mine coal from surface deposits at Suquash, transporting it in canoes along the east coast of Vancouver Island to Fort Rupert, in addition to assisting with construction.

This arrangement changed with the arrival of professional coal miners from Britain contracted by the HBC to further investigate coalfields in the region — in many instances working alongside the Kwakwaka'wakw.

By late fall, as many as one hundred Kwakwaka'wakw were working at times for the establishment (independent of the Suquash coal mines), but in short order once-friendly relations became stressed. The newly arrived British miners essentially broke the Kwakwaka'wakw labour monopoly asserted back in 1836.

With the introduction of foreign miners, Blenkinsop recorded in the journal pages of the Fort Rupert post the first-ever labour strike in what is now British Columbia: "Indians today refuse to work till more pay is given."

With coal shafts now being sunk in the interior reaches of the Island, in consequence of the poor and repeated test results along the coast, a new understanding was required for both the HBC and Kwakwaka'wakw.

Ultimately, the HBC was forced to soothe this ongoing labour strife by concluding the Fort Rupert Treaties — the only two such treaties on northern Vancouver Island.

FORT RUPERT AND THE MYSTERY OF THE FORT VICTORIA TREATIES

Why did Governor Douglas rush this treaty process — before even getting the terms from his superiors?

ONE OF THE ENDURING MYSTERIES of the Fort Victoria Treaties (a.k.a. Douglas Treaties), initiated in the early 1850s with the Indigenous peoples of southern Vancouver Island, is why chief factor James Douglas (later governor) inaugurated these agreements before receiving the formal treaty language promised by Archibald Barclay, secretary of the Hudson's Bay Company (HBC).

And indeed, the HBC ultimately sent Douglas the land transfer agreement form (similar to that used in New Zealand with the Maori people) to use as a guide. Douglas had been waiting for this form for some time. He had instructed his officials to collect the Chiefs' X's — as a sign of consent — on a blank sheet of paper for later application, once the official Barclay text was in hand. But all of a sudden he was prompted to call the Chiefs to Fort Victoria for impromptu treaty councils.

Why didn't Douglas continue to wait? This is one of the great mysteries of B.C. history.

To my mind, the founding of Fort Rupert in 1849 on northern Vancouver Island provides a compelling explanation.

As described in "Fort Rupert and the Forgotten Coalfields of Suquash," the introduction of professional British miners to early Fort Rupert led to work stoppages by the Kwakwaka'wakw people employed by the HBC to collect coal. In short order, work stoppages in demand for greater pay led to demands for payment of Indigenous lands.

Fort Rupert (Tsaxis) in 1885.

Though HBC authorities had been discussing the need to purchase Indigenous title for years, HBC employee George Blenkinsop was compelled to take action himself with the Kwakwaka'wakw stopping work and subsequently shutting down expansion of Fort Rupert itself. He recorded the unified presence of the Kwakwaka'wakw, April 15, 1850, with regard to the Queackar and Quakeolth Tribes' stated ownership of Beaver Harbour and the surrounding landscape of Fort Rupert:

> This afternoon we were stopped by all the Chiefs from working in the Garden on the lower part of the Fort. They told us we should inclose [sic] no more of their lands as we had not paid them for it, and that it blocked up their roads to the forest for wood &c. Knowing it to be had in contemplation by the authorities that the land was to be purchased of them, I thought it advisable to make each of them payment for the land necessary for garden purposes &c. They willingly sold me all right to the land in the neighbourhood of the Fort for a Blanket

and a shirt each. I made them all put their marks to an agreement drawn out to that effect, so we may now consider ourselves the sole owners of the land, or at least appropriate to our use as much as we may require for gardens, mining purposes, &c. They seemed highly pleased with the arrangement, and said in putting their marks to the document, "Loweelaa Seesaanee," which being interpreted means, "We have no more to say and no further demands to make on you for our lands."

Without further consultation with Douglas, Blenkinsop had concluded the early treaty arrangements on northern Vancouver Island before the treaty councils of southern Vancouver Island were convened some four months later.

The treaties concluded on southern Vancouver Island involved inviting the local Chiefs to Fort Victoria for consultation, but far-flung Fort Rupert had infrequent communications delivered from a substantial distance by the SS *Beaver*.

The *Fort Rupert Journal* next recorded that two Chiefs of the Kwakwaka'wakw subsequently travelled to Fort Victoria just three days after signing these land deeds. Blenkinsop wrote:

> Thursday 18th April [1850] . . .
>
> Dispatched a canoe this afternoon with Bottineau [one of the fort's Interpreters], Tizer, 2 miners, and 8 Indians, also [Head Chief] Waawaatie and [Chief] Jim, to Fort Victoria with letters to the Board [of Management]. Provided them all with muskets, ammunition, and provisions necessary for the voyage. Terms of payment to be found in the letter-book.

Unfortunately, the letter-book for Fort Rupert is nowhere currently to be found. But the fact that two Chiefs (and eight other Indigenous peoples) and one of the fort's interpreters left in a canoe just three days later for Fort Victoria is an important point to be considered.

Departing April 18, 1850, these Chiefs and other members of the Kwakwaka'wakw (specifically the Queackar and Quakeolth Tribes) started out just eleven days before the first Fort Victoria Treaty was concluded on southern Vancouver Island. This suggests their arrival would have been contemporaneous with the first treaty-making councils held at Fort Victoria, and more probably they had arrived just before the first meeting.

This is significant. It would mean that the earlier Blenkinsop transaction, rather than the treaties concluded with southern First Nations, was the first HBC land purchase conducted in British Columbia.

Examining the original copies in the B.C. Archives in 1969, anthropologist Wilson Duff prepared an analysis of the Fort Victoria Treaties: "Douglas was no longer waiting for Barclay [the HBC Secretary] to send out 'the proper form' but had evidently written the remainder of the text himself, following in part the wording of his own May 16, 1850, letter to Barclay. He had, in fact, settled on the wording of the texts by 1851, when he wrote the complete texts of the Fort Rupert treaties at a single sitting."

Again, why did Douglas not wait for the exact language promised by the HBC?

Once Douglas obtained the legal language extracted from New Zealand, he did not reconvene the treaty councils of Fort Victoria to have the Chiefs re-sign and mark their X's anew. The blank sheets carrying these marks were simply attached, or perhaps transcribed, to the newly prepared treaty language.

It's possible that Douglas would have prepared the Fort Rupert Treaties with Blenkinsop's original transaction (and the Chiefs' marks of consent) having been already obtained. This offers a potential explanation for the intervening ten or so months between Blenkinsop's purchase on April 15, 1850 and the formal treaty later prepared by Douglas himself on February 8, 1851.

But to my mind, the arrival of the Kwakwaka'wakw Chiefs with news of the earlier Blenkinsop transaction threatened to upset all of Douglas's planned treaty-making on southern Vancouver Island. From an HBC perspective, if word leaked out about the land purchases in the north, this conceivably could inflate demands in treaty-making efforts in the south.

We know that Douglas was upset about what Blenkinsop had done. In fact, the principal reason Douglas decided to initiate treaty-making in and about Fort Victoria before obtaining the Barclay language was primarily due to what he must have viewed as Blenkinsop's precipitous actions.

Wilson Duff's analysis of the northern Island treaties concludes that "The payments ... [were] at a higher rate and in a greater variety of goods ... in the Fort Rupert transactions."

Given that the Queackar and Quakeolth Tribes had initiated negotiations and demanded payment for their lands at Fort Rupert (as opposed to the other Fort Victoria Treaties inaugurated by Douglas himself), the unexpected arrival of Chiefs from Fort Rupert carrying the more costly Blenkinsop land purchase agreements would have been the key reason for Douglas to quickly gather the Chiefs of southern Vancouver Island. He had to, before word got out that the proactive stance of the Kwakwaka'wakw had secured a greater variety of trade goods.

Douglas wasted no time with the unexpected arrival of the Kwakwaka'wakw Chiefs and quickly collected the southern Chiefs' X's, giving verbal guarantees through HBC interpreters — but without any formal legal document.

This, then, is the likely explanation to the mystery of why Douglas hastily convened the southern Vancouver Island treaty councils before having secured formal treaty language from the HBC.

THREE:
BECOMING
BRITISH COLUMBIA

WAR IN THE NEW EL DORADO AND THE BIRTH OF BRITISH COLUMBIA

How did we get where we are today?

FROM MY OWN RESEARCH ON Indigenous-newcomer conflict in the North Pacific Slope region and particularly in British Columbia, the central preoccupation of Governor James Douglas was the ever-constant threat of Indigenous warfare on fledgling non-Indigenous settlements.

This was the main concern of the imperial government, too. Herman Merivale, the permanent undersecretary of state for the colonies, wrote (while professor of political economy at Oxford University), "The history of the European settlements in America, Africa, and Australia presents everywhere the same general features — a wide and sweeping destruction of native races by the uncontrolled violence of individuals, if not of colonial authorities, followed by tardy attempts on the part of governments to repair the acknowledged crime."

This threat of Indigenous-newcomer violence and warfare is a recurrent theme throughout the early history of the colonies of Vancouver Island and of British Columbia, and most certainly south of the forty-ninth parallel in Washington Territory.

As such, Douglas — either in his capacity as chief factor of the Columbia Department of the Hudson's Bay Company (HBC) or as a colonial governor — was always careful to enact policies that ensured peaceful relations with Indigenous peoples. Predicated in large measure on earlier and successful fur trade/HBC practices (negotiated for the most part within pre-existing Indigenous systems of law), his policies largely stemmed violent conflict until the critical and catastrophic year of 1858, when the mainland Crown Colony of British Columbia was formed.

Douglas had repeatedly warned the imperial government that violent conflict would likely occur with the expansion of the California mining frontier into British (let alone Indigenous) territory. Old Oregon had been partitioned in 1846 between American and British interests and confirmed in the Treaty of Washington, but by the time of the Fraser gold rush in 1858, the border had still not been fully surveyed and remained, as the Duke of Newcastle, Henry Pelham-Clinton, secretary of state for the colonies, considered, "an imaginary boundary" that neither defined the Indigenous world nor stopped the violent warfare directed largely from south of the border.

Border Obelisk, Point Roberts, U.S. Boundary Commission, c.1859–1861.

Ethnographer James Teit and Nlaka'pamux wife Antko, Spences Bridge, B.C., 1897.

Douglas had already witnessed the violent confrontations increasingly occurring in Washington Territory prior to 1858, where the "Indian Wars" continued well into the 1870s, considered the last great such conflicts in the United States.

In the summer of 1858, as Douglas had predicted, wholesale conflict erupted along the Fraser and Thompson River corridors due to the invasion of non-Indigenous gold seekers onto Indigenous lands along the southern section of the Fraser River corridor below the fifty-first parallel. These large paramilitary-like companies of foreign miners carried, along with the requisite pick, pan and shovel, the extermination practices of the California mining frontier. Mining — the single greatest disruptor of Indigenous lands in the American West — created a frontier defined and segregated by race. This frontier did not recognize the British-American border and effectively shaped the Fraser River landscape in its own image.

The sudden invasion broke the back of Indigenous control over access and use of their territories and resources, shaped the landscape into a series of foreign, ethnically defined mining enclaves and precipitated the formation of Indian reserves even before the British proclaimed the Crown Colony of British Columbia in the fall of 1858.

Among the Indigenous Nations that bore the brunt of the expansion of the California mining frontier into B.C. were the Nlaka'pamux, Syilx (Okanagan), and the Secwepemc (Shuswap) peoples — who were in the process of forming a confederacy to drive out all foreign-born gold seekers.

Ethnographer James Teit recounted some forty years later the dire circumstances of this war and the Indigenous response to it:

> Hundreds of warriors from all parts of the upper Thompson country had assembled at Lytton with the intention of blocking the progress of the whites beyond that point, and, if possible, of driving them back down the river. The Okanagan had sent word, promising aid, and it was expected that the Shuswap would also render help. In fact the Bonaparte, Savona, and Kamloops bands had initiated their desire to assist if war was declared For a number of days there was much excitement at Lytton, and many fiery speeches were made. CuxcuxesqEt, the

> Lytton war-chief, a large, active man of great courage,
> talked incessantly for war. He put on his headdress of
> eagle feathers, and, painted, decked and armed for bat-
> tle, advised the people to drive out the whites.

In 1859, the year after the conclusion of the Fraser Canyon War, Douglas remained concerned about the possibility of "having the Native Indian Tribes arrayed in vindictive warfare against the white settlements." In further reporting to Lord Lytton, secretary of state for the colonies, Douglas — from his long years of experience — cautioned about the importance of maintaining peaceful relations: "As friends and Allies the native races are capable of rendering the most valuable assistance to the Colony while their enmity would entail on the settlers, a greater amount of wretchedness and physical suffering, and more seriously retard the growth and material development of the Colony, than any other calamity to which, in the ordinary course of events, it would be exposed."

Douglas understood this threat well. Without the active participation of Indigenous peoples in the fur trade, HBC operations on the Pacific would have been severely hampered — if not entirely impossible.

While the gold rush of 1858 seemingly changed everything — having eclipsed the fur trade — the new economy was still ultimately dependent in large measure on the involvement of Indigenous peoples. "Take away the Indians from New Westminster, Lillooet, Lytton, Clinton," stated member of the legislative assembly Thomas B. Humphreys during the Confederation debates just twelve years later, "and these towns would be nowhere ... Take away this trade and the towns must sink. I say, send them out to reservations and you destroy trade, and if the Indians are driven out we had all best go too."

Douglas's repeated warnings to the imperial government about the likelihood of Indigenous-newcomer conflict were recorded in colonial dispatches that, in many instances, were printed for British Parliament. These published warnings were subsequently viewed by the influential Aborigines' Protection Society (APS) — borne of William Wilberforce's anti-slavery movement — which in short order expressed great concern to the Colonial Office that exterminationist campaigns against Indigenous peoples in California was about to be repeated. The APS urged immediate action.

As such, Lord Lytton demanded that all necessary steps be taken to protect the Indigenous peoples of British Columbia from a similar fate and sent the APS letter to Douglas on September 2, 1858:

> It appears, from all the sources of information open to us, that unless wise and vigorous measures be adopted by the representatives of the British Government in that Colony, the present danger of a collision between the setters and the natives will soon ripen into a deadly war of races, which could not fail to terminate, as similar wars have done on the American continent, in the extermination of the red man.

> The danger of collision springs from various causes. In the first place, it would appear from Governor Douglas's Despatches, as well as from more recent accounts, that the natives generally entertain ineradicable feelings of hostility towards the Americans, who are now pouring into Fraser and Thompson Rivers by thousands, and who will probably value Indian life there as cheaply as they have, unfortunately, done in California.

The APS and indeed British policy sought to stem the violent tide of the California mining frontier and encouraged "some guarantee that the promised equality of the races should be realized ... and instead of obstructing the work of colonization they [Indigenous peoples] might be made useful agents in peopling the wilderness with prosperous and civilized communities, of which they one day might form a part."

In my opinion, the APS letter forwarded by Lytton to Douglas provided the new governor with the essential spirit of the Indigenous protection policy that had evolved. Indigenous peoples were to be treated as equals, and the method to secure this goal — from the imperial perspective — was to ensure that land reserves were set aside and protected from newcomer encroachment.

These Anticipatory Reserves, as Douglas called them, were a safe refuge in which to prepare Indigenous peoples for entry into the "civilized life" and served the express purpose of forestalling further conflict.

From our modern perspective, these policies that had Liberal humanitarianism as their foundation appear as solidly Eurocentric and self-justifying, but nevertheless were a concerted attempt to halt the exterminationist practices of previous centuries, particularly the atrocious results of U.S. cultural assumptions still prominent during the nineteenth century.

Even after the Fraser Canyon War, Douglas continued to be concerned about further Indigenous-newcomer violence, writing about it to the Duke of Newcastle on October 9, 1860, in the aftermath of the 1858 Fraser War:

> I had the opportunity of communicating personally with the Native Indian Tribes, who assembled in great numbers at Cayoosh [Lillooet] during my stay.
>
> I made them clearly understand that Her Majesty's Government felt deeply interested in their welfare, and had sent instructions that they should be treated in all respects as Her Majesty's other subjects; and that the local Magistrates would tend to their complaints, and guard them from wrong ... and that on their becoming registered Free Miners, they might dig and search for Gold, and hold mining claims on the same terms precisely as other miners; in short, I strove to make them conscious that they were recognized members of the Commonwealth.

The commonwealth Douglas spoke of was based on policies of inclusion (not surprising considering what had occurred to HBC families south of the border); it was a "British California" that made sure to distinguish itself from the discriminatory practices found south of the forty-ninth parallel.

Douglas met with the assembled Chiefs at Rock Creek, B.C., with the object of determining what grievances they might have that could "induce them to make reprisals on the white settlers." The governor was to discover that:

> There was one subject which especially pre-occupied their minds ... namely the abject condition to which the cognate Native Tribes of Oregon have been reduced by the American system of removing whole Tribes from their native homes into distant reserves where they are compelled to stay, and denied the enjoyment of that natural

freedom and liberty of action without which existence becomes intolerable.

They evidently looked forward with dread to their own future condition, fearing lest the same wretched fate awaited the native of British Columbia. I succeeded in disabusing their minds of those false impressions by fully explaining the view of Her Majesty's Government, and repeating in substance what . . . was said on the same subject to the Assembled Tribes at Cayoosh [Lillooet] and Lytton.

Those communications had the effect of re-assuring their minds and eliciting assurances of their fidelity and attachment.

Douglas protected the rights of Indigenous peoples to the best of his abilities. In post-1858 British Columbia, First Nations (women included), along with Chinese, were the main miners operating along the Fraser and Thompson Rivers. Unlike their U.S. counterparts, they were not targets of eradication.

For instance: "From about 150,000 native people still living in California at the time of the [1848] gold discovery," states historian Jim Sandos, "that number had plummeted to 30,000 in 1860, an 80 per cent decline in just twelve years." And Sandos attributes "the systematic murders of Indians by whites ... [as] the greatest single cause of death after 1848."

While Douglas assured Indigenous people that relocation from traditional lands was not part of the B.C. Indian reserve policy, the governor had originally agreed with Lord Lytton as to its possibility. Lytton had pondered in a draft reply to Douglas whether "the desirable thing would be to remove them, by argument, agreement, & reasonable terms from the [gold] Diggings most thronged to by the whites."

Lytton subsequently instructed Arthur Blackwood, senior clerk in the North American department of the Colonial Office, to soften the language of the draft dispatch from expressing Lytton's own view of the desirability of removal to a query to Douglas as to "would it be possible." The final dispatch sent to Douglas was modified accordingly and asked whether it "might be feasible to settle them permanently in villages."

Lytton's inspiration with regard to Indigenous removal from traditional lands clearly came from the work of Sir George Grey, governor of the Cape Colony in South Africa. Throughout his colonial career, Grey was also the governor of South Australia, twice governor of New Zealand and later the premier of New Zealand. Referring to Grey's work as a model for consideration, Lytton stated to Douglas:

> Sir George Grey has thus at the Cape been recently enabled to locate the Kaffirs [derog. Black Africans] in villages, and from that measure, if succeeding Governors carry out, with judgment and good fortune, the designs originated in the thoughtful policy of that vigorous and accomplished Governor, I trust that the posterity of those long barbarous populations may date their entrance into the pale of civilized life.

Douglas initially responded enthusiastically to Lytton's query:

> I have the honour to acknowledge . . . the policy to be observed towards the Indian tribes of British Columbia, and moreover your instructions directing me to inform you if I think it would be feasible to settle those tribes permanently in villages . . . I have much pleasure in adding, with unhesitating confidence, that I conceive the proposed plan to be at once feasible, and also the only plan which promises to result in the moral elevation of the native Indian races, in rescuing them from degradation, and protecting them from oppression and rapid decay.

Of course, Grey's relocation of Black Africans was the basis for the apartheid system in South Africa. In my opinion, Douglas — while seeming to have agreed initially with Lytton — ultimately did not institute a similar policy, realizing it would precipitate further and greater Indigenous-newcomer warfare.

Douglas was always cognizant of the threat of warfare. This ever-present threat of Indigenous-newcomer conflict not only informed the establishment of early Indian reserves, but also is one of the key contexts that explains and helps define the so-called Douglas system of early colonial Indigenous policy. More importantly, the peace concluded in 1858 in the aftermath of the Fraser Canyon War was bolstered by Douglas's strong commitment that Indigenous peoples "should be treated in all respects as Her Majesty's other subjects ... that they were recognized members of the Commonwealth."

Some seventy years later the words of B.C.'s mixed-race governor were reiterated by the province's mixed-race premier, Simon Fraser Tolmie. On June 15, 1930, Premier Tolmie (son of HBC senior employee William Fraser Tolmie) met with two hundred members of the Nlaka'pamux Nation in Lytton at the Spintlum Memorial in a ceremony that recognized the extraordinary peacemaker role played by Chief David Spintlum in 1858. On that blazing hot sunny day, Chief Jimmy Anderson stated, "Spintlum, he was my friend, the great chief. He made an agreement with the white men to shed no blood. It has been carried out. I am very glad. I stretch out my hand and I cling to this treaty with the whites. I am very happy that the great chief [Tolmie] has come to us, for his father we knew well and loved him."

Mrs. Tolmie laying a wreath at Spintlum Memorial.

Premier Tolmie replied, "I am glad to meet you here for you are my father's friends. Whitemen and Indians own this province together. Let us develop it together. My advice to your young men, as to the young men of my own people, is to educate yourselves to take a strong and good part in the development of our country."

Here was the promise of Governor Douglas — the guarantee of a B.C. commonwealth — restated to all assembled and translated into their own language (*Province*, June 16, 1930), a response to the chaos of the gold rush and the promise of a future together in marked contrast to the fate of our neighbours south of the international divide.

Clearly, today, the words of both Douglas and Tolmie should not only be remembered — but fully enacted.

"The Peculiar Circumstances of British Columbia"

B.C.'s colonial land policy was an experiment — and a response to the "imaginary boundary" with the United States.

SOME OF HISTORY'S MOST CRUCIAL turning points have since fallen from public knowledge. For example, the application of an imperial "land disposal" policy that the Colonial Office was unsure how to apply to the peculiar circumstances of British Columbia.

This was in large measure due to the unknown and chaotic conditions of the Fraser gold rush and failed land policies practiced elsewhere in the British Empire but more particularly British Columbia's close proximity to the United States, where a preemption system allowed settlers to obtain free land in advance of formal government surveys. If B.C. charged settlers for land it was deemed likely that prospective settlers would not establish themselves north of the border.

Almost two years would unfold before preemption as a means of Crown land disposal would be enacted in British Columbia, and this delay was due to an internal debate within the Colonial Office. This internal debate was very much evident in communications between the Colonial Office and the Imperial Emigration Board.

The Duke of Newcastle (who succeeded Lord Lytton as secretary of state for the colonies) had increasingly seen the dilemma of British Columbia. But before consenting to Governor James Douglas's anxious request to institute a preemption system, Newcastle required further in-house expert opinion.

One such expert was Thomas W.C. Murdoch, chairman of the Colonial Land and Emigration Commission. Writing to Herman Merivale, undersecretary for the Colonial Office, on September 23, 1859, Murdoch was adamantly opposed to the institution of a preemption system in British Columbia:

> It appears to me that nothing but the clearest necessity should induce the Government to have recourse to such an arrangement. It may perhaps be unobjectionable in the case of isolated adventurers in tracts of Country far removed from actual settlement, and where no other rights have grown up or are likely to be immediately created. But in a Country like British Columbia and as a means of meeting the demands of a large body of settlers it could not fail to introduce great confusion and uncertainty of title and lay the ground for future disputes and litigation.
>
> From the nature of the case there would be no definition of the boundaries of individual settlers, and it is impossible to believe that under such circumstances rival claims to the same land would not continually spring up. And in a Country where superficial improvements are so easily made and as easily obliterated, the decision of such claims would involve very great difficulty; not only to the Executive Government, who would first be called upon to decide them, but even to Courts of Law.
>
> The History of every new Colony shows the embarrassment and loss which has arisen from a careless or indiscreet system of disposal of the Crown Lands in the first instance ... This was the case in Ceylon and Natal where land was granted with great laxity and without reference to any General survey, and the records of the Colonial

Office contain ample proof of the confusion and expense which has been caused in Ceylon ...

Upon the whole I would recommend that no countenance should be given to Governor Douglas' proposal to sanction the occupation with preemptive rights of unsurveyed land.

Murdoch's lengthy assessment was reviewed by Arthur Blackwood, the Colonial Office's clerk in the North American department. In an inter-office note to Merivale on September 26, Blackwood openly wondered whether the unique circumstances of British Columbia would call for a strict application of land policies practiced elsewhere:

The Commrs opinion [Murdoch] is that it will be more advantageous for the Colony in the end not to sanction Governor Douglas' plan of holding Land under a preemptive right, even though that plan be temporary.

But has he sufficiently adverted to the consideration (which the Duke of Newcastle entertains) that the vicinity of the Americans makes it almost impossible to maintain the system of disposing of Land in the Colonies which is so easily indoctrinated at Whitehall. Home views on this point are sometimes carried to excess — irritate the Colonists — and retard the success of a settlement ...

It will deserve Consideration which plan to adopt — whether to insist on the rigorous adherence to principles which, though sound in themselves, are not applicable in all cases, or to sanction a departure from them under the peculiar circumstances of British Columbia.

Herman Merivale seemingly agreed with Blackwood, particularly as the United States had already instituted a preemption system that continued to offer new settlers a substantially more attractive land disposal policy. It would be British Columbia's potential undoing if the imperial government continued to demand formal and expensive surveys before country lands could be settled. In his own inter-office note, on September 27, Merivale stated, "Nothing can be sounder than Mr. Murdoch's reasoning, but how are we to exclude squatters in Brit. Columbia, when in Oregon, on the other side of an imaginary line, every man (as I under-stand the case) can select 160 acres of Country land where he pleases with a certainty of never being disturbed until the Government Surveyor reaches him, perhaps years afterward, & perhaps the prospect of not hav-ing to pay even then?"

This was the peculiar circumstance of British Columbia. With each sub-sequent review of the Murdoch report, the Colonial Office was increasingly of the opinion that the preemption system advocated by Douglas should be sanctioned and the governor "instructed to press on surveys, even of a rough kind, as rapidly as possible" to expedite immediate settlement.

In the race to compete with the United States, Douglas continued to wait — likely with impatience — for Britain to confirm his final plan. Newcastle, though largely in agreement, remained concerned that poten-tial American settlers would quickly take the best of B.C.'s lands, noting on October 2:

> I am very unwilling to set aside the opinion of Mr. Murdoch on such a Matter as this — especially when I cannot hes-itate to admit the soundness (in theory) of his arguments. I believe however that two such opposite systems as the English and American cannot co exist on two sides of an imaginary boundary, and it is certain that the U.S. Citizens will not adopt ours. It must not moreover be forgotten that in such a Colony as B.C. population is wealth, and every new Settler will soon add much more to the Revenue than it will lose by diminution (for a time) of Land Sales.

In the end, needing to get settlers on the ground even without formally completed surveys, Douglas waited no longer. As on previous occasions, he acted unilaterally in advance of receiving final approval and proclaimed the Preemption Act of 1860.

Murdoch and Rogers in the Emigration Office were dismayed, imme-diately expressing regret and disapproval to Merivale on February 7, 1860:

> We, therefore, think it a matter for regret that Governor Douglas should have adopted the course he now reports. Without denying that under the peculiar circumstances of British Columbia, it may be more important not to

discourage persons disposed to settle on the Land, then to maintain strictly the rule which forbids the sale or grant of unsurveyed Crown Land, we think that the relaxation of that rule should have been restricted to the absolute necessity of the case, and should not have been made general with the view to invite Settlers. Probably the effect will not be sufficiently extensive to create any very serious difficulty, but we would suggest that Governor Douglas should be recommended to withdraw the general Instructions which he has issued and should not sanction the grant of unsurveyed Land on preemptive right except on special application.

While members of the Land and Emigration Commission urged that Douglas withdraw his ordinance, the Colonial Office disagreed. T. Frederick Elliot, assistant undersecretary, noting on February 9 in response, "This the Com[missione]rs regret, but their views on the subject in their former report were not adopted at this Office, and therefore this regret cannot be expressed to the Governor. It was intended, if I understand aright, to leave him a wider discretion to meet the pressure for lands in the best way he could, and I presume that under that view of the case his proceeding will be tacitly acquiesced in by way of experiment."

Did Douglas ever know that his plan to meet the chaos of the gold rush received such opposition? Difficult to say, but this was very much an experiment that reflected all the uncertainties of a frontier gold rush where Douglas's policies and practices did not fit any formal models of land management found elsewhere in the empire.

The wait-and-see provisional nature of the colony and the governorship were reflected in Douglas's temporary Crown land policies and the wide discretionary powers he held. The provisional nature of these policies was particularly evident with the institution of the Anticipatory Reserve system: rough surveys marking out a potential Indian reserve to be formalized at a later date — the very flip side of the preemption system of formally surveyed boundaries — hastily allotted for one main and immediate purpose: to forestall non-Indigenous preemption of Indigenous lands earmarked for protection, which is to say, to forestall any possibility of Indigenous-newcomer warfare again erupting.

The Anticipatory Reserve system did just that. It anticipated the potential for grievances over the paucity of highly prized, agriculturally rich lands that constitute today only about 3 percent of the entire province, but it has also left a legacy of disputes — particularly with regard to the formation of these early Indian reserves. Was it worth it?

The Hudson's Bay Company knew the trail that connected B.C. with Fort Vancouver (on the lower Columbia River near Portland, Oregon) was no longer about annual HBC fur brigades from New Caledonia (the HBC fur-trading district comprising the north-central portions of present-day B.C.), but had the potential to convey thousands of newcomers in search of arable land.

James Douglas also knew this. Not only had he rightly predicted the 1858 conflict during the Fraser River gold rush — in which thousands of foreign gold seekers travelled through the Okanagan and Shuswap valleys, in many cases setting off conflict — but with the introduction of the American-style system of land preemption in 1860, Douglas also well knew that conflict over land was inevitable and could easily cross the border again.

It is this mentality that needs to be fully understood.

Douglas was most concerned about the pronounced cultural mindset south of the border that included an exterminationist attitude with respect to Indigenous peoples, a mindset that did not end with the Fraser Canyon War of 1858 and was prevalent throughout his governorship. By way of example, a "Special Dispatch" to the *Colonist* newspaper in Victoria, dated October 24, 1865, reported:

> A special order has been issued from headquarters for the re-arrest of Captain John Hill, of the 6th infantry, C[alifornia] V[olunteers], who is on trial before a military court martial on a charge of murder, alleged to have been committed in Nevada ... It is charged that when his company were on their way through Nevada they found the dead body of an Indian woman with a living child clinging to it. Hill ordered the dead woman to be scalped and not satisfied with this cold blooded act, ordered the infant to be torn from the bosom of its dead mother and dashed over a precipice. The fall not completely killing the child, its brains were dashed out with stones by orders of Capt. Hill.

Today, this story is foreign, distant and utterly repugnant, but it was common in Douglas's day, common enough to cause the Aborigines' Protection Society of London to lobby the British government to protect the Indigenous peoples of British Columbia.

An exterminationist attitude is what Douglas had sought to prevent and what he contended with throughout his governorship.

The Anticipatory Reserve system policy was also a response to any potential confusion caused by a lack of formal surveys, so as not to risk the colony's fiscal insolvency. While the Colonial Office had expressed fears about land policies that could lead to later confusion and expensive litigation — or block settler progress — Douglas's remedy was to have signs and corner posts roughly marking out the potential Indian reserve that would not be formalized until a later date.

Let's remember, the cost of the formal survey process simply could not be undertaken at this time. Therefore, this policy anticipated the potential for both reserves and non-Indigenous settlement while striving to avert conflict — and operated within the seemingly contradictory poles of Queen Victoria's goals of protection and progress.

"UNEMBARRASSED BY A SHILLING OF DEBT"

Why are B.C.'s land claims such a problem today? In part it's due to confused and contradictory colonial policy.

VIEWING THE 1858 B.C. gold rush from the other side of the world, Colonial Office officials in London could only see so much.

They had little information about the rapid flow of some thirty thousand-plus gold seekers who had quickly crossed the forty-ninth parallel.

Sir Edward Bulwer-Lytton, secretary of state for the colonies, addressed the British Parliament on July 8, 1858, during a debate on the Government of New Caledonia bill:

> This is not like other colonies which have gone forth from these islands; and of which something is known of the character of the colonists ... As yet the rush of the adventurers is not for land but gold, not for a permanent settlement but for a speculative excursion. And, therefore, here the immediate object is to establish temporary law and order amidst a motley inundation of immigrant diggers, of whose antecedents we are wholly ignorant, and of whom perhaps few, if any, have any intention to become resident colonists and British subjects.

Lord Edward Bulwer-Lytton

The immediate institution of "temporary" law and order invites the question: Why did the imperial government not mandate fully constituted law and order?

Once again, Lytton's words are indicative of the clouded realities of a colonial project mired in the chaos of a frontier gold rush.

Put simply, the imperial government did not have sufficient information to form hard and fast policies; its sole aim — as advocated by the influential Aborigines' Protection Society — was to assert British sovereignty and the spirit of liberal humanitarianism (though waning) against a rapacious mining frontier in order to save Indigenous lives.

Unlike the earlier Crown grant of Vancouver Island to the Hudson's Bay Company (HBC) — stipulating that the monopoly was responsible for promoting an orderly agricultural settlement — the protection of Indigenous peoples on British Columbia's mainland was the sole and paramount concern. Permanent land disposal policies that defined settlement would have to wait until a clearer picture emerged out of the chaos of the gold rush.

"[T]he most pressing and immediate care in this new colony," argued Lytton in the House of Commons on July 8, "will be to preserve peace between the natives and the foreigners at the gold diggings."

Indeed, Henry Labouchere, Lytton's predecessor as secretary of state for the colonies, warned Parliament the same day that "there was one circumstance which constituted the main danger of disorder, and that was the strong aversion which the Indians entertained towards the Americans."

"This colony was not like Australia or New Zealand," warned the Duke of Newcastle in the House of Lords on July 26, "as remote from great Powers as from England — it was near to great Powers, but remote from us."

The mainland colony's situation did not fit the formal models of colonialism practiced elsewhere in the British Empire. The close proximity of the United States and the "great danger" of Indigenous-newcomer conflict spreading across the border necessitated, as Lytton urged his fellow members of Parliament on July 19, giving "all the power they could to the only authority at present in the colony — the Governor."

The establishment of the Crown Colony of British Columbia was a hastily fashioned attempt to provide temporary law and order and to assert British sovereignty as quickly as possible.

The gold-seeking community the British government sought to rein in was, in the words of Lytton in the House on July 8, "so miscellaneous, perhaps so transitory, and in a form of society so crude" that James Douglas's appointment was provisional until a clearer picture had been gained of the foreign population whose sympathies were "decidedly anti-British."

Lytton, a member of Lord Derby's new cabinet, joined a ministry deeply suspicious of the HBC's commitment to further colonization on Vancouver Island. But at the same time, HBC policy and their centuries-old relations with Indigenous peoples was deemed successful and held by imperial authorities in high esteem.

Because of this, James Douglas — through his long years of association with the fur trade — was ultimately chosen to be governor, instead of choosing a British-born career civil servant.

In the first year, the imperial government issued only two main directives for Douglas to follow: (1) ensure the welfare and protection of Indigenous peoples (as opposed to the California experience); and (2) in formulating any Indian reserve policy (for which Douglas was given complete authority), ensure that non-Indigenous settlement take precedence and the material progress of the colony not be thwarted in any way.

This last point was made plainly clear by the colonial secretary of the imperial government, Lord Carnarvon: "Whilst making ample provision under the arrangements proposed for the future sustenance and improvement of the native tribes, you will, I am persuaded, bear in mind the importance of exercising due care in laying out and defining the several reserves, so as to avoid checking at a future day the progress of the white colonists."

These were Douglas's primary instructions during the critical first year of B.C.'s development as a provisional colony. Neither the proprietary Colony of Vancouver Island nor the Crown Colony of British Columbia were excluded from the paradoxical policy "to protect the poor natives and advance civilization."

Britain's Derby government was committed to enforcing a policy of self-sufficiency on newly emerged colonies like British Columbia. Lytton adamantly encouraged Douglas to practice "the strictest thrift at the onset" so that when responsible institutions were finally inaugurated in B.C. the colony would be "unembarrassed by a Shilling of debt."

Self-sufficiency and economic retrenchment were central tenets of the new Derby government, so much so that Lord Lytton expounded on the necessity of adopting these thrifty measures:

> I cannot too early caution you against entertaining any expectation of the expenses of the colony under your charge being met at the outset by a considerable Parliamentary Grant ... I am fully satisfied that parliament would regard with great disfavor any proposal of a gift or a loan to the extent you suggest ... But I cannot avoid reminding you, that the results, even if the object could be attained, would, according to all past experience, be of a very questionable character. The lavish pecuniary expenditure of the Mother Country in founding new Colonies has been generally found to discourage economy, by leading the minds of men to rely on foreign aid instead of their own exertions, to interfere with the healthy action by which a new community provides step by step for its own requirements; and to produce, at last, a general sense of discouragement and dissatisfaction.

> For a Colony to thrive and develop itself with steadfast and healthful progress it should from the first be as far as possible self supporting. I can assure you that in bringing these general considerations under your notice, I by no means overlook the special circumstances of the case of British Columbia, nor do I at all under estimate the difficulties and the anxiety which they must occasion you. But I need not impress on one so accustomed as yourself to the details of public business and the conduct of financial enterprises that, even under more unfavorable prospects than those of a Colony of which the resources, along with the necessities are rapidly augmenting, there

is room for exercising the control of a judicious economy, and for adapting your objects to such means of
attaining them as you may possess.

To Lytton's mind, if colonial finances were lacking, then Douglas
must adapt his policies to fit the financial restrictions.

With the imperial government providing no grants or loans yet still
demanding that costly road-building be implemented immediately,
Douglas did indeed adapt his policies to the limited means at his disposal.
At times, economic circumstances meant that Douglas had to severely
cut expenditures to the bare bones. In 1863, Douglas did not even draw
his personal salary in order to sustain Vancouver Island's elaborate road-
building program, that year's single largest budget expenditure.

Queen Victoria's paradoxical policy of protecting Indigenous people
while promoting progress presented colonial administrators like Douglas
with an onerous task: to interpret and implement two mutually exclusive
imperial goals.

In part, this dilemma explains the infirm and often contradictory nature
of early Indian reservation policy during the colonial period. The Indian
reserve was considered both a refuge for Indigenous peoples from newcomer encroachment and an impediment to progress. Consequently, the
administration of crown lands might shift and adapt its focus, depending
on a given administrator's interpretation.

The limited economic means better explains the historical context of
colonial Indian reserve policy in British Columbia. More succinctly, if
there was little to no financial resources available, it makes sense that neither settler lands nor Indian reserves would be formally established and
legally confirmed until the colony could afford them.

Consequently, Douglas announced the system of Anticipatory Indian
Reserves in 1859 and the Preemption Act of 1860; both preceded formal
surveys but were clearly adaptations to severe financial strictures.

Shielding Indigenous people from the onslaught of newcomers was
described in the language of welfare and protection, while "progress" in
newly emergent British colonies was predicated on two main land management goals: (1) the requirement for formal land surveys in advance of
settlement; and (2) the quick development of routes of communication,
particularly road-building.

The Colonial Office deemed formal surveys and the construction of roads and bridges to be the highest priority; without them, the provisional colony of B.C. would remain just that — provisional — or conceivably no colony at all.

A fully surveyed and accessible land base was the only means by which a colony would succeed within the limits of imperial policy.

The imperial government was no longer prepared to foot the bill, so the sale of lands was seemingly the only means by which revenue could be raised to pay for surveying and construction of roads. The adjacent Colony of Vancouver Island was hampered by the Wakefield system — a theory of systematic colonization which had been practiced in Australia — and compounded by the close proximity of the U.S., which had instituted a preemption system that forestalled the need for expensive and formal surveys; hence inexpensive land was readily available. The American Donation Land Claim Act of 1850 stipulated that a married immigrant couple "could acquire a 640-acre tract of farmland" for little to no expense.

As such, new immigrants were not particularly attracted to Vancouver Island prior to 1858 due to land prices being high (one pound sterling per acre). Douglas knew a similar policy in the mainland colony would not foster agricultural settlement. Internal debate within the Colonial Office realized that the land policies adopted in Australia would not work in B.C., but at the same time, they were anxious that expediting settlement prior to formal surveys would ultimately lead to confusion and future litigation — how prophetic!

By 1860, the stark realities of a provisional colony still without any formal land disposal policy suggested to Douglas the only means by which the temporary colony might become permanent.

In the absence of a settled imperial land disposal policy, Douglas exercised his local authority and instituted the American-style Preemption Act and the Anticipatory Reserve system. Both solved the immediate problem of the need for expensive and formal surveys, even at the risk of precipitating future confusion and "expensive litigation."

As we all know, expensive litigation, has become one of the legacies we continue to grapple with today!

THE ALEXANDRA BRIDGE CONTROVERSY

Sometimes, a bridge connects more than two banks of a river.

IN MY TRAVELS OVER THE YEARS through the goldfields of the Lower Fraser River, I have frequently hiked down to one of the great remaining markers of British Columbia's past — the historic Alexandra Bridge in the Fraser Canyon.

On one occasion I stood at the centre of this amazing span with then premier of British Columbia Gordon Campbell — having been asked to explain the history of the Fraser Canyon War of 1858 prior to his attending a naming ceremony for the new Chief David Spintlum [Cexp'nthlEm] Bridge, which crosses the Thompson River in Lytton, in recognition of the Chief's role as peacemaker during the tumultuous conflict.

But I want to talk about a different conflict, now forgotten, that government officials grappled with and had to do with the Alexandra Bridge itself, which was owned by Joseph Trutch, an engineer, surveyor, politician and, later, British

Joseph Trutch

The original 1863 Alexandra Bridge and toll house of the Cariboo Road, c. 1868.

Columbia's first lieutenant governor. Though "Trutch's Bridge" is remembered as an amazing technological feat, the Trutch name lives in infamy for having reversed many of Governor James Douglas's land policies with regard to Indigenous peoples.

In 1863 Trutch contracted San Francisco-based engineer Andrew S. Hallidie to both design and erect a wire suspension bridge, the latest technology then available, in preference to previous wooden constructions.

Hallidie's pivotal construction role is rarely acknowledged. He was subsequently the father of San Francisco's famous cable trolley system and had already completed at least eight substantial cable suspension bridges in California, "bridges that were able to withstand the ferocious floods that decimated the region during the early 1860s." Hidden in the California Historical Society's archives are Hallidie's recollections of the arduous Alexandra Bridge project and the great difficulties of transporting the heavy California-made iron and steel components to Yale — the height of steamboat navigation on the Fraser River. Not well known to British Columbians (although he has both a building and a plaza named for him in San Francisco), the Californian engineer recalled:

> Everything of iron or steel for the bridge was prepared
> in San Francisco and shipped by steamer to Victoria,
> Vancouver Island — which at that time was a free port

— thence by [another] steamer to New Westminster on the Fraser River and thence by light-draft steamers to Fort Yale. These latter steamers were owned by Captain [Thomas] Wright, who was generally called Bully Wright.

The material for the bridge formed a pretty good load for the stern-wheel steamer, but everything went well until on the third day we reached Emery's Bar, about three miles below Yale — here the stream proved too much for her. Spring lines were run out, and every device known to steamboat men tried without success — even a barrel of pitch was broached and fed into the furnace to keep up steam and a sixty-three-pound bundle of wire was hung on the safety valve. The heat of the fires blistered the paint and drove the passengers clear aft, but all without effect, and the captain, one of Bully Wright's sons, decided to land his cargo on the Bar, and returned to New Westminster, where his father gave him a blessing and sent him back with instructions to land the freight at Yale [even] if he made a dozen trips.

Wright's son did as his father told him, reducing the cargo weight to one-fourth the size, and made several more attempts to reach Yale with still no success. Finally, the steamship captain enlisted the services of local Indigenous peoples to get the job done, highlighting the crucial role that First Nations played in the building of B.C.'s gold rush trail. As Hallidie recorded, "He [Wright] then arranged with Indians to canoe the material up the river to Yale . . . In course of time the material was all landed at the site of the bridge, which was a long distance from anywhere or any place where anything could be obtained, hence great care had to be exercised in providing everything that was likely to be required for the work. The work of bridge building required long exposure to the elements and lengthy absences from San Francisco."

Apparently, this was Hallidie's last bridge-building experience. Evidently the difficulties encountered with the Fraser River project hastened his decision "to devote himself exclusively to the development and manufacture of wire rope" — certainly a much sought after commodity during the silver mining rush of the famous Comstock Lode in Nevada.

The SS *Reliance* at Yale on the Fraser River.

Shortly after the completion of the new toll bridge in 1863, Joseph Trutch was appointed B.C. chief commissioner of lands and works by Governor James Douglas. Trutch was also confirmed as surveyor-general by the secretary of state for the colonies, the Duke of Newcastle. Indeed, there were many high testimonials with regard to Trutch's professional capabilities.

Douglas's decision to recommend Trutch's appointment prior to the arrival of his newly appointed replacement, Frederick Seymour, from Britain suggests to me that the soon-to-be former governor believed Trutch would continue the land policies Douglas had inaugurated and was someone capable of transitioning the once-provisional colony into a formally surveyed legal entity.

Governor Seymour confirmed the Trutch appointments, but also questioned the contravention of well-established Colonial Office rules. The "Rules and Regulations for Her Majesty's Colonial Service" stipulated that "No Public Officer is to undertake any private agency in any matter connected with the exercise of his public duties."

Trutch had, in fact, alerted his colleagues to the potential conflict during the first session of the B.C. Executive Council:

I feel it necessary at once to request you to bring to the notice of His Excellency the Governor that I hold Private interests in the Public Works of the Colony, which might perhaps be deemed to conflict with the Public duties of an officer in charge of the Lands and Works Department ...

Should His Excellency consider that my retaining these Charter rights would detract from my official usefulness I am prepared to negotiate for the transfer to the Government of my interests, for an equivalent in money — the amount to be determined by appraisement or by a decision of a referee in the usual manner of business.

I would add however that, having reflected maturely on this subject, I have come to the conclusion, that my continuing in position of these Toll-rights is not incompatible with the faithful discharge of my official functions, and that I should not hesitate therefore to enter upon the duties of my office whilst still retaining my existing interests.

I desire however to submit this matter, most respectfully, for the decision of His Excellency the Governor.

The executive council was of the unanimous opinion that Trutch could not hold public office while retaining his private interests, particularly in the Alexandra Toll Bridge.

Governor Seymour agreed to Trutch's proposal to contract an independent appraiser to assess the value of projected tolls during the remainder of the government charter, in order to calculate compensation. The manager of the Bank of British Columbia was selected and calculated conservatively that the revenue from the bridge would be fifty-eight thousand pounds over the seven-year period and recommended that Trutch accept forty thousand pounds from the government. The executive council unanimously rejected this proposal.

The Trutch offer to sell his bridge must be placed in historical context.

First, his dual appointments would pay him an annual salary of eight hundred pounds. Clearly, without appropriate compensation for his toll-bridge interests, Trutch would consider this a huge personal loss. Second, the Colony of British Columbia was in no position to purchase the bridge;

it had little in the way of revenue and nothing but increasing debt (the most compelling reason for B.C. to ultimately join Canada) due to ambitious road-building projects undertaken to serve and supply the ever-shifting gold rush centres of early B.C.

Throughout the early history of British Columbia it was always difficult to attract qualified civil servants at considerably lower wages than what could be potentially made in the gold rush. Compounding this problem was the nature of competing routes of communication in the colony, whereby private interests might be attached to one road over another. Trutch's interest in the Fraser River corridor was, in effect, in direct competition with the Harrison-Lillooet route that had been completed earlier in order to completely bypass the treacherous Fraser Canyon.

With the toll bridge valued high and government coffers seemingly low, the issue was, in effect, deadlocked. Trutch's solution was essentially to transfer all his private toll-bridge interests to his brother John — yet Governor Seymour still had reservations about this new arrangement. His deputy, Arthur N. Birch, responded on behalf of the colonial government that "I do not consider that Mr. Trutch's arrangements with his brother in any way alters his interest in the Alexandra Bridge." Nevertheless, "I do not consider that there is a[nother] gentleman in this Colony capable of filling the appointment."

Meanwhile, the Cariboo rush to the north (in addition to the Big Bend gold discovery on the Columbia River) increasingly captured the imagination of the economically depressed colony, and quick action demanded immediate road-building expertise. Trutch was dispatched without delay.

Seymour solved his dilemma, for the moment, by the expedient solution of limiting the powers given to Trutch, effectively denying him jurisdiction — and indeed influence — in the area from Harrison River in the south to the hub town of Clinton in the north.

Seymour further elaborated to the Duke of Newcastle on May 19, 1864:

> There are two great routes from New Westminster to the gold mines of the Cariboo. They run together up the Fraser to the mouth of Harrison's River. The 'Douglas Lillooet' line here diverges and follows the last named river into Harrison's Lake. By 'portages,' Lillooet, Anderson's and Seton's Lakes are successfully reached; then the

THE ALEXANDRA BRIDGE CONTROVERSY

line rejoins the Fraser which it crosses and runs over land to Clinton where it forms a junction with the conflicting 'Yale-Lytton' route. From this point there is but one established road to Cariboo. The alternative mode of proceeding from the mouth of Harrison's River to Clinton, is by navigating the Fraser as far as Yale, and then travelling by the great trunk road which crosses the main river at Spuzzum, and Thompson's River a little above Lytton. Both of the rival routes are kept up by tolls. Vested and conflicting interests having sprung up in each line ... if the traffic on the first named line be impaired, the profits on the Second increase . . .

Mr. Trutch has been appointed Surveyor General. He retains his property, in the bridges for the present. I will therefore only employ him in works above the Clinton Junction or below the mouth of Harrison's River. He will, with such assistance as I can afford, at once lay out the line of road into Cariboo.

With these renewed confirmations of the Trutch appointments, though circumscribed, Birch instructed Trutch on June 22, 1865, accordingly: "The Public will expect from the Government, independent of the Surveyor General a special supervision over the claims of those living on the Douglas-Lillooet or Hope-Kootenay ['Dewdney Trail'] lines of road. The Governor will inform the Secretary of State that he has made the best arrangement he could under the circumstances and that he has no wish that they should be interfered with. But he trusts that you will not relax in your efforts to find a purchaser for the Alexandra Bridge."

No purchaser for the bridge was forthcoming during these years, perhaps due in part to the "boom and bust" nature of B.C.'s early gold rush economy.

But in 1894, not even Andrew Hallidie's bridge engineering — originally designed to withstand the flooding of California rivers in the 1860s — could survive that year's massive rise of the Fraser River. The bridge (a 268-foot span, with a 90-foot clearance from the river and a 3-ton load capacity) was destroyed, and portions of the Cariboo Road were swept away. The remaining structure was subsequently dismantled, the railway now superseding the Old Cariboo Wagon Road. Not until the dawn of the automobile era was the Alexandra Bridge reopened, in 1926. It was built upon the original 1863 pilings, while the new bridge was elevated a further ten feet.

This second Alexandra suspension bridge was used by automobile traffic until 1964, when a third bridge of the same name was built farther downstream on Highway 1, along the Gold Rush Trail.

Today, there is a growing community-based movement by both the Spuzzum First Nation (the bridge stands in the traditional territory of the Nlaka'pamux people) and the New Pathways to Gold Society to save the historic 1926 bridge.

Since 2009 the New Pathways organization has partnered with the Spuzzum Nation "to save the historic 1926 Alexandra Bridge and develop the adjacent 55-hectare Alexandra Bridge Provincial Park site's heritage tourism potential" — recognizing that the iconic bridge is situated on an ancient Indigenous crossing point that "has been a transportation hub for 10,000 years, making it B.C.'s original Gateway Project."

This is indeed true. Hopefully Alexandra Bridge will not suffer the same fate as the demolished Spences Bridge, farther north.

Concurrent with the public's growing demand to save the Alexandra Bridge is a similar concern to save the old Alexandra Lodge, a roadhouse property that includes the historic Chapman's Bar gold mining site of 1858

"Burial place and idols of the Frazer River Indians." Lithograph by Californian artist Henry George Burgess.

and quite possibly the location of the lost Indigenous village of Tikwalus that was set ablaze by miner-militias during the Fraser Canyon War.

There is a small cemetery by the old lodge (just next to Highway 1) that contains many members of the Chapman family, their grave markers mute testimony to the family's earlier presence there; to my mind they are the likely descendants of the Tikwalus village.

If memory serves, I recall once examining the Indigenous testimony taken by the McKenna-McBride Commission (1913–16) with regard to the Alexandra Lodge property and that there were, at one time, three conflicting claims of ownership to this historic property.

During the Fraser gold rush, an earlier version of this roadhouse once stood, and with it possibly a Crown grant or preemption right to the land was issued. But by the time of the railway, this earlier claim had been largely lost to memory, the Cariboo Road was defunct and a second claim — the transfer of the railway corridor from B.C. to Canada — technically had included this property. The McKenna-McBride Commission, charged with investigating the previous Indian reserve cutbacks initiated by Joseph Trutch, subsequently discovered a third claim to this property that predated the others, and that was the claim made by the Chapman family. The commission collected evidence that suggested their occupation dated to the time of the gold rush (and undoubtedly far beyond that).

Perplexed about how to deal with three competing claims, the commission ultimately assigned a new Chapman's Bar Indian Reserve farther up the river, while confirming the right of the original roadhouse ownership. The Alexandra Bridge and lodge of the same name are, to my mind, like bookends in the early history of the Fraser River gold rush.

James Douglas's Secret Mission to Find Gold

The Vancouver Island Exploring Expeditions of 1857 and 1864 recorded more than just the elusive metal.

Gold! This was the quest of not one but two expeditions that crossed Vancouver Island from east to west during the mid-nineteenth century — both starting from Cowichan Bay and along the river of the same name to Kaatza (meaning the "Big Lake" in the Hulqu'mi'num language) and beyond in search of the elusive metal.

When the first "Indian diggings" were confirmed by Hudson's Bay Company (HBC) chief factor James Douglas in the interior of what would become British Columbia, he soon wondered whether gold might also be found on Vancouver Island.

This was a year or two before the 1858 Fraser River gold rush. Certainly, there had been a limited gold rush to Haida Gwaii in the 1850s, but no serious gold reconnaissance of Vancouver Island by non-Indigenous exploring parties, even though the founding of the Colony of Vancouver Island in 1849 had been the direct result of the massive California rush of the same year.

While Douglas, who was also the governor of Vancouver Island, was excited by discoveries on the mainland, apparently most were not! The governor's son-in-law and Speaker of the colonial legislature, Dr. John Sebastian Helmcken, recalled that "the Governor attached great importance to [those mainland discoveries] . . . and thought it meant a great change and a busy time. He spoke of Victoria rising to be a great city — and of its value, but curiously enough this conversation did not make much impression."

Some few weeks later, Douglas was shown further gold collected by the Nlaka'pamux Indigenous people, this time "a soda-water bottle half full of scaly gold," yet Helmcken recorded that the Vancouver Island House of Assembly "took no heed of these discoveries."

Helmcken's reminiscences, gathered by archivist and researcher Dorothy Blakey-Smith, show just how far removed the officials of the small colonial outpost were from the mainland discoveries that would ultimately reshape the coast. Nevertheless, Douglas remained undaunted and soon found reason to mount an expedition to cross the Island in search of gold.

Shortly before sunset on September 2, 1857, the expedition steamed into Cowichan Bay aboard HMS *Satellite* and anchored near the mouth of the Cowichan River. According to one member of the expedition, Lieutenant Thomas Sherlock Gooch, "a few hours later she was joined by the Hudson's Bay Company steamer *Otter*, having on board His Excellency James Douglas, Governor of Vancouver's Island."

Apparently, the stated object of Douglas's visit to Cowichan was to confer with the S'amunu' people (a tribe of the Cowichan Nation). Only much later would it become known the governor had an additional, hidden motive.

The following day Douglas, accompanied by several naval officers, HBC officials and an escort of fifty seamen and Royal Marines, travelled up the river for the ancient village of the S'amunu' people.

As described by Gooch, "The entire tribe turned out to welcome the Governor. They were not demonstrative, but were undoubtedly pleased to see Mr. Douglas. This remarkable man was a born administrator, and his name was held in fear and respect by every tribe on the north-west coast of America." The Chief of the village, "a handsome, well-set-up, and dignified man of about thirty-five" led the official party about two miles farther to an open campground, where the governor's base was set up, with Swuq'us (meaning "dog" and related to an ancient Cowichan story), known today as Mount Prevost, looming in the distance. Apparently ponies had also been shipped from Victoria to use in the party's explorations of the valley's agricultural potential (perhaps an ominous sign for the local Indigenous peoples).

Gooch's account becomes more interesting as to Douglas's hidden intention:

> Late this evening (September 4th) Mr. Joseph Pemberton, Surveyor-General of the Colony, accompanied by two young Americans and an Iroquois in the pay of the Hudson's Bay Company, and several Somanos [sic] Indians to act as porters, left the camp without the knowledge of any of our party, except the Governor, with the intention of crossing the Island to the Pacific side. It was not generally known, but Douglas knew that gold had recently been discovered on the mainland. He wished to quietly ascertain whether it also existed on the Island. Hence the attempted secrecy.

Before the expedition was underway, the S'amunu' people, many apparently hired as packers, abandoned the project. This shortage of people led Royal Marines like Lieutenant Gooch to immediately enlist. This was 1857; the smallpox epidemic of 1862 had yet to sweep the coast. Indigenous populations, such as the Cowichan, were not only numerous but had already taken more than one determined stand against the colonial government — which had not engaged in any treaty-making in the Cowichan Valley as it had on southern Vancouver Island.

History records that the Cowichan people were naturally aggrieved they had not been paid for their traditional lands, and though the larger settlement by non-Indigenous people was yet to occur (five years later, with the arrival of HMS *Hecate*), it seems likely that Douglas would have been confronted on this issue.

Whatever the reason the S'amunu' people had to abandon their support of the expedition, colonial authorities learned from S'amunu' intelligence of the existence of "a large lake in the centre of the Island" and this became the expedition's first goal — to find Kaatsa.

As the Surveyor-General Pemberton's party headed up through the Cowichan River lands for the "unknown" lake, the story was of tough terrain, travel, weather and hardships. "Through thick masses of wild rasp-berry bushes and other underwood ... With our packs and our rifles it was a scramble getting down," Gooch admitted, "but at last, with torn clothes and bleeding hands, the lowland was gained."

Yet through it all they continued to look for gold: "Some ravines, with torrents from the north, were crossed, and in the beds of the streams gold-bearing rocks were found, and specimens obtained."

Governor Douglas would have been pleased.

The expedition was undoubtedly at a great disadvantage without the S'amunu' to not only pack for them but, more critically, to guide them. What success they did have was aided immeasurably by one mixed-race individual by the name of Tomo Antoine, the legendary Haudenosaunee (Iroquois) hunter and HBC interpreter. Gooch described this extraordinary individual:

> As Antoine was an important member of our party he deserves a description. About forty-five years old, he was a slight, actively built man, with a dark, copper-coloured face, lit up by keen, intelligent blackeye ... By birth an Indian of Lower Canada, he spoke the French dialect of that province well, and also English, and many Indian languages. His reputation as a huntsman and axeman stood high, and from his intimate knowledge of back wood life and of the customs of Indian tribes Antoine was a valuable addition to any pioneering expedition in North America. Further, although of a rather suspicious and peppery temperament, the Iroquois was a cheerful, socia-ble fellow, and spun us many amusing yarns when seated round our campfire at night.

The "Tomo" referred to here is none other than Thomas Quamtany, one of Douglas's most favoured interpreters, employed in this role at Fort Victoria through the treaty-making councils of the 1850s.

After further hardship and toil, the expedition party finally "had their eyes gladdened by the sight of a large sheet of water glistening in the rays of the setting sun." Wrote Gooch, "This was at once pronounced to be the great central lake described by the Somanos Indians."

Glad to leave the bush, the exploring party set out to inflate a thirty-foot "Indian rubber boat" — surely the first such inflatable boat to have been used in British Columbia. "It was blown out, duly named the Pioneer, [and] launched on the waters of the Cowichin."

Pemberton's party also "spent eleven hours" building a sizable raft which they named the "Saucy Jack" and both these craft were put into play exploring the great inland lake of Cowichan.

The expedition surveyed the surrounding countryside, eventually making it to Nitinat and the west coast of the Island, but no further mention is made of gold discoveries. Reporting to Douglas on November 12, 1857, Pemberton wrote, "The principal instruments and chronometer I carried myself, but as the country is heavily timbered, after passing Mount Prevost, and the fallen trees slippery to walk on, occasional falls was a thing unavoidable, which so damaged the instruments that I regret to say the observations, though taken with the utmost care, proved useless, and the map annexed a compass sketch."

And as to gold, the object of the original secret mission, all the Pemberton Report could say was "gold-bearing rocks are met with in the mountains" and "trusting that the circumstances mentioned in the earlier part of this report will somewhat excuse its incompleteness."

So ended the first attempt by non-Indigenous people to cross the interior of the Island in the pursuit of gold. Douglas would have undoubtedly been disappointed; the expedition had been launched with great fanfare and at considerable cost.

While the HBC had already staked claim to coal reserves at places like Suquash and Fort Rupert on northern Vancouver Island (and subsequently Nanaimo), significant gold discoveries remained outside the jurisdiction of the Island Colony and entirely within the Indigenous country lands of mainland New Caledonia — the HBC fur trade world as yet to be reconstituted as the Crown Colony of British Columbia. Undoubtedly, here was another motive for Douglas as governor of the separate Colony of Vancouver Island: to essentially assert sovereignty over the Mainland in advance of any authority from Britain.

Seven years would transpire before another attempt would be made to cross the Island from Cowichan to Nitinat, and as before it was a hunt for the elusive gold. But by this time Governor Douglas had retired, a new governor presided, smallpox had overwhelmed the Quw'utsun (Cowichan) and their reduced numbers were used to justify reducing their reserve lands.

Chief Kakalatza (Kakalatse), who guided the 1864 Vancouver Island exploring expedition.

While the 1857 reconnaissance had met with indifferent results, the Vancouver Island Exploring Expedition of 1864 achieved much greater success, particularly in its search for gold — and this time with the active participation of Chief Kakalatza [Kakalatse] of the S'amunu' people.

Dr. Robert Brown

The expedition followed a similar path to Cowichan Lake under the command of Dr. Robert Brown, a young botanist who awarded Chief Kakalatza special recognition. In *Robert Brown and the Vancouver Island Exploring Expedition*, John Hayman notes Chief Kakalatza's importance to the expedition both for his intimate knowledge of the river landscape through which they travelled and also for the ethnographically important stories shared with members of the expedition:

Brown's most rewarding period as a collector of myth and legend was probably during the four months of the Vancouver Island Exploring Expedition in 1864, and he was later to acknowledge his indebtedness to … Kakalatza, a joint chief of the Somenos [S'amunu'] who accompanied the exploratory party from Cowichan Harbour to Cowichan Lake. "Every dark pool suggested a story to him," Brown remarked, "every living thing had a superstition, and hour after hour we lay awake listening to the strange story of Kakalatza, Lord of Tsamena."

I know descendants of Kakalatza [Kakalatse]; they are proud to know the story of their famous ancestor.

Yet, there was another pivotal expedition member: "Tomo, who joined the expedition at Cowichan Harbour and remained with it until the conclusion." Tomo (Thomas Quamtany), the mixed-race guide and interpreter considered by Governor Douglas to have been indispensable in so many early explorations, was the only individual to accompany both expeditions, in 1857 and 1864.

The Brown Expedition left Victoria by boat on June 7, 1864, and arrived at Cowichan Bay that same day. On June 9, they left the village of Comiaken and arrived at the "Great Cowichan Lake" on June 15. Of the river, Brown wrote:

> The Cowichan River is about 40 miles in length, and is a most tortuous stream; a straight line from the mouth of the lake would not probably be more than 29 miles; it is exceedingly rapid, there being hardly any smooth water with the exception of short distances in the canyon, and about two miles at the height of the river before joining the lake. Its banks, some distance from the sea where the sea breezes do not affect them, covered with magnificent forests of the finest description.

And as to the existence of gold, Brown provided much more detail than did Pemberton's problem-plagued expedition of 1857: "The color of gold we found everywhere, and in one or two places from X cent to IX cents to the pan was reported to me, in other places sufficient pay dirt to last for a long period. I may call to the recollection of the committee that white men have since then been reported as making as much as $5.00 per diem on this same river."

In addition, this expedition was now able to collect identifiable Indigenous names at every point, Chief Kakalatza pointing out to Brown himself the long-time place names found throughout the river corridor. Wrote Brown:

> A trail is here and there found along the banks with occasional fishing lodges, and camping ground such as (above Samena), Tsaan (the 'torn-up place'); Saatlaan (the place of 'green leaves'); Klal-amath (two log houses); Qualis (the 'warm place', Latitude 48 degrees 45 min. 37 seconds north); Kuchsaess (the 'commencement of the rapids'); Quatchas (the canyon); Squitz (the 'end of the swift place'), a most picturesque series of rapids with Indian lodges of which we secured a sketch, and so on until we came to Swaen-kum, an island where the Indian deposits the poles by which he has hitherto propelled his canoe up the rapid stream for now we have come into Squakum, the still waters, the commencement of the lake, where the current is no longer perceptible.

On Friday, June 10, 1864, Brown described the expedition:

> Sent the canoe with Tomo, Kakalatza, Lemon [son of Comiaken Chief Locha], in charge of Mr. Buttle, up the River with the provisions, appointing an Indian fishing village called Saatlaam as the rendezvous, the exact situation of which had been described to me by Tomo & said to be reached by tolerably good Indian trail. To lighten the canoe each of us took our personal [belongings] though this was somewhat compensated by the amount of personal baggage Kakalatza took — amongst others his hat and incredible to say a hat case to hold it which he had got from some young Englishman who had 'gone through the mill' in Cowichan since the halcyon days of Regent Street. His villagers gathered out to

see him off. He wished to take one of his young men with me but I declined. With the rest of the party I started off, taking with us an Indian boy Selachten to put us on the trail.

The exploration having begun, Brown remained alert to any information about gold: "On a creek a little further up, gold has been found in paying quantity it was said by Mr Jas. Langley who prospected it in company with Harris & Durham in 1860 [following Pemberton's confirmation in 1857], but we now know better what pay [is] in placer diggings & I am assured by Harris that it would not pay. It yielded according to our washing about 8 colours to the pan, but I have no doubt but that more could be got."

Not unlike the earlier Pemberton Expedition, Brown's party was often "losing the trail frequently and tearing our hands & feet through thick undergrowth of crabapple & raspberries." And sometimes when he inquired of the Indigenous name of a particular locale, it was so ancient that "the meaning we could not learn, as it was named in days long gone by, by the old people from something they could not understand, just like places in our own country."

Unlike the Pemberton Expedition, the 1864 exploration sought more than geographical information or intelligence of gold. Tomo, like Kakalatza, often spent the evenings in camp telling stories — undoubtedly like those told to Lieutenant Gooch in 1857, but the difference was that Brown recorded them.

> Moonlight night — late to rest — stood round the camp fire listening to Tomo's description of Indian astronomy and was struck with it as similar to the Arabian in the similitudes they draw between constellations and known objects. The handles of the plow are two men in a canoe, the Pleiades are a collection of fishes, Four stars (The Plow?) are an elk. The Moon they think travels and has a frog inside of it (Is this worse than our Man in the Moon?) The stars are little people. A strange people are these Indians. The more you know of them the more can you appreciate their shrewdness — the curious store of lore and traditions they possess; to judge them as you

see them "loafing" about the white settlements is like judging a man by the coat on his back. Few ever take the trouble to learn about them and still fewer know anything bad about them tho' loudest in their general dogmatic denunciation of them.

As the party continued up the Cowichan River, gold was never very far from their minds. The expedition even employed an experienced American gold seeker who was constantly dipping his pan into the various streams and sand and gravel bars they encountered. In fact, American gold seekers often played a pivotal role in the early development of this province. Brown wrote of this experienced gold miner:

> Foley (a very experienced Miner) prospected a bar & found about 1/2 cent to the pan & thinks pay might run ahead of the prospect and that Chinamen might by using Blankets and quicksilver make $1 to $1.50 per diem which would be a great thing for the country. On every creek and bar yet we have found the colour of gold and plenty of black sand but too fine. Hitherto the River has been bordered by flats (more or less wooded) & it is not likely that good prospects can be got on bars in their vicinity. What gold comes down the hills lands on the flat where an equally good prospect can be got. When the hills come down to the water that is the time for prospects.

As the expedition continued to map and record their journey, heavy rains compelled them to take shelter in two Indigenous lodges at Skutz Falls shown to them by Kakalatza. "These lodges were empty just now," recorded Brown. "Three young men & two women having gone (so old Kakalatza said) to hunt elk at the great Lake. We accordingly took possession of the best lodges — & as our trousers were very wet, we took them off & fastened our blankets round our legs Indian fashion & stretched our length upon mats belonging to the 'three hunters of Kaatsa' in which position Mr. Whymper took a rough sketch of the party."

Though the rain continued unabated, Tomo continued to hunt and bring fresh game, and the expedition continued the next day, Tuesday, June 14, in the direction of Lake Cowichan.

"Now we appreciate our waterproof sheets," Brown commented on the deluge they had experienced, "It seemed true as Macdonald [an expedition member] declared that 'the devil was whipping his wife' &, if we may judge from his frequent allusions to that gentleman, he appears to be on terms of considerable intimacy."

The American miner, Foley, continued to prospect, next panning "an old bar & found 1 cent to the pan, fit to pay a good miner with a rocker $2.50 to $3.00 per day. It is on the old bars of the river that we have found the best prospects & hence the best gold."

To give these wages some perspective, standard pay for a labourer at the time was about one dollar per day. Brown recommended for the future that "men who have the means & the inclination with appliances superior to ours, & more time at their disposal, to test further a river which we have proved to yield more gold than any other place yet tested in Vancouver Island."

Brown was convinced of their success:

> Foley is a very experienced Californian & British Columbian Miner & may be relied on. I particularly cautioned him against the slightest approach to exaggeration, telling him that I was not at all anxious to swell out my report with reports of gold but only want the naked— even underestimated — statement of the truth. He assured me that he had gone under rather than over, when he stated the prospect at from 3/4 to 1 cent the pan. A very experienced miner can wash out 300 pans a day. Call it $2.00 a day. I saw many Chinese on Fraser River last autumn between Lillooet & Yale — particularly about the far-famed Boston Bar weighing out their day's earnings, and dividing from 55 cents to $2.50 to each — & yet they were contented, notwithstanding the privations of these out of the way places, & the high rate of provisions.

"So exciting is gold hunting," enthused Brown, "that men are willing to leave the certainty of good wages to take the uncertainty of poor ones, led away by the hopes of striking large ones. Nothing but this could ever make them endure the hardships & disappointments of their work."

Finally, Brown's party approached Lake Cowichan, and in a little clearing somewhere before the lake "found on a cedar tree divested of a piece of the bark, written in pencil fresh as the hour its being written 'Harris, Langley & Durham Augt 1st/60' marking the limits of their exploration. We added our autographs to this memorial tree."

Just beyond, Chief Kakalatza was waiting with their canoe and about a mile farther along Brown was greeted by "a blazing fire" where other expedition members were found busy cooking supper, "which we soon encircled to dry & warm ourselves, until the heat made us retreat to a respectable distance from it." Brown continued:

> The Indians say "You White Men are fools. You build a fire to warm yourselves but you make it so big that you cannot get round it," & I daresay they are quite correct. A White man's camp you can know for years. He cuts down trees, he heaps on logs, & altogether he makes a very 'tall' fire, but the Indian manages things better, & saves himself a great deal of trouble. He gathers a few sticks, saves his axe, makes a small fire & crowds round it, warming without burning themselves.

In short order the expedition travelled the great Lake Cowichan and Kakalatza soon returned to S'amunu', having fulfilled his promise to guide them to the lake. The Brown party inspected the vast terrain, sampled the creeks for gold and ultimately ventured to Nitinat on the west coast, but not before breaking into two separate parties.

Under the command of Lieutenant Peter Leech, Royal engineer, the breakaway party headed down into the Sooke Lake watershed and finally struck the kind and amount of gold that Governor Douglas had so hoped for on the Leech River, a tributary of the Sooke River — and it was some of the coarsest gold yet found. With this discovery, the Island's own gold flurry commenced – the Leech River gold rush — some six years after the Fraser River rush of 1858.

Leech River gold fever was immediate. Before the end of 1864 there were a total of six general stores, thirty saloons, and about twelve hundred miners in these goldfields.

How gold has — and continues — to change the world. Between 1857 and 1864 not only had a smallpox epidemic hit and an instant gold rush town been created, but also increased numbers of non-Indigenous settlers moved into the Cowichan Valley. While Robert Brown's expedition had been a success, for Indigenous people it represented vastly more than a mere mixed blessing. Throughout the 1864 journey, Brown widely conversed with the Quw'utsun (Cowichan) people and recorded the substantial ill-effects on their people. "The Indians are complaining of the conduct of the whites," wrote Brown at Cowichan Bay on June 9, 1864.

> They say "You came to our country. We did not resist you — you got our women with children & then left them upon us — or put them away when they could have no children to keep up our race (a fact or nearly amounting to as much). You brought diseases amongst us which are killing us. You took our lands and did not pay us for them. You drove away our deer & salmon & all this you did & now if we wish to buy a glass of firewater to keep our hearts up you will not allow us. What do you white men wish?"

> This is in part very true. The Indians have not been treated well by any means. There is continually an empty boast that they are British subjects, but yet have none of the privileges or the right of one. Their lands have never been paid for in these districts at least. They are not taxed nor yet vote. They are confined in their villages to certain places. Nor are any means taken to protect their rights of fishing & hunting.

In the years since a sympathetic Brown itemized the complaints of the Quw'utsun (Cowichan) peoples, the fact remains that "their lands have never been paid for."

While the names of Pemberton and Brown are immortalized in history, the success of these two colonial exploratory parties depended quite significantly on Chief Kakalatza and Thomas Quamtany, a.k.a. Tomo. Their names certainly warrant inclusion, indeed a much more prominent place, in the history books of our province — in addition to the outstanding grievances of these Indigenous people for the last one-and-a-half centuries.

BRITISH COLUMBIA'S FORGOTTEN GOVERNOR

How seventy-five pounds of gold dust sparked the transformation of the B.C. Interior.

SOME YEARS AGO, I started a mission of exploration.

I headed to the small community of Seymour Arm (previously Ogdenville, Seymour City) in Shuswap Lake country in search of a trail built by my great-great-great-uncle William during the Big Bend gold rush of 1865–66 for the Crown Colony of British Columbia.

For years, I wondered whether it still existed. The trailhead apparently started at the instant gold rush town of Seymour City and crossed the Monashee Mountains to the Columbia River.

I was also determined to find out more about the Big Bend gold rush, it seeming to have escaped larger notice. Indeed, the forgotten Big Bend gold flurry was the signal event that reshaped the Interior grasslands of British Columbia — promoted by a remarkable Colonial Office official, Arthur Nonus Birch, who was parachuted into B.C. to kickstart the failing economy.

A career civil servant, impeccably well-connected within Colonial Office circles in London, Birch came to British Columbia in 1864 with the newly appointed governor, Frederick Seymour, the successor to James Douglas.

The Colonial Office List for 1877 reveals Birch intimately knew and worked for some of the highest authorities in imperial governance, including

Governor Frederick Seymour

four separate cabinet members who had been sec-retary of state for the colonies. Birch's brother, the Reverend H.M. Birch, had been tutor to the Prince of Wales.

With respect to the new governor of British Columbia, Birch recalled that "Fred Seymour, who I knew as Governor of Honduras, a brother of General Sir Francis Seymour, was appointed first Governor, and specially asked that I should be allowed to leave from the Colonial Office to go out with him and start the new Government on Down-ing Street lines."

Before leaving for British Columbia, Birch had co-edited the Colonial Office List for 1863 — an annual publication that included the *Rules and Regulations for Her Majestys Colonial Service* — thus testifying to his expertise in such matters.

Seymour appointed Birch the colonial secretary — considered the high-est official within the B.C. executive council — giving him all responsibility and authority for the administration of the colony.

Arthur Nonus Birch

Prior to the Big Bend rush, there had been significant gold strikes in the vicinity of Rock Creek, which compelled Governor Douglas to construct a viable trail from Hope to the Similkameen District ("The Dewd-ney Trail") to prevent the gold from being diverted south of the forty-ninth parallel, always a problem for colonial authorities.

In 1864, the year of his arrival, Arthur Birch commanded an official exploratory party to the Kootenay region to see first-hand the new gold diggings of Wild Horse Creek, to the south of Big Bend, but also was particularly concerned to establish an all-British route to these mines. In the Colonial Secretary's unpublished reminiscences, the threat of Amer-ican annexation of this new gold district once again demanded action:

> We received Californian papers reporting great gold
> discoveries on the spurs of the Rockies in the Koote-
> nay district. As far as we could gather from old maps,
> the country described was in British territory. The rude
> maps of those days made it very difficult to decide sat-
> isfactorily ... [but we] became anxious, with the idea
> that if the reported mines were in or near the boundary,
> Americans would annex them ... I suggested that, as I
> had been a prisoner in New Westminster for some four
> months, I should undertake a journey of discovery.

As happened with the Fraser rush of 1858, American interests were
again threatening to siphon off the lucrative trade south of the border
— and Birch's expedition confirmed that the only way to get there was
through the United States.

At this juncture in B.C.'s development, no practicable British route
existed to the Columbia River region. This became the driving necessity
of the Seymour/Birch administration.

When the official Kootenay Expedition returned, Birch and his
exploring party delivered seventy-five pounds of gold dust into the trea-
sury, colonial revenue they had quickly collected from the Wild Horse
goldfields. In Birch's words: "We were the first Gold Escort direct from
the Rocky Mountains to the seaboard of the Colony."

The delivery of such incredible wealth immediately drew the attention of both colonial and imperial authorities, along with the local press. The
British Colonist published the entire report and agreed with the need for
an all-British route:

> The trail by way of Rock Creek is not the one which will
> enable the traders of Vancouver Island and British
> Columbia to compete with their American neighbors
> ... we could not, with our present routes, however
> improved, place goods in the Kootenay mines anything
> like so cheap as the packers and traders from Oregon.
> It devolves, therefore, on the Government of the neigh-
> boring colony to discover if possible a line of transit that
> will reduce the land travel nearly one-half.

Ultimately, as gold discoveries moved from the Wild Horse diggings towards the Big Bend, Birch favoured connecting the Columbia gold-fields via Kamloops and Shuswap.

The government was compelled to plot an all-British route to the mines via Kamloops and Shuswap and open the agricultural capabilities of the Interior to supply the goldfields, instead of continuing to import everything from the United States.

If the colony was to survive and thwart American expansion, land settlement had to occur quickly.

The gold colony had reached its critical moment.

Birch subsequently became acting governor during Seymour's lengthy absence from British Columbia, and during this time Birch both largely instigated and authorized all public works connected with this new gold rush. Writing to the Colonial Office on March 12, 1866, Birch confirmed, "I have the honor to report that extensive Gold fields have been discovered on that portion of the Columbia River commonly known as 'Big Bend' ... The excitement prevailing in California and throughout the neighbouring Territory convinced me of the necessity of opening communication with these mines without delay and in time to enable the Merchants to throw in supplies before the 'rush' of miners fairly commenced."

Thus, a new gold rush mania swept British Columbia, with the local press trumpeting upwards of ten thousand gold seekers anticipated in the summer of 1865. The *British Columbian* newspaper proclaimed in January 1866, "The Big Bend diggings are the all absorbing theme. Everybody talks about them, thinks about them, dreams about them, and every available human being is going to them at the earliest possible moment."

The general mania that propelled the colonial government both secured and built the new "Big Bend Highway" that branched off the better-known Cariboo Road at Cache Creek to Savona, then by steamship through the Kamloops and Shuswap territories, ultimately to the instant town of Seymour City. From here a trail was then constructed to the Columbia, with the added possibility of connecting the whole road system not only to the Fraser network but with Canada itself.

As with much of my ground-truthing historical research, serendipity struck.

Having made it to the little community of "Seymour City," I surveyed the landscape for clues to its gold rush past.

The pilings for the wharf constructed to accommodate the arrival of steamships remained — but where was the trail?

I asked questions at the local pub, but no one seemed to know — until I met a third-generation trapper who knew the country intimately.

He was rather shocked to discover my interest, quickly rolled out his maps and, pointing with a finger, directed me on how best to find the original trail bed. Apparently, he was the only remaining person in Seymour Arm to know of its existence!

The very next day, a colleague and I bushwhacked off the road and quickly found ourselves standing on a remnant of this long-forgotten route!

Though the Big Bend gold flurry rivalled the better-known Cariboo goldfields only for a brief period, this flurry of activity was crucial. It brought increasing awareness of the absolute importance of fostering agricultural settlement to undercut American interests. From this moment, the ranching industry took off, while at the same time becoming the impetus for reducing the size of early Kamloops and Secwepemc (Shuswap) Indian reserves. The validity of these reductions are still being argued in court today.

From the colonial perspective, non-Indigenous settlement had been slow, as gold rushes were notorious for quickly booming and suddenly busting. But with Birch, the progress of the colony had seemingly been jump-started and "Downing Street lines" considered it all "a very excellent performance for a Colony 8 years old."

In my opinion, the significance of this gold rush has not been given the attention it deserves. The colonial administration was under huge pressure to succeed (as previously under Douglas), and building roads to new goldfields continued, even at the risk of incurring further debt.

The alternative, of course, was thousands of Americans ready to assert their own sovereignty north of the forty-ninth parallel if the British did not.

As for acknowledging Indigenous sovereignty and land claims by Indigenous peoples across Canada — the struggle continues to this day.

FOUR:
BRITISH COLUMBIA
AND THE
CALIFORNIA
CONNECTION

THE THIRD GREAT "DEVIL-DANCE"

B.C.'s gold rush was a rush indeed, as massive numbers of fortune seekers picked up stakes in California and headed north.

AS A GOLD RUSH HISTORIAN, I have always been fascinated by the immense excitement and profound mania that swept through mid-nineteenth century gold seekers in California, Australia and British Columbia. The 1849 California rush was referred to as "Gold Fever," the "California Fever," the "Yellow Fever" and "Gold Mania."

In Ancient Greek the word *mania* (μανία) means, quite simply, madness or frenzy. The Fraser River gold rush of 1858 — considered the third great mass migration of gold seekers in search of a new El Dorado — was no different.

The Californian historian Hubert Howe Bancroft in his nineteenth-century history of B.C. wrote of "the infection which spread with such swift virulence in every direction" — an absolute mania that had gripped the Golden State — "the third great devil-dance of the nations within the decade" following the Californian (1849) and Australian (1852) gold rushes. "At one leap British Columbia had become the rival if not the peer of California herself," concluded Bancroft.

"Never, perhaps, was there so large an immigration in so short a space of time into so small a place," wrote the Reverend R.C. Lundin Brown. Many in California felt that the delirium was reminiscent of, if not exceeding, the old glory days of 1849 so missed by thousands of old sourdoughs who had been left behind in the wake of capital- and labour-intensive mining developments.

"The desire to become rich suddenly ... spread like an epidemic throughout the state," alerted the *San Francisco Bulletin* in an April 20, 1858 article, "Eight Hundred Miners for Frazer River." Abraham Lincoln's future secretary of war, Edwin Stanton declared on June 19, 1858, "A marvellous thing is now going on here ... [that] will prove one of the most important events on the Globe."

Stanton was not the only American swept up by the excitement of the Fraser River gold rush. Wild suspense continued to build about the "New Yellow Fever," noted the *Bulletin*, as "knots of old experienced miners, verdant new-comers, excited youths, wild spectators, with a sprinkling of 'Micawbers' and bummers, were seen ... discussing the chances of accumulating a 'pile' by a few months of hard toil."

Nor was the general panic created by B.C. gold limited to San Francisco. The interior gold camps of California, hundreds of them dotted along the Sacramento, Yuba and Feather rivers, were on the march by the middle of May 1858.

"In the stage, from Murphy's to Stockton, little else was talked about yesterday," exclaimed an excited gold seeker, quoted in "Union Gone In!" in the *Bulletin* on June 12, 1858. "And every time the persons inside (several of whom were old miners) passed acquaintances on the way, they were saluted with, 'Halloa, John, (or Tom), on your way to Frazer River?'"

The general impression, reported the *Bulletin*, was that when a man was seen travelling, he must be on the route to the new mines. At Oroville, Marysville and Sacramento, ten thousand miners were reported as preparing to leave. The *San Francisco Newsletter* believed that at least fifty thousand would join the rush within ninety days. "These figures are not written at random," the newsletter claimed in "A Summary of Events from 20th May to 5th of June, 1858," "but from positive information obtained from the interior of the northern, central and southern sections of this State."

Californians were not only pouring in but staying, reported the *Bulletin* on June 7, 1858, in "The Fraser River Gold Fever in San Francisco." And

"The Frazer River Thermometer," 1858 Broadsheet produced in San Francisco, California.

the few that did return apparently had "a good deal of gold to exhibit," which was likened to "oil upon the fire already lighted."

The result was instantaneous. The Fraser River goldfields were a reality and, according to newspapers of the day, they "created a much more general and violent excitement" than had ever been experienced in the eastern states during the days of '49. "Excitement of this kind is infectious," wrote the *Bulletin*'s editor. "A person who does not run out and listen to the talk on the streets, in the bar-rooms, in business stores ... can have no idea of the alarming state of the Frazer river excitement at the present moment in San Francisco."

Certainly the San Francisco business community understood the "alarming" state of things and made the most of it. Whisky, wine, beer, pork, picks, pans, shovels, gold scales, boots, books, packs, maps, medicines and miracle cures were all repackaged for special use on the Fraser River.

Charts of varying quality, accuracy and technical detail were immediately offered for sale. A.C. Anderson's *Handbook and Map to the Gold Fields* (1858) would sell an unprecedented three thousand copies in just three days!

Warm woollens refashioned for the Fraser River's northern climate became the selling card of many a clothier: "We have a large stock of heavy and coarse Coats, Pea-jackets, Pants, Shirts, Socks, &c, just suitable for ... miners visiting those mines." The Quincy Hall Clothing House proclaimed in large bold type that it was closing out its immense stock: "GOT THE GOLD FEVER AND BOUND FOR FRAZER RIVER!" Grocery stores warned of the scarcity of provisions up north and suggested that miners bound for the Fraser River stock up with supplies before departing.

Merchants such as Thomas Hibben were even more determined to capture the full extent of the new trade. Hibben quickly dissolved his partnership in the Noisy Carriers' Book and Stationary Company to relocate to Victoria.

Wells, Fargo and Company also established an express headquarters in Victoria, while Nichols and Company's Express for Frazer River was just one of several smaller mail carriers to notify Californians of their intended move north.

Even the *San Francisco Bulletin* printed a timely run of "The Bulletin for The North," which had as a special feature an extensive, very useful listing of Chinook Jargon with equivalent translations in both English and French.

Clearly, there was money to be made in "mining the miners." Although the interior reaches of California were hit particularly hard by the sudden outflow, for a time San Francisco profited from the mania. As the main point of departure for the new goldfields, San Francisco and its business community had substantial motivation to fuel the Fraser River fever and thus benefit through increased merchandising and transportation of gold seekers.

California was "'knocked endways' by this outrageous gold excitement." Manton Marble in the New York–based magazine the *Knickerbocker* outlined the frenzied pace of change to his Eastern audience when he wrote:

> During this brief period, ten steamers, making the round trip between San Francisco and Victoria in ten days, had been plying back and forth at their best speed, taking five hundred passengers and full freights up, with only thirty passengers and no freights down. Clipper-ships, and ships that were not clipper built, in scores, were crowded alike — the Custom-House sometimes clearing seven in a day. Many of the steamers and vessels went up with men huddled like sheep — so full that all could not sit or lie down together ... Nothing else was discussed in the prints, nothing else talked of on the street; all the merchants labelled their goods 'for Fraser River:' there were Fraser River clothes and Fraser River Hats, Fraser River shovels and crowbars, Fraser River tents and provisions, Fraser River clocks, watches, and fish- lines, and Fraser River bedsteads, literature, and soda-water. Nothing was saleable except it was labelled 'Fraser River.'

Friends and family once considered lost were now presumed to have headed for the Fraser River. "On further inquiries about Richard Bullis, the man who mysteriously disappeared on last Friday," the *Bulletin* snitched, "we learn that there are reports that he was suddenly taken with the Frazer river fever ... As nothing whatever has been learned of him direct, and as he was not exempt from the new contagion, it is probable that young Bullis is now rowing up towards Fort Hope."

Indeed, the Fraser River had captured the imagination of California gold rush society. The *San Francisco Newsletter* peppered its pages with tantalizing stories of the new diggings: of William Price, "a boy who went fortune hunting," and told of three men who had taken $1,800 in the short space of a month; or at Kerrison's Bar where Saint Marie and Charles Hanna got four ounces in just half a day's work with a rocker; or at Hill's Bar, where men anxiously awaited quicksilver in order to accumulate $10 to $12 dollars a day, though predictions by old timers suggested the possibility of $50 to $100 to the hand; and Captain Daniels' eyewitness account of a lone Frenchman having made the extraordinary pile of $10,000 in five quick weeks.

The editor of the *Bulletin* declared: "What a tremendous effect will the news now going home have upon the people at the East and in Europe! Talk about $10, $20 and $50 per day to men who work for these sums a whole month or a year — why, if people get wild here [California], they will run mad there."

"Noon on the Frazer," Kinahan Cornwallis, *The New El Dorado; Or British Columbia*, 1858.

People from every walk of life in San Francisco appeared to be leaving: "The Frazer Infection in the Police Department" sent officers Berham, Hanford, Quackenbush, Guyton, Riley, Dennison, Parks, Bovee and Captain Donellan flying north with the greatest of haste, while the "Dwindling of the Fire Department from Frazer Fever" was blamed on two hundred members of the force having bolted. James Moore, a member of No. 8 Fire Company (the "Pacific") was one of the first Californians up the Fraser

River, having taken part in the infamous Hill's Bar strike. "Give my regards to all of '8's' fellows," he wrote to a friend, having also sent a sample of Hill's Bar gold from the ten to thirty-two dollars a day he had averaged while there.

Even the notorious American politician Edward McGowan, narrowly escaping the long arm of California law, was said to have made "his stealthy exit" on the Sierra Nevada to the foreign gold mines.

While California "dominated the first decade of mining in the West," states the American historian Duane Smith, "only a few small gold discoveries of local significance, primarily in Washington, Oregon, Arizona, and Nevada, [had] challenged this dominance. Then in the spring of 1858 came news of gold discoveries along the Fraser River in British Columbia." Smith agrees that the Fraser River fever not only "swept San Francisco and the Mother Lode country," but also "perhaps more than 30,000 rushed to the new El Dorado; [though] we will never know the exact numbers."

Smith is correct. There is absolutely no way to accurately determine just how many Californians flooded the Fraser and Thompson River corridors in 1858, but suffice to say that it was well in excess of the thirty to thirty-three thousand people given as the usual conservative estimate.

With no colonial government established in New Caledonia (the name the region was known by before becoming a Crown colony), records of the myriad number of miners who chose to travel through the inland corridors of the Pacific coast have undoubtedly been underestimated. We have been left records from the infamous and literate few, but what of the untold thousands of unknown miners who left no trace? Even many of those who chose to travel using maritime routes of communication are uncounted.

While larger steamships might provide passenger lists (though usually such ships sailed in excess of their recorded capacity), Smith rightly notes that other gold seekers "commandeered anything that would float" — presumably small-scale water craft that were also unrecorded.

For some Californians, it was not even the allure of mineral wealth as much as the sense of joining a rare human adventure of gold seekers who had grown accustomed to excitement.

And so, British Columbia, unlike any other province in the Canadian Confederation, was born of this wide-scale and sweeping mania — British Columbia gold fever!

B.C.'S PERMEABLE BORDER

The blinding influence of a political divide sometimes keeps us from seeing our full history.

WHENEVER I TRAVEL up the No. 1 Highway through the Fraser-Thompson Corridor, I am amazed at the impact the gold rush had on Indigenous communities, and that so much has been forgotten about Washington State's involvement in the early development of the province.

Travelling by such lesser-known places as the Chapman's Bar, Boothroyd and Cook's Ferry Indian reserves often leads me to wonder who were the name-sakes of these Indigenous lands and why do we know so little about them?

I decided to try and find out.

In my view, the historical exploration of transboundary regions, such as the Pacific Northwest (or dare I say, Canada's Southwest!), has been largely undermined by preoccupations with nation-building history in two separate countries that has encouraged the blinding influence of a political divide.

Cross-border migrations across the forty-ninth parallel were nothing new for Indigenous peoples, fur traders, gold seekers or, indeed, my own grandfather, who, during the late 1920s, drove from B.C. to Mexico on two separate occasions — once in a 1928 McLaughlin-Buick motorcar!

B.C. was part of a natural north-south world — the Pacific Slope — where previously the Spanish, Russians, British and Indigenous Nations once moved quite freely west of the Rockies — until the United States and Canada commenced their new nation-building narratives to encompass their recently claimed portions of the Pacific coast. These east-west reconfigurations had little interest in stories of the previously natural north-south flow, and the transcontinental nationalism of the U.S. and Canada effectively severed Pacific Slope communities from a shared history, now largely forgotten.

Canadian historians often fail to recognize that the Pacific province does not fit any simple Laurentian thesis, whereby Canada's gradual westward expansion was based upon the commercial fur trade and economic system of the St. Lawrence region.

One of the goals of Confederation was to reorient these connections into an East-West alignment, but it was not always so.

In 1858, ignoring Governor Douglas's concerns, Britain countered that it was not the policy of Her Majesty's Government "to exclude Americans and other foreigners from the goldfields."

"On the contrary," cautioned the colonial secretary, Sir Edward Bulwer-Lytton, "you are distinctly instructed to oppose no obstacle whatever."

Soon tens of thousands of American miners moved north across the still-unmarked international divide; many believed the new goldfields were actually in American territory.

Gold seekers from Washington Territory were some of the very first to arrive.

One such person was Captain George Wesley Beam, later a member of the Washington Territorial legislature, who, when just south of Yale, wrote in his diary that "The [Fraser] river bears south much more than you have an idea."

During the transformative year of 1858, there was literally no parallel marked out on the ground to separate British Columbia from Washington. The forty-ninth parallel was of little consequence; many Americans either hoped or assumed the U.S. Boundary Commission would establish the goldfields south of the international divide.

George Wesley Beam

Until the boundary was located and confirmed, many American gold seekers left their mark in the form of place names in the goldfields.

John Chapman, for instance, the founder of Steilacoom City in Washington Territory in the early 1850s, was the undoubted namesake of Chapman's Bar (near Alexandra Lodge) in the Fraser Canyon, the name later used by colonial surveyors in defining the Chapman's Bar Indian Reserve.

Likewise, George Washington Boothroyd, a member of Major Mortimer Robertson's 1858 Yakima Expedition to the Fraser Mines, travelled through the American and Canadian Okanagan region as part of a large-scale militia determined to fight Indigenous peoples in their bid for gold, later building his roadhouse at what became known as Boothroyd's, near today's Boothroyd Indian Reserve.

But it was American Mortimer Cook who perhaps provides the best example of this forgotten history between B.C. and Washington State.

Like many other gold seekers to B.C., Cook had previously fought in the American war with Mexico before travelling to the California gold rush in 1849, where he partnered with John Warner. These two subsequently heeded the call of the Fraser River gold excitement.

By 1861, Cook and Warner built Cook's Ferry, one of the first crossings of the Thompson River at today's Spences Bridge — named after road builder Thomas Spence, also a veteran of a filibustering raid into Mexico.

During the time of the "Cook's Ferry" community, Warner apparently married a member of the Cook's Ferry band of the Nlaka'pamux Nation possibly named Ellen Thompson, and as the online *Skagit Valley Journal* notes, "she was rumored to be the daughter or sister of the chief of the tribe."

On this side of the forty-ninth parallel, the name of Mortimer Cook is known for building the ferry across the Thompson River, but it was certainly news to me to discover more from sources south of the border.

Ten years after the establishment of Cook's Ferry, he went on to construct another ferry — and then a toll bridge — near Topeka, Kansas. From there, Cook established one of the first gold banks in Santa Barbara, California, becoming mayor on two separate occasions in the 1870s. Cook amassed significant wealth but lost his banking fortune in about 1878, and ultimately returned to Washington State, where he founded the old town and logging community of Sedro (known today as Sedro-Woolley).

Why do we in British Columbia know nothing about Cook's later accomplishments or the fact that he was responsible for founding two different communities on either side of the border?

Bridge built by Thomas Spence at the original location of Cook's Ferry.

Never did I imagine that there was such a link to this side of the border, nor to today's Cook's Ferry Indian Band.

During those early years, the forty-ninth parallel wasn't much of a dividing line, but national myths on both sides ignore these early linkages. Put quite simply, these north-south connections didn't fit the new Canadian national narrative.

We can't just blame Ottawa. More often than not, historians of British Columbia have denied the role of the American presence in shaping our social, political and economic life.

It seems to me that the north-south orientation of B.C. was part of a larger Pacific Slope puzzle, a piece that has never properly fit the stories we tell ourselves.

In the meantime, I suspect there's yet more historical evidence waiting to be found south of the border to explain these seemingly anomalous place names in British Columbia.

Must be time for another road trip.

B.C., Latin America and the Monroe Doctrine

How close did British Columbia come to U.S. annexation? Closer than you think.

In 2019, Venezuelan President Nicolas Maduro accused the United States of plotting a coup against him. Regardless of how accurate or justified that may have been, some pundits openly wondered whether the Monroe Doctrine was about to be dusted off.

What is the Monroe Doctrine? During the nineteenth century, President James Monroe asserted a U.S. protectorate over the entire western hemisphere. This policy declared that any involvement by European nations in North, Central and South American countries would be viewed as "the manifestation of an unfriendly disposition toward the United States."

Subsequent presidents such as Ulysses S. Grant, Theodore Roosevelt, John F. Kennedy and Ronald Reagan maintained this position and their perceived right to be involved in the affairs of their "backyard."

Latin American countries were not the only ones potentially affected by the United States' imperial gaze. In fact, during the mid-nineteenth century, both British Columbia and Nicaragua became preoccupied with the threat of potential annexation, which was being encouraged by two American agitators with a shared history of urging United States expansion.

William Walker

Those two agitators had another, very different, shared history — for a time, they were co-editors of the *San Francisco Herald* newspaper.

They were John Nugent and General William Walker, the notorious filibusterer who led militias in the takeover of Nicaragua. During the 1858 gold rush, President James Buchanan appointed Nugent as special U.S. Agent to the Fraser River to assert and protect American interests.

Nugent's appointment was feared by many as indicative of possible American intentions to annex British Columbia, especially when he invoked the United States' Nicaragua Policy with regard to "protecting" American citizens in B.C.

Nugent argued that Americans had been denied proper justice and that the Hudson's Bay Company (HBC) had been supplying their Indigenous allies with weapons to protect against the incursion of American gold seekers.

The close association of the HBC with their longstanding Indigenous trade allies was always suspect in the eyes of many Americans steeped in the notion of manifest destiny.

Nugent's unpublished orders from U.S. secretary of state Lewis Cass expressed great interest in the gold deposits of the Fraser River. The feeling in California was "that Uncle Sam sadly blundered when he yielded Lewis Cass' ultimatum of '54° 40'."

John Nugent

Cass, who had urged the annexation of Texas and the whole of the Oregon Territory, as well as the occupation of Mexico, advised Nugent accordingly: "The President desires to be accurately informed with respect both to the locality and extent of these discoveries, the mode in which they are improved ... the quality of the gold discovered ... means of access to the gold region ... and generally all information on that subject of a reliable character."

Nugent's appointment was greeted by the *San Francisco Bulletin* with total disdain. "That he will permit the occasion of his official career to pass without getting Brother Jonathan into a collision with John Bull, is hardly possible."

"Americans and Englishmen cannot mix," asserted a letter writer to the *Bulletin*, "and but little will be needed there on Frazer river to provoke a crisis — a sort of independent California fight which will involve the two nations, even if the British cruisers on the other side do not."

With the discovery of Fraser River gold, friction between British and American navy ships commenced off the coasts of Cuba, Nicaragua, Costa Rica and Panama.

In the summer and fall of 1858, the British Navy took it upon itself to haul over U.S. vessels and search them for both slaves (having outlawed slavery) and American filibusters.

American officials were incensed with what they regarded as the highhanded practices of the British government, patrolling the American hemisphere to prohibit the trade in slaves.

One agitated American looked forward to the day when miners bound for the Fraser River "might become the conquerors of Vancouver Island," believing that his fellow citizens would "thunder a welcome to the new State of Vancouver."

If anything, the British naval decision to conduct a right of search aboard American vessels served to fuel the filibustering mood among American communities along the Pacific Slope. An even greater provocation came later, with British plans to support the Nicaraguan and Costa Rican governments against the filibustering raids of General William Walker.

Though Britain was about to relinquish its territorial claim to the Mosquito Protectorate, their departure was forestalled by the discovery of gold on the Fraser River. The Central American routes gained more importance to British interests with the creation of the Crown Colony of British Columbia.

As the American minister to Britain, G.M. Dallas, hypothesized to Lewis Cass, "The discovery of the golden sands in Frazer River, leading to the creation of the new colony of British Columbia, has increased the solicitude of Isthmian routes of transit."

With the goldfields of the Fraser River seemingly offering untold riches beyond those of California, British interests required a strong presence in Central America. With the appointment of John Nugent, the actions of the Royal Navy off Nicaragua sent a strong message: regardless of the self-serving pretensions of the Monroe Doctrine, whether in Nicaragua or potentially in British Columbia, filibustering would be met with strong opposition.

James McIntosh, the commander-in-chief of the U.S. Home Squadron, felt that the inspection of his ships by a foreign power was an invasion of national sovereignty. Writing aboard the flagship USS *Roanoke*, off the coast of San Juan del Norte, Nicaragua, McIntosh informed the secretary of the U.S. Navy, Isaac Toucey:

> It looks like a renewal of the scenes which lately occurred
> around the Island of Cuba, changed only to filibusters
> for Africans. You may rely on my taking prompt and
> efficient measures to protect the honor of our flag should
> it become necessary; and, if really her Britannic Majesty's
> officers have instructions to board and examine American
> merchant ships for filibusters, under the very guns of the
> ships of my squadron, the time must be very short before
> the most serious consequences may be anticipated.

McIntosh was of the opinion that the British Navy had abrogated the terms of the Clayton-Bulwer Convention, agreed to by both countries, which stipulated that "neither will ever erect or maintain any fortifications commanding the same, or in the vicinity thereof, or occupy, or fortify, or colonize, or assume or exercise any Dominion over Nicaragua, Costa Rica, the Mosquito Coast, or any part of Central America."

Yet the American commander was to have a frank discussion with a British officer who "distinctly declared that England had never abandoned the protectorate."

Fraser River gold had undoubtedly delayed Britain's departure.

General M.M. McCarver, a member of the California legislature, gave as his considered opinion that the discovery of gold on the Fraser River "on the line which divides the territory of two of the most powerful nations on earth ... may be the means of producing blood as well as gold."

There were reports as far away as England that Walker himself might have "possible intentions in British Columbia on the part of the Americans — with or without direct support from their Gov't."

As it was, the determined stance of the Royal Navy off the coasts of both B.C. and Nicaragua thwarted American ambitions. With Cass's

Nicaraguan directive being applied to the colonies of Vancouver Island and of British Columbia, little wonder that Britain reinforced its presence in Central America.

Luckily for Governor James Douglas, Nugent determined that the richness and extent of British Columbia gold was limited and did not warrant the continued influx of American miners. Had it been otherwise, American policy may have favoured annexation.

Nugent concluded:

> The Americans, it is true, were in sufficient force any time within the first six months to make successful any movement on their part towards the seizure of the colonies ... It is true that, in all probability, both will eventually cease to be under European control.

> Their ultimate accession to the American possessions on the Pacific coast is scarcely problematical — but in the meantime their intrinsic value either of locality, soil, climate, or productions, does not warrant any effort on the part of the American government or the American people towards their immediate acquisition.

British Columbia escaped a possible American takeover, but in the twenty-first century the Monroe Doctrine still hasn't entirely disappeared into history.

"Dead Broke, a Borrowed Coat and Six Squashed Pies"

How a Fraser gold seeker became the foremost economic thinker of his time.

I REMEMBER THE FIRST TIME I had a good look at the fabled Golden Gate Bridge.

It was the mid-1980s; fortune had struck when a friend invited me to spend the summer in California. There we were, on the beach below the historic Presidio in an immense crowd of San Franciscans celebrating the fiftieth anniversary of that hugely symbolic bridge — a gateway marking the entrance to a harbour jam-packed with gold rush history.

Just off the beach, legendary crooner Tony Bennett was singing "I Left My Heart in San Francisco," and the warm blue sky belied Mark Twain's observation that the coldest winter he ever experienced was the summer he spent in San Francisco.

That gorgeous long summer was my chance to explore firsthand the historic connection between British Columbia and the Golden State. Wandering around old San Francisco felt familiar — after all, the 1850s iron-façade buildings on Wharf Street in Victoria were manufactured in California.

View of San Francisco, formerly Yerba Buena, in 1846–7.

My mission was to locate two historic markers. One was the site of the Hudson's Bay Company's (HBC) California headquarters established in 1841, when San Francisco was still known as Yerba Buena and was not part of the United States.

But more particularly, I wanted to find a well-known hotel that once existed about four hundred feet away from the HBC store, a hotel established in 1852 with the city's first public library and reading room, known as the "What Cheer House."

Standing on the former site of the hotel that day I wondered just how many gold seekers must have stayed here? Who would have read in this first library during the time of the Fraser River exodus (the third greatest mass migration of gold seekers in human history)?

Here is the singular story of one such would-be miner, Henry George, subsequently "the most popular American economic thinker of the 19th century" — a populist before populism had a name. The word *populism* — coined in 1890 — meant opposition to a monopoly on wealth held by businessmen and bankers, and this is a rags-to-riches story of the gold rush of a very different sort!

Henry George

A young eighteen-year-old typesetter, Henry George travelled from Pennsylvania via the Strait of Magellan aboard the USS *Shubrick*. He arrived in California in late May of 1858 after a journey of 155 days and just as the Fraser River excitement was peaking.

About an hour after the *Shubrick* anchored, the ship was visited by Henry George's cousin, James George, a bookkeeper for the retail clothing firm of J.M. Strowbridge and Company, who had already travelled to California. Work prospects for young Henry were in rather short supply, and with increasing news of the Fraser gold excitement, he had made his decision to travel north and seek his fortune.

Henry's son, Henry George Jr. (later a member of the U.S. House of Representatives from New York), wrote a biography of his famous father entitled *The Life of Henry George* (1900), in which he described that decision.

> For in June [1858] had come the thrilling news of large gold discoveries just over the American line, in the British possessions, on the Frazer River, not far from its mouth. There was much excitement in San Francisco, especially among that multitude of prospectors and adventurers, who, finding all the then known placer lands in California worked out, or appropriated, and not willing to turn to the slow pursuits of agriculture, had gathered in the city with nothing to do. A mad scramble for the new fields ensued, and so great was the rush from this and other parts that fifty thousand persons are said to have poured into the Frazer River region within the space of a few weeks. Indeed, all who did not have profitable or promising employment tried to get away, and the Shubrick's log shows that most of her officers and crew deserted for the gold fields.

Though Henry's cousin had been doing well with the clothing house, like thousands of others he got swept up by the Fraser Fever and "thought

"Ho! For Frazier River," illustration by J. Ross Browne from "A Peep at Washoe" in *Harper's Monthly Magazine*, December 1860.

he saw a chance for a fortune in the sale of miner's supplies," entering into partnership to establish a store in Victoria.

In Henry's case the proposed plan was for him to head to the Fraser goldfields and in the event mining prospects fell short, his cousin promised employment as a clerk in the new Victoria-based store.

"Henry George's hopes burned high," recorded his son, and Henry wrote home to Philadelphia on August 15, 1858, of his "golden expectations," which were met with dismay by his mother.

I think this money-making is attended with too many sacrifices. I wished it all in the bottom of the sea when I heard of your going to Victoria, but since it had been explained to me I feel better ... I shall never feel comfortable until you are settled down quietly at some permanent business. This making haste to grow rich is attended with snares and temptations and a great weariness of the flesh. It is not the whole of life, this getting of gold. When you write explain about the place and how you are situated. Then we will look on the bright side.

Henry George sailed through the Golden Gate and out of San Francisco, employed as a seaman aboard "a topsail schooner," landing in Victoria at the height of the rush north. The old HBC fort "suddenly swelled in population, until it was estimated that at times ten thousand miners, in sheds and tents, gathered about the more substantial structures."

But George's arrival at Victoria was the most inauspicious time to continue towards the goldfields, as the "melting snows on its great mountain water-sheds swelled high its volume, came tearing down its long, twisting course and rushed through its rocky gorges like a roaring flood of destruction, earning the name sometimes given it — 'The Terrible Frazer.'"

The goldfields had come to a standstill, thousands of gold seekers left waiting for the river to drop before mining operations could resume. So George subsequently found employment in his cousin's newly established miner's emporium on Wharf Street.

The store was apparently a one-storey rough wooden structure with a makeshift loft situated beside the "Victoria Hotel" and facing the Inner Harbour. Henry George worked very hard there, sleeping in the loft during these tumultuous times. "He fastened a note outside the street door inviting customers who came out of the regular hours to 'Please give this door a kick.'"

In a letter to his sister, December 6, 1858, he described further the conditions. "You innocently ask whether I made my own bed at Victoria. Why, bless you, my dear little sister! I had none to make. Part of the time I slept rolled up in my blanket on the counter, or on a pile of flour, and afterwards I had a straw mattress on some boards. The only difference between my sleeping and waking costumes was that during the day I wore both boots and cap, and at night dispensed with them."

After some months of hard toil it appears that George had enough of the place. He left his cousin's shop to go live in a tent with fellow San Franciscan George Wilbur, who was determined to make a second attempt in the Fraser goldfields, "but before they could set off they were daunted by stories of failure that returning miners were bringing down." The lure of gold had tarnished and they abandoned the project.

George's "golden expectations" were now dashed, and without employment he decided to return to San Francisco, borrowing passage money from George Wilbur and others. He was truly destitute, as described by Wilbur.

> He had no coat; so I gave him mine. An old fellow named Wolff peddled pies among the tents, and thinking that Harry would enjoy these more than the food he would get aboard the ship, we bought six of them, and as he had no trunk, we put them in his bunk, and drew a blanket over them so that nobody would see them and steal them. He wrote me from San Francisco when he got down that first night out he was so tired that he threw himself down on his bunk without undressing, and that he did not think of the pies until the morning, when he found that he had been lying on top of them all night.

George had left Victoria "dead broke" along with a borrowed coat and six squashed pies. It seems his northern adventure had not amounted to anything but for some key facts. "Arriving in Victoria in August 1858, Henry George observed conditions which formed the genesis of his economic theories that would garner worldwide acclaim."

Having returned to California, his own economic conditions, while improving, were a mixed bag — he was even reduced to begging at one point in the 1860s — but for two key developments.

First, his experience as a typesetter landed him a job and started his career in newspapers and as a writer. Second, George's income now provided the kind of lodgings beyond the tent or shack he had inhabited in Victoria.

The next letter home to his sister announced his sense of prosperity after the hardship endured in British Columbia: "I am boarding now, and have been for the past two weeks in the 'What Cheer House,' the largest, if not the finest, hotel in the place. I pay $9 per week and have a beautiful

What Cheer House advertisement published by Lawrence and Housewoorth, 1866.

little room and first rate living. I get $16 per week the way I am working now, but will soon strike into something that will pay me better."

The What Cheer House advertised not only "an extensive library of choice works," but that "To be a man in the world" one must observe that "Economy is the only sure Road to Wealth."

Apparently, the What Cheer House had several hundreds of books in its library, including some economic works such as Adam Smith's *Wealth of Nations*. George's "solid reading was begun in this little library." In fact, when George continued to be down on his luck, he "spent much of his time when out of work in that little room and that he had read most of the books."

George made good use of this library even while experiencing rather desperate poverty at times. By 1865 he had become a journalist and founded the *San Francisco Daily Evening Post*, where he became a critic "of speculation in public lands, the illegal actions of monopolies, and the exploitation of new Chinese immigrants in California." He proposed economic reforms, public ownership of utilities that included such industries as railroads and the telegraph system and popularized the "single-tax" reform movement, though he never embraced the ideology of socialism.

His major work was *Progress and Poverty* (1879), which he infused with his strong moral passion for justice and his hatred of poverty, like he had experienced in British Columbia. It was George's first book and sold several million copies during the 1890s, exceeding all other books sold in the United States except for the Bible. In this volume, George stated of the nineteenth-century gold rushes:

> There is no mystery as to the cause which so suddenly and so largely raised wages in California in 1849, and Australia in 1852. It was the discovery of placer mines in unappropriated land to which labour was free that raised the wages of cooks in San Francisco restaurants to $500 a month, and left ships to rot in the harbour without officers or crew until their owners would consent to pay rates that in any other part of the globe seemed fabulous. Had these mines been on appropriated land, or had they been immediately monopolised so that rent could have arisen, it would have been land values that would have leaped upward, not wages.

Progress and Poverty has been described as "a treatise on the questions of why poverty accompanies economic and technological progress and why economies exhibit a tendency toward cyclical boom and bust."

"We see it all over the world," stated George in *Progress and Poverty*, "in the countries where land is high, wages are low, and where land is low, wages are high. In a new country the value of labour is at first at its maximum, the value of land at its minimum. As population grows and land becomes monopolised and increases in value, the value of labour steadily decreases."

Less well known was the inspiration for these social and economic theories: George's experience as a gold seeker in the Fraser River excitement of 1858. More than thirty years after his time in Victoria, George gave a speech in San Francisco (February 4, 1890) that traced "the genesis of his thought on social questions."

"I came out here at an early age, and knew nothing whatever of political economy," stated George. "I had never intently thought upon any social problem. One of the first times I recollect talking on such a subject was one day, when I was about eighteen, after I had come to this country, while sitting on the deck of a topsail schooner with a lot of miners on the way to the Frazer River."

George continued:

> I remember, after coming down from the Frazer River country, sitting one New year's night in the gallery of the old American theatre — among the gods — when a new drop curtain fell, and we all sprang to our feet, for on that curtain was painted what was then a dream of the far future — the overland train coming into San Francisco; and after we had shouted ourselves hoarse, I began to think what good is it going to be to men like me — to those who have nothing but their labour? I saw that thought grow and grow. We were all — all of us, rich and poor — hoping for the development of California, proud of her future greatness, looking forward to the time when San Francisco would be one of the great capitals of the world; looking forward to the time when this great empire of the west would count her population by millions. And underneath it all came to me what that miner on the topsail schooner going up to Frazer River had said: "As the country grows, as people come in, wages will go down."

It is said that during his lifetime, George became the third most famous person in America, behind Thomas Edison and Mark Twain. He was one of the most important voices of the Progressive Era; his supporters included Leo Tolstoy, Albert Einstein, Winston Churchill and John Dewey. The ideology of "Georgism" dominated the social and economic thinking of the day — and many of his insights seem prophetic today. About 150 years ago, George spoke of a rising populism that had swept the country:

> The most ominous political sign in the United States today is the growth of a sentiment which either doubts the existence of an honest man in public office or looks on him as a fool for not seizing his opportunities. That is to say, the people themselves are becoming corrupted.

Thus, in the United States today is republican government running the course it must inevitably follow under conditions which cause the unequal distribution of wealth. Where that course leads is clear to whoever will think. As corruption becomes chronic; as public spirit is lost; as traditions of honor, virtue, and patriotism are weakened; as law is brought into contempt and reforms become hopeless; then in the festering mass will be generated volcanic forces, which shatter and rend when seeming accident gives them vent. Strong, unscrupulous men, rising up upon occasion, will become the exponents of blind popular desires or fierce popular passions, and dash aside forms that have lost their vitality. The sword will again be mightier than the pen, and in carnivals of destruction brute force and wild frenzy will alternate with the lethargy of a declining civilization.

The prediction is all the more remarkable, considering its foundations came from a young lad who had experienced the chaotic, frenzied Fraser River excitement of 1858 firsthand, followed by an informal education in the What Cheer House hotel. Clearly, this is a very different sort of rags-to-riches story! And more to the point, this is a story that once again places British Columbia's early history — before the coming of transcontinental railways — squarely within the north-south world of the expansive Californian mining frontier.

B.C. AND THE CALIFORNIA "BONANZA KINGS"

How Cariboo Gold launched the richest men in the world.

The Bullion Mine, Virginia City, Nevada, c. 1875-77.

I REMEMBER TRAVELLING YEARS AGO into the sublime landscape of the Comstock Lode country of Nevada, anticipating my soon-to-be quenched thirst — for a drink, but also for history. This had been the nineteenth century's "Silicon Valley" — a place so rich in silver it made some of the wealthiest entrepreneurs of their day — the legendary Bonanza Kings of California.

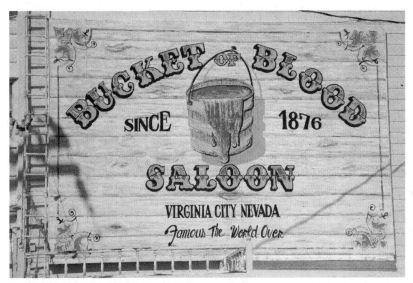

The Bucket of Blood Saloon, Virginia City, Nevada.

Rolling past the ruins and passing Boot Hill cemetery, we made our way to an old saloon in historic Virginia City — a quite wonderfully preserved gold, or more accurately, silver rush town — a boomtown that sprung up shortly after the Fraser River gold rush of 1858.

So many who flooded into British Columbia during the Fraser and Cariboo gold rushes made their next stake in Nevada's White Pine District in the 1860s. Samuel Clemens had lived here for a time; in fact, in Virginia City he adopted his more famous nom de plume, Mark Twain.

"What saloon should we go to next?" I asked my colleague Alan. We both felt a bit parched, having just come from the Western Historical Association conference in Reno. "That one!" He pointed to the other side of Main Street, and so we crossed, imagining the thousands of miners who had frequented this once bustling town. We now entered the oldest watering hole of this legendary city — the rather ominously named Bucket of Blood Saloon.

Mark Twain once wrote, "To be a saloon-keeper and kill a man was to be illustrious" — indeed, the wild west! Before us was a long wooden bar, old slot machines spinning and pints frothing, surrounded by a land drenched in hard-rock mining history. What an immense place to contemplate the past, and the amazing transitory, transboundary mining societies that once ranged from California to Australia to British Columbia, and subsequently to such places as Nevada and beyond.

I have always been fascinated by the stories of my ancestors who chased "the golden butterfly" to California in 1849 and then to the Fraser River goldfields in 1858 — part of a natural north-south world that continued well into the early twentieth century; that is, before the reorienting effects of the transcontinental national dream (yes, Sir John A. Macdonald's vision) shapeshifted B.C. into the east-west alignment of the new Canadian state.

Meanwhile, my friend had heaped his own small fortune atop the bar. "Another round?" he asked, winking at me. Alan was feeling quite flush, having "broke the bank" at the previous saloon on a gigantic one-armed bandit. I remember the rush of coins spilling out, accompanied by the theme of the TV series *Bonanza* (which starred Canadian Lorne Greene as the iconic Pa Cartwright).

Second pint in hand, I was soon back in the nineteenth century, thinking about these roving miners and the rags-to-riches stories that were all too frequent in the chaotic and often lawless days of the California mining frontier.

So many who had joined the Fraser and Cariboo rushes were subsequently found south of the border in mining towns throughout the American West, taking with them substantial amounts of B.C. gold that, in many instances, financed later and even greater bonanzas — defined as "exceptionally large and rich mineral deposits" or as time went on, "events that create a sudden increase in wealth, good fortune, or profits."

Here is one such intriguing bonanza story.

Written under the title of "A Thing not Generally Known" in Victoria's *British Colonist* newspaper, February 6, 1878, the story told of a Cariboo gold miner Jim Wade, "a thrifty, good-natured Irishman, who had made $50,000 or $60,000, by mining and packing at Cariboo, and had visited San Francisco to see the 'sights' and invest his money." For perspective, sixty thousand in 1860s dollars is roughly equivalent to one million dollars today.

In other words, Jim Wade had struck it rich.

Upon his return to San Francisco, one of the first things he did was to visit his old friends and fellow Irishmen James Flood and William O'Brien, who ran a saloon called the Auction Lunch in the financial district on Washington Street. Apparently Flood and O'Brien had moved their saloon on three different occasions, each time closer to the California stock exchange. Their eatery had become a favourite among stock brokers and mining developers who, while having a few drinks, would offer tips to the barkeeps, who began to invest the little money they had in the new Comstock Lode of Nevada.

It takes money, of course, to make money. So, with the arrival of Jim Wade (and his wallet), the two barkeeps hatched a plan: borrow some of their old friend's newfound wealth and take advantage of a particularly hot tip. The *Colonist* reported: "From this man Flood & O'Brien borrowed $35,000 and invested the amount in a low priced stock on which they had obtained 'points' from the operators . . . The stock rose steadily from $2 to $3 dollars a share until it touched an almost fabulous figure and then the fortunate Bonanza kings sold out and realized a cool $500,000 apiece. This transaction laid the foundation of the fortunes of these men."

There were in fact four such Bonanza Kings. Flood and O'Brien, the saloon keepers, had formed an association with two experienced Comstock Lode miners: James Graham Fair, a mine superintendent; and John William Mackay, a mining engineer. Consolidating their interests, these four in short order "accumulated $200,000,000, own two banks, the best

San Francisco Exchange Building on the corner of Battery and Washington Streets, c. 1856.

business real estate in San Francisco, and five of the principal mines on the Comstock Lode, and rule the San Francisco stock market."

It was further reported in the *Colonist* that "'no dog dare bark on California Street', without the permission of Flood & O'Brien." All set in motion by Cariboo gold! The *Colonist* declared with this remarkable turn of events: "A thing generally not known is that on the basis of gold dug from our Cariboo mines has been reared the colossal fortunes of Flood, O'Brien, Mackay and Fair — the Bonanza kings — probably the four richest men, viewed by their present and prospective wealth, in the wide world."

David W. Higgins, one-time editor and owner of the *British Colonist*, former owner of the *San Francisco Call* newspaper (and Speaker of the B.C. legislature) expanded further the story of how Cariboo gold created these Bonanza Kings. In his book *The Passing of a Race and More Tales of Western Life* (1905), Higgins wrote of learning the tale of Jim Wade's gold from Thomas B. Lewis, a native of Virginia, "and a heavy loser by the failure of the Harrison-Lillooet route" that had been backed by the B.C. colonial government as an alternative transportation corridor to the arduous Fraser Canyon route.

After Lewis's financial misfortune in B.C., he returned south of the border and found employment behind a saloon bar:

> He had known Flood and O'Brien when they kept the Auction Lunch, a "bit" grogshop near the waterfront at San Francisco. He told me that, while tending bar one day, the partners overheard two brokers, who had dropped in for a beer and a lunch, discussing in a confidential tone a plan for advancing to $100 the price of shares in a certain Washoe mine. A few days before, a packer, named Jem Wade, had arrived from Cariboo with $65,000 in gold. This sum he deposited in Flood & O'Brien's safe. "If only we had a few thousand dollars," quoth Flood to O'Brien, "we could make a fortune."
>
> "Let's ask Wade to lend us his gold for a few days," suggested O'Brien. The idea was acted upon. Wade was asked, and, being an old friend, he consented, and the stock in the mine was secured with Wade's money. Before the firm sold out, the stock rose to nearly a thousand dollars a share.

The shares, having been bought on a margin, the liquor dealers realized nearly a million dollars from the investment of $65,000 of Cariboo gold. The next day the Auction lunchrooms were offered for sale, and in the course of a few weeks Flood bought a seat on the stock exchange and became one of the most important men on the board.

Indeed, all four of these Bonanza Kings made huge, fast wealth. For three years after the discovery of the "big bonanza," their mines produced three million dollars per month. Over twenty-two years of operation, they yielded more than $150 million in silver and gold. Former saloon keeper James Clair Flood had particular success, ultimately becoming the president of the Bank of Nevada, based in San Francisco.

James Clair Flood

An article entitled "How a Poor Lad became one of the great Money Kings," in the February 22, 1889 edition of the *Daily Alta California*, states that Flood had first travelled to California during the 1849 gold rush and mined on the Yuba River before entering the liquor trade.

Linden Towers, mansion of James Clair Flood, Menlo Park, California, c. 1880.

However, his rags-to-riches story came not from the hard work of sluicing for gold dust — or even serving booze behind a bar — but from being a savvy stock manipulator.

Flood was considered one of the one hundred wealthiest Americans of his day, amassing an enormous fortune, and is still known today for having built two great mansions: the James C. Flood Mansion at 1000 California Street in San Francisco; and the incredible Linden Towers in Menlo Park that stood until 1936.

The impact of Jim Wade's Cariboo gold went well beyond the wealth (and mansions) of James Flood. Along with the former '49er's increased power and wealth came a fight for financial dominance against rival W.C. Ralston, head of the Bank of California.

David Higgins relates:

> One of the pursers on the Nicaraguan line of steamships was W.C. Ralston. He made a lucky turn in stocks, and went on the [stock exchange] board about the same time that Flood made his appearance there. They made heaps of money, and for a long time pulled together. But the day came when Ralston, who meanwhile had become cashier of the Bank of California, was "short" on one of the Comstock stocks. Knowing that Flood had a great many shares in the company, he sent for him, and asked him to lend him a sufficient number to make up the deficiency. Flood, who had long secretly disliked Ralston, and now saw an opportunity of "downing" him, refused to grant his request. Ralston flew into a towering passion, and in his rage exclaimed: "Look here, Flood, I'll send you back to sell liquor at a 'bit' a glass."
>
> "If you do," retorted Flood, "I'll sell it over the counter of the Bank of California."

Apparently, Ralston (portrayed by Ronald Reagan in a 1965 episode of *Death Valley Days* called "Raid on the San Francisco Mint") covered up for many months that he had massively overdrawn his account at the bank, in excess of some four million dollars — again, a truly staggering amount of money at the time. Ultimately, he was given twenty-four hours to make good on the debt.

Higgins recorded what happened next:

> He left the bank and went straight to a place where he was accustomed to take a salt-water plunge daily. He disrobed and put on a pair of trunks, all the time conversing and joking with the attendants and a few friends whom he met on the bathing-float. Then he entered the water and swam about two hundred feet from the shore. No one appeared to take much interest in his movements. Certainly not a soul thought for a moment that the good-natured, jovial man who had left the bathing-house a few moments before with a smile and a joke on his lips, was about to dive into the great sea of eternity that circles the world about, and would be seen no more of men ... That was the last ever seen alive of the banker and broker who for so long a time had controlled the financial interests of San Francisco. A few minutes later he was observed to be floating with the tide, helpless, his face downward, his body partially submerged.

Ralston was dead, seemingly having died by suicide and abetted by James Flood's refusal to bail him out. The story is even more remarkable, considering this chain of events was set in play by wealth taken from the Cariboo goldfields.

W.C. Ralston

Mark Twain jested in his famous work *Roughing It* that "The cheapest and easiest way to become an influential man and be looked up to by the community at large, was to stand behind a bar, wear a cluster-diamond pin, and sell whisky." Perhaps Twain had James Flood in mind, as "no great movement could succeed without the countenance and direction of the saloon-keepers." This classic rags-to-riches story of '49er James Flood is indeed about the so-called Californian Dream.

And what became of British Columbia miner Jim Wade? Once again, the *British Colonist* provides the clue. Apparently as of 1878 he was living on a ranch in southern California "prosperous and happy" — but talked "of revisiting the Cariboo during the coming summer to try and make a new strike and, perhaps, create a few more Bonanza kings."

And this makes me wonder — just how many others must have slipped across the forty-ninth parallel with their own quiet bonanzas in past times? It seems to me that we will never fully know.

FIVE: CANADA ON THE PACIFIC SLOPE

CANADA'S WESTWARD EXPANSION TO THE PACIFIC SLOPE

B.C., Rupert's Land and the Terms of Union

How did we get here?

Just how did B.C. and Rupert's Land come to be part of a Canada?

The Colony of British Columbia joined Canada in 1871, but Canadian designs to include B.C. into the coast-to-coast federation began years earlier — particularly with the Fraser River gold rush of 1858.

Access to the Pacific Ocean was the driving force of federal ambitions to compete with the United States. Canada's considerable knowledge of, and interest in, British Columbia is a point worth emphasizing. Many have advanced the argument that Canadian representatives negotiated the B.C. Terms of Union without full knowledge of the unique aspects of the colony's geography and policy developments — especially with regard to Indigenous lands management issues. From a historical perspective this view is largely incorrect.

It has also been contended that B.C.'s previous and longstanding position of not recognizing Indigenous title was not known. Therefore, it remains an unpaid debt and ongoing dispute.

On the contrary, Canada's knowledge of B.C. was quite substantial. There were many Canada–British Columbia connections that existed prior to 1871. Captain John Palliser explored west towards the Rocky Mountains (1858–60) in search of a practicable route to the Pacific Ocean that built on earlier explorations such as those of Simon Fraser (1808) and Alexander Mackenzie (1793). Then, Fraser River gold became an important impetus for a transcontinental British North America, the "all Red Route" that would ultimately span from coast to coast.

The Fraser rush was considered the third great mass migration in pursuit of gold, following the gold rushes in California and Australia. Not unlike the American government, the Canadian government was quick to learn all about the two Pacific coast colonies (Vancouver Island and British Columbia) as part of its larger plans for westward expansion.

American westward expansion had already begun, with its acquisition of Oregon and California. The need to link these states to the east by building a transcontinental railway was soon considered and eventually realized. In particular, the incredible mineral wealth of California was a great impetus for immediate U.S. expansion. If Canada were to compete with the U.S., it would also need to expand westward and acquire further lands for colonization, settlement, markets and resources — and perhaps most importantly, access to the Pacific Ocean.

This necessitated union with British Columbia. Without B.C. there would not be a Canadian equivalent to the American transcontinental nation.

As the historian E.E. Rich concluded, "the discovery of gold on the Fraser ... made the British and Canadian governments alike more aware of the importance of preserving the route across the prairies" to link with the Pacific Slope.

Englishman Kinahan Cornwallis in *The New El Dorado* (1858) gave glowing accounts of B.C. in 1858 and concluded, "as to the probability of a railway being constructed from Canada to some point in British Columbia ... there can be little doubt."

Alfred Waddington, a member of the Vancouver Island legislative assembly and author of *The Fraser Mines Vindicated* (1858), was one of the chief proponents of a transcontinental railway linking Canada with the Pacific coast. But in 1857, at approximately the same time gold discoveries were announced on the West Coast, a select committee of the British House of Commons agreed in principle to Canada's "just and reasonable wishes" to annex the Hudson's Bay Company (HBC) lands or the northwestern territories comprising Rupert's Land, the vast land drained by rivers flowing into Hudson's Bay, and further, the huge contiguous HBC fur-trading districts that reached all the way to the Rocky Mountains.

This acknowledgement of Canada's claim to the territory west of the Great Lakes heightened aspirations for westward expansion. Gold was discovered in the Fraser River that same year and practical notions of a transcontinental state began to take shape.

The Fraser gold rush drew many notable Canadians to British Columbia, including future B.C. premiers George Anthony Walkem, Robert Beaven, John Robson and Amor De Cosmos. Equally important, early migrants such as Walkem and Robson acted as political informants to prime ministers John A. Macdonald (Conservative) and Alexander Mackenzie (Liberal).

In the same year that Captain Palliser reached Fort Victoria, a number of Canadian-sponsored business enterprises sprung up, intending to profit from a new transcontinental connection. For example, the Canada Agency Association Limited proposed it be made sole agent for the sale of Crown lands on Vancouver Island and in British Columbia.

The issue of harmonizing currencies was discussed by the British Colonial Office, "the wisest course to be adopted in the case of the currency of British Columbia will be to assimilate it to that of Canada." The British War Office acknowledged a letter from the Governor of Canada that a volunteer calvary corps in Upper Canada solicited "permission to raise a force of one hundred men for service in British Columbia."

They were by no means alone. The North West Navigation and Railway Company of Canada offered to run a postal service across the continent. Lord Carnarvon saw the "great political advantages" of this scheme, which would "probably go far to facilitate the erection of colonies, the development of natural resources & the consolidation of B.N. America as part of the Empire."

Arthur Blackwood, senior clerk in the North American department of the Colonial Office, believed that a transcontinental route was an invaluable asset if relations between the United States and Britain worsened in Central America. "If a war should break out with the U. States interrupting our maritime communication with V.C. Isl[an]d & B. Columbia we have the consolation of knowing that we can still fall back upon this overland route."

Clearly, from the Canadian perspective, B.C. was not the *terra incognito* claimed by later federal governments.

British Columbia was encouraged by both the Canadian and imperial governments to join Confederation. The colony ultimately accepted, primarily for relief of its accumulated debts due to its extensive road-building program and for the additional incentive of a continent-wide railway system.

The federal government of Prime Minister John A. Macdonald met, if not exceeded, all of British Columbia's conditions for political union. Where there might be disagreement during negotiation, such matters were largely left unresolved in order to win B.C.'s acceptance of the final terms of the union.

In other words, Macdonald's government made a number of offers and concessions that effectively ignored difficult questions that might impede immediate political union. I want to explore the terms of the union in greater detail, specifically Article 7 (Canadian system of tariffs), Article 11 (the transcontinental railway), and Article 13 (federal responsibility for Indigenous peoples). Each article highlights Canada's strategy of delay to secure its main objective of access to the Pacific coast.

The Canadian system of tariffs was the most contentious issue, by far, that concerned members of the B.C. colonial legislature. With its introduction came huge losses to the agricultural interests of the new province.

The Colony of British Columbia's own tariff policy was favoured by many British Columbians, as it provided more protection for agricultural and business owners who feared being inundated by cheaper Californian imports. Extensive debate on this issue alone raised the policy of tariffs to equal, if not greater, status than the most scrutinized demands for the introduction of responsible government and a transcontinental rail link with Canada. Article 7 (tariffs) stated that the old B.C. tariff should "continue in force in British Columbia until the railway from the Pacific Coast and system of railways in Canada are connected unless the Legislature of British Columbia should sooner decide to accept the Tariff and Excise Laws of Canada."

Effectively, Article 7 postponed any decision on modified tariffs. Canadian negotiators realized the immediate introduction of their policy would seriously jeopardize B.C.'s entry into the union and Canada's expansionist ambitions. For Canada's immediate purposes, B.C. tariff policy, though at odds with the Canadian position, was allowed to stand. Harmonization would have to wait.

Governor Anthony Musgrave

In the case of Article 11, the Canadian government committed itself to the construction of a transcontinental rail link. Prior to Confederation, the people of Victoria had petitioned Governor Anthony Musgrave that Vancouver Island should not be left out of any future plans for a cross-country rail line. An eight-to-two vote of the colonial legislative council on February 10, 1871, reaffirmed the desire for some kind of Island connection with Canada.

And yet, in the same way that Article 7 left tariffs an open question, Article 11 did not specify the rail route through B.C., nor the location of a western terminus. The railway clause read in part, "The Government of the Dominion undertake to secure the commencement simultaneously, within two years from the date of Union, of the construction of a Railway from the Pacific towards the Rocky Mountains, and from such points as may be selected, east of the Rocky Mountains, towards the Pacific to connect the seaboard of British Columbia with the Railway system of Canada; and further, to secure the completion of such Railway within ten years from the date of Union."

As with the tariff clause, the terms of Article 11 were written so that final decisions on the divisive issue were effectively postponed. If the Canadian government had demanded that B.C. accept the Canadian tariff immediately, or set an exact location for a western terminus, it is unlikely that B.C.'s decision to join Canada would have occurred so quickly — if at all.

Article 11 allowed all regions of the "United Colony" (the separate colonies of Vancouver Island and of British Columbia had merged in 1866) to believe they were destined for commercial greatness as profits from railway surveys and ultimate construction were assured to each region by various representatives of Canada.

As a result, B.C. politicians divided into self-interested camps. Many potential rail corridors were projected in an elaborate federal survey program that seemed to have no end in sight. Through it all, the Canadian government exacerbated old divisions of "Island versus Mainland" that flared up over whether the western rail terminus would end at either Esquimalt or Burrard Inlet.

Obviously, Canada ultimately chose to bring the railway down the Fraser River. (Contrary to current historical thought, the Bute Inlet route favoured by Vancouver Island was deemed a practicable route — another great untold story, found in the next chapter, "The Battle of the Routes.")

"The Terms, the Full Terms, and nothing but the Terms" was the rallying cry as Islanders, in particular, rightly viewed that the B.C. Terms of Union had been breached by the Canadian government. Article 11 was ultimately a railway promise that fractured B.C.'s political landscape and fuelled the threat of secession.

Finally, consider Article 13 — federal responsibility for Indigenous peoples. Once again (!), the negotiators for the Dominion postponed any immediate harmonization of two distinctly different Indigenous lands management policies. Much like Article 7 established that B.C. could not dictate changes to the Canadian tariff structure, Article 13 enshrined a similar relinquishment of B.C.'s authority with respect to Indigenous peoples.

The British Columbia conception of Indigenous lands management was outlined by Joseph Trutch to Governor Anthony Musgrave on January 29, 1870, and conveyed to Lord Granville, secretary of state for the colonies, during the Confederation debates and negotiations with Canada.

> The Indians have, in fact, been held to be the special wards of the Crown, and in the exercise of this guardianship Government has, in all cases where it has been desirable for the interests of the Indians, set apart such portions of Crown lands as were deemed proportionate to, and amply sufficient for, the requirements of each tribe; and these Indian Reserves are held by Government, in trust, for the exclusive use and benefit of the Indians resident thereon.

> But the title of the Indians in the fee of the public lands, or any portion thereof, has never been acknowledged by Government, but, on the contrary, is distinctly denied. In no case has any special arrangement been made with any of the tribes of the Mainland for the extinction of their claims of possession; but these claims have been held to have been fully satisfied by securing to each tribe,

as the progress of the settlement of the country seemed
to require, the use of sufficient tracts of land for their wants
for agricultural and pastoral purposes.

Canadian Indigenous policy had, in certain instances, recognized a
form of Indigenous title. This was not the policy of British Columbia with
the exception of the "Fourteen Agreements" — or Fort Victoria Treaties
— concluded by James Douglas under the auspices of the Hudson's Bay
Company (HBC). The B.C. policy was established on the principle of continuous use and occupation, with Indigenous peoples confirmed in their
traditional village sites and "cultivated fields."

The grant of reserve acreage neither followed a general quota per cap-
ita allowance, nor endeavoured to relocate Indigenous peoples to larger
reserves outside traditional lands (as practiced in the United States and
Canada). Instead, the B.C. policy recognized the (perceived) needs of
Indigenous peoples while recognizing the larger practicalities of colonial
settlement — constrained by the relatively small amount of arable land,
approximately 3% of B.C.

With Canadian Indigenous policy, the amount of arable land was more
considerable, and reserves established east of the Rockies were greater in
size. Also, where Canada had concluded treaties, compensation was offered
and annual annuities paid. Indigenous title had not been recognized in all
cases by the Canadian government, but with Canada's westward expansion into Rupert's Land, the federal government began to apply a uniform
policy of compensation based on past usage. This appears to have been
largely a made-in-Canada policy. Neither imperial nor HBC practices had
been uniform, nor had the prior policies of the Dominion government.

At the time of the Fraser River gold rush Herman Merivale, permanent undersecretary of state for the colonies (responding to a missionary
who urged the necessity of treaties), wrote about the case of the Red River
Settlement:

> This letter alludes to one matter which is new to me ...
> I mean claims of the Indian tribes over portions of Lord
> Selkirk's land [Red River Settlement] & generally over
> the territories comprised in the [HBC] Charter — The
> Americans have always taken care to extinguish such
> rights however vague — We have never adopted any

very uniform system about them. I suppose the H.B.C. have never purchased from such claimants any of their land. And I fear (idle as such claims really are, when applied to vast regions of which only the smallest portion can ever be used for permanent settlement) that the pending discussion are not unlikely to raise a crop of them.

The question of imperial recognition of Indigenous title was further elaborated upon by Merivale — asserting typical English property notions of the time — with regard to the Red River territory.

In the old days no one ever thought of recognizing 'territorial rights' in Indians. Charles the second simply made over to the [Hudson's] Bay Company the freehold of the soil in their Charter territory. According therefore to English real property notions, the Indians had no 'territorial rights' within that territory at all … I think it might be pretty safely assumed, that no right of property would be admitted by the Crown as existing in mere nomadic hunting tribes over the wild land adjacent to the Red River Settlement. But that agricultural Indian settlements (if any exist) would be respected and that hunting grounds actually so used by the Indians would either be reserved to them or else compensation made.

In Canadian parliamentary debates, Indigenous title was noted in a joint address to the governor general (for transmission to Britain) that requested the transfer of Rupert's Land and the Northwestern Territories to Canada. Dated December 11, 1867, it stated "that upon the transference of the Territories in question to the Canadian Government, the claims of the Indian Tribes to compensation for lands required for the purposes of settlement, will be considered and settled in conformity with the equitable principles which have uniformly governed the British Crown in its dealings with Aborigines."

George-Étienne Cartier (Macdonald's Quebec lieutenant and de facto deputy prime minister) and William McDougall (representing the HBC) were subsequently appointed as delegates to participate in London-based negotiations with the imperial government for the transfer of these HBC

Sir George-Étienne Cartier

lands. In the final agreement negotiated between these three parties, no clear directive was made to the Canadian government that compensation of Indigenous claims was required.

As Merivale noted previously, Britain negotiated the Dominion's acquisition of Rupert's Land without making any explicit directive to extinguish Indigenous title. And in the case of Rupert's Land and the greater Northwest Territories, the imperial government negotiated and confirmed its future participation in Indigenous lands management decisions. Of Britain's authority in this regard, Cartier — on behalf of Canada — stated:

> His Lordship [Lord Granville] subsequently requested us to communicate to him any observations which we might desire to offer upon this reply of the Company, and upon certain counter proposals which it contained. We felt reluctant, as representatives of Canada, to engage in a controversy with the [Hudson's Bay] Company concerning matters of fact, as well as questions of law and policy, while the negotiations with them was being carried on by the Imperial Government in its own name and of its own authority.

Lord Granville viewed the Rupert's Land Order (which he personally negotiated) in a largely undefined way with regard to Indigenous peoples, and consistent with previous imperial policy. Welfare and protection of Indigenous peoples was guaranteed, but no explicit directive issued. Writing to the governor general of Canada, John Young, on April 10, 1869, Granville stated:

> I am sure that your Government will not forget the care which is due to those who must soon be exposed to new dangers, and, in the course of settlement, be dispossessed of the lands which they used to enjoy as their own, or be confined within unwontedly narrow limits.

This question had not escaped my notice while framing the proposals which I laid before the Canadian Delegates and the Governor of the Hudson's Bay Company. I did not, however, then allude to it, because I felt the difficulty of insisting on any definite conditions without the possibility of foreseeing the circumstances under which these conditions would be applied, and because it appeared to me wiser and more expedient to rely on the sense of duty and responsibility belonging to the Government and people of such a country as Canada.

With Canada's acceptance of the Rupert's Land transfer agreement it effectively adhered to Britain's direction and dropped any reference to Indigenous rights or compensation. The Canadian Parliament resolved "that upon transference of the territories in question to the Canadian government, it will be the duty of the Government to make adequate provision for the protection of the Indian tribes whose Interests and well-being are involved in the transfer."

Nonetheless, Canada subsequently ratified a treaty with the Chippewa and Swampy Cree Tribes, on August 3, 1871, at Lower Fort Garry (Manitoba), where compensation was paid "as a present of three dollars for each Indian man, woman and child belonging to the bands" and then further annual payments of fifteen dollars per family of five.

This was, it seems, the start of a uniform Canadian policy that — independent of clear imperial direction — advanced treaty payments to maintain peaceful relations.

While Lord Granville oversaw applications of Canadian Indigenous policy to what would become western Canada, he also used his influence to urge the Colony of British Columbia towards union. It is important to remember that Indigenous policies, whether in Canada or Rupert's Land, were at the forefront of Canadian politics during the British Columbia Confederation debates. In fact, the B.C. debates of union with Canada were approximately simultaneous with the transfer of Rupert's Land (1869), the creation of the Province of Manitoba (1870) and the Lower Fort Garry Treaty (1871).

Lord Granville subsequently wrote to the last governor of British Columbia, Anthony Musgrave, on August 14, 1869 (while the Rupert's Land negotiations were being finalized), that it was time for British Columbia to give fuller consideration to union with Canada.

> The question, therefore, presents itself whether this single Colony should be excluded from the great body politic which is thus forming itself. On this question the Colony itself does not appear to be unanimous. But as far as I can judge ... I should conjecture that the prevailing opinion was in favour of union. I have no hesitation in stating that such is also the opinion of Her Majesty's Government ... The constitutional connexion of Her Majesty's Government with the Colony of British Columbia is, as yet, closer than any other part of North America; and they are bound, on an occasion like the present, to give, for the consideration of the community and the guidance of Her Majesty's servants, a more unreserved expression of their wishes and judgement than might be elsewhere fitting . . . It will not escape you, that in acquainting you with the general views of the Government, I have avoided all matters of detail, on which the wishes of the people and the Legislature will of course be declared in due time.

> I think it necessary, however, to observe that the constitution of British Columbia will oblige the Governor to enter personally on many questions — as the condition of Indian tribes and the future position of Government servants, with which, in the case of a negotiation between two Responsible Governments, he would not be bound to concern himself.

The Granville letter contains a three important considerations. First, B.C. had not achieved responsible government and, therefore, the imperial government was required to act on their behalf in framing the Terms of Union with Canada, as Granville had done with Rupert's Land.

Second, with respect to "the conditions of the Indian tribes," Granville (in consultation with Governor Musgrave), played the central role as negotiator in lieu of the B.C. legislative council.

Third, the letter highlights Granville's acknowledgement that he was well acquainted with the B.C. dispatches that had reached him, and was obviously well apprised on British Columbia matters. This is worth stressing in that one of the dispatches detailed the conditions of Indigenous peoples in B.C. The memorandum prepared by Joseph Trutch was also included with this dispatch and stated that "the title of Indians in the fee of the public lands, or any portion thereof, has never been acknowledged by Government, but, on the contrary, is distinctly denied."

Lord Granville was the central figure in all negotiations with regard to Indigenous peoples in both B.C. and Rupert's Land. In both instances Granville reserved the right to imprint and enshrine Indigenous policy according to rather loose imperial standards. Even though Joseph Trutch confirmed that Indigenous title was "distinctly denied" by British Columbia, no objections were forthcoming from the secretary of state for the colonies while negotiations were underway. It can be argued B.C. was not out of step with the imperial policy of the time.

Governor Musgrave subsequently conveyed Granville's pivotal role in any Confederation negotiations to the B.C. legislative council. "Any arrangements which may be regarded as proper by Her Majesty's Government can I think best be settled by the Secretary of State, or by me under his direction, with the Government of Canada." Yet, certain members of the B.C. legislative council were anxious that the application of the Canadian Indigenous policy to B.C. would adversely affect both Indigenous peoples and the colony's economy.

Henry Holbrook — the main advocate of entrenching Indigenous welfare and protection within the B.C. Terms of Union — spoke of Indigenous peoples residing in his riding of New Westminster.

"The Indians of the Lower Fraser are intelligent, good settlers," asserted Holbrook. "I ask that they receive the same protection under confederation as now."

MLA Thomas Humphreys debates when he stated unequivocally that Indigenous peoples of many B.C. towns were the foundation of those places. He spoke of how badly the settlers had treated them when all they wanted was to be treated fairly. "I say, send them out to reservations and you destroy trade, and if the Indians are driven out we had all best go too."

Dr. John S. Helmcken, who represented B.C. in the Confederation negotiations, agreed. "I think it right to get the best terms we can, and point out the difficulties," he stated. "I say if the Indians are to be stuck in reservations there will be a disturbance. I think, sir, that it will be well that there should be some opposition." Years later, in 1887, Helmcken expanded upon this view:

> It was the "policy" of the Govt. of Vancouver Island not to remove any tribe or family from their village sites — but to make reserves of land immediately around and including their habitations. The Indians to-day occupy the same sites they did when I first arrived in 1850. None have ever been removed and so by the same token have never been removed to "reserves", using this term in the Canadian or American sense. It was never intended that the Indians should be a separated community ... It must therefore be evident that the Indian policy of Vancouver Island differed altogether from that of Canada. In fact it was knowingly framed seeing the great disadvantages of that system.

B.C. Confederation delegates Dr. John S. Helmcken (L) and Dr. Robert W.W. Carrall (R), Niagara Falls, c. 1870.

These members of the B.C. legislative council expressed a view that the Canadian system would serve to banish Indigenous peoples to distant reserves, pay them annuities, and prevent their active involvement in the B.C. economy. This prediction seems correct; in later years Indian reserves in the Prairie provinces followed this model of relocation, in addition to not being allowed outside reserve boundaries without obtaining a pass from the Indian agent (following the North-West Resistance).

Holbrook's motion to enshrine protection of Indigenous peoples in the Terms of Union failed twenty to one, not because of the intent of the motion, but because it conflicted with Lord Granville's directive that responsibility for Indigenous peoples was within sole federal jurisdiction.

Henry Crease, the colony's attorney general, bolstered this view when he stated that "the honorable gentleman must have forgotten the direction of the Imperial Government." Other members agreed. "We have the full assurance in Lord Granville's despatch that Indians must be protected," stated Dr. Robert W.W. Carrall (who, along with Helmcken and Trutch, represented B.C. in Ottawa during the Confederation negotiations).

At the conclusion of the Confederation debates, a draft Terms of Union that included no specific article governing Indigenous peoples was ratified by members of the B.C. legislative council. Article 13 was inserted into the final terms after B.C. delegates negotiated directly with the Canadian government in Ottawa:

> The charge of the Indians, and the trusteeship and management of the lands reserved for their use and benefit, shall be assumed by the Dominion Government, and a policy as liberal as that hitherto pursued by the British Columbia Government, shall be continued by the Dominion Government after the Union.
>
> To carry out such policy, tracts of land of such extent as it has hitherto been the practice of the British Columbia Government to appropriate for that purpose, shall from time to time be conveyed by the local Government to the Dominion Government in trust for the use and benefit of the Indians on application of the Dominion Government; and in case of disagreement between the two Governments respecting the quantity of such tracts of

land to be so granted, the matter will be referred for
decision of the secretary of state for the colonies.

The phrase, "a policy as liberal as that hitherto pursued by the British
Columbia Government," did not suggest that Indigenous lands manage-
ment policy in B.C. was similar to (or more advantageous than) the
Dominion's policy. Many have interpreted the word *liberal* as British
Columbia's way of hiding the true nature of the B.C. Indigenous policy.
It has also been suggested that had the Canadian government fully known
the B.C. position, such wording would not have been agreed to. But this
is not the case.

The "liberal policy" guaranteed that Indigenous peoples were not to be
isolated onto reserves and prevented from continuing as active partici-
pants in the B.C. economy. The word *liberal* speaks of "liberty of action"
as promised by Governor James Douglas to Indigenous Nations in the
aftermath of the Fraser Canyon War of 1858, and the guarantee that
Indigenous peoples in B.C. would not be relocated from traditional lands.

It is also unlikely that Article 13 can be attributed to Joseph Trutch, as
many have suggested. Though Trutch was one of three delegates appointed
to negotiate the terms of Confederation, Lord Granville and George Cartier
are the likely authors. Granville had defined his exclusive role with respect
to Indigenous peoples in B.C. (precluding B.C. legislative council participation). George Cartier, senior Canadian negotiator in determining
B.C.'s Terms of Union (in addition to the elevation of Manitoba to provincial status), had also represented Canada in the Rupert's Land transfer
with Granville that included guaranteeing welfare and protection for
Indigenous peoples.

The Confederation diary of Helmcken stated, "The clause about Indians was very fully discussed. The Ministers thought our system better
than theirs in some respects, but what system would be adopted remained
for the future to determine."

As with Articles 7 (Tariffs) and 11 (Railways), Article 13 was left to
future governments to clarify. As Cartier subsequently stated to the Canadian House of Commons, "the only guarantee that was necessary for the
future good treatment of the Aborigines was the manner in which they
had been treated in the past."

The Dominion government, like the British imperial government, had knowledge of the B.C. position on Indigenous land policy before, during and after the Terms of Union were ratified — and the potentially divisive issue was left unresolved in order to secure union with Canada.

As for Indigenous peoples in B.C., the British government was complicit in claiming sole authority to negotiate on behalf of the Crown Colony of British Columbia.

In doing so, it effectively sidestepped the issue of Indigenous title that continues to claim the B.C. landscape today.

THE BATTLE OF
THE ROUTES

The great untold story about competing railway routes, Vancouver Island and the national dream.

WHEN I WAS YOUNG, I travelled with my grandparents to Comox, on the east coast of Vancouver Island, to take the ferry to the Mainland for a short camping excursion. We were all excited to go, but then the weather changed — a fierce rain and windstorm — and as often happens, the ferry was shut down to "the Continent."

My grandfather was so very disappointed. "Damn it all!" he complained, "They should never have blasted Ripple Rock to oblivion — we could have had a bridge to this Island!"

I had never heard of Ripple Rock. As the old boy told me, the rock was located near Campbell River, and the fearsome whirlpool it created had taken down many a ship — and more than one hundred lives. A navigational hazard, it was removed in 1958 with what was then the world's largest non-atomic blast!

Old Gramps, puffing away on his pipe excitedly, blamed the steamship company — they wanted to make "damn sure" that a bridge to Vancouver Island would never be built. The immense rock submerged in the middle of Johnstone Strait was viewed as the key pillar-point to support a lengthy bridge span to Vancouver Island.

The blasting of Ripple Rock, c. 1958.

Ever since, I have been fascinated to learn more about this once proposed fixed link from the Island to the rest of Canada via the now defunct (what a shame!) Esquimalt & Nanaimo (E&N) Railway. Both were part of the same grand vision to connect the Island with the "ribbons of steel" promise of John A. Macdonald's national dream.

It has generally been accepted by historians that the present-day Fraser Canyon route of the transcontinental railway was the only practicable line. But this assertion ignores a technically superior route via Bute Inlet that — although supported by a majority of members of the B.C. legislative council — was dropped by the federal government in favour of the Fraser Canyon route. Ever since, the Bute Inlet route has been relegated to an inferior position, and Prime Minister Macdonald's original support for Bute Inlet and Esquimalt Terminus is seen today as a mere political ruse.

It was not always so. Bute Inlet No. 6 and Burrard Inlet No. 2 were once viewed as the "great rival routes" for connecting the new province with Canada. Under the Terms of Union, July 20, 1871, the federal government committed itself to the construction of a transcontinental rail link to the Pacific Slope, though it wrote Article 11 in such a way that final decisions on divisive issues were effectively postponed.

Perhaps this kind of procrastination was typical of the "Old Tomorrow" tactics of John A. Macdonald. In the case of railways, Article 11 seemingly allowed all regions of British Columbia to believe they were destined for the spoils of railway development. In total, twenty-one survey parties were deployed from Ottawa to the Pacific coast — shrewd Canadian agents that quietly plotted rail corridors throughout the province.

A practicable line that descended the Thompson and Fraser Rivers was discovered in 1871 — through "imperfect exploration" — yet Chief Engineer Sanford Fleming first declared that "the difficulties … appeared so great that a recommendation to adopt the route discovered, could not be justified until every effort had been exhausted."

The Canadian government surveys of 1871, which focused primarily on routes to Burrard Inlet, caused considerable consternation on Vancouver Island, especially in Victoria and Esquimalt. Many believed their favoured route of Bute Inlet, across Johnstone Strait and the treacherous Ripple Rock of Seymour Narrows, had been entirely ignored.

Survey operations were subsequently reorganized in 1872 to look beyond the immediate choice of the Fraser-Thompson Corridor. The Canadian government sent three survey parties to Bute Inlet and the Valdez Islands that was the only possible site for a fixed rail connection between Vancouver Island and the continent.

The extremely able engineer Marcus Smith, formerly with the Inter-colonial Railway of Canada (whose diaries are held by the B.C. Archives), was sent to supervise all survey parties in the province. As the deputy engineer-in-chief to Sanford Fleming and the resident engineer for British Columbia, Smith (second cousin of economist Adam Smith) took an immediate interest in the Bute Inlet route. The Canadian government had purchased the plans of former road-builder Alfred Waddington that outlined a route from the head of Bute Inlet in Xwémalhkwu (Homalco Nation) country (the undeveloped town site of Waddington), up the Homathko River and ultimately across the Cascades through Tŝilhqot'in (Chilcotin) traditional territory to the Cariboo goldfields.

Waddington's earlier attempt to construct a bridal trail along the steep banks of the Homathko Canyon was roundly condemned by Lower Main-land authorities, who realized that, if successful it would move the wealth of the Cariboo to Victoria and away from the Fraser Canyon and New Westminster. The Canadian government was not deterred and supplied Marcus Smith with copies of Waddington's reports from 1862. Of course, this was the earlier colonial road-building project that had sparked the infamous Chilcotin War.

Smith considered Waddington's prior work both arduous and "honestly prepared." After further inspection, a practicable route was located by survey crews. In addition, a further survey continued from the north side of Bute Inlet to the Valdez Group of islands and crossed a selection of sea channels, including Seymour Narrows, to a point on Vancouver Island just north of today's Campbell River. The line was not an easy trek, but was nevertheless one of the first established possible western sections of the "all-red route."

By contrast, on July 21, 1872, Marcus Smith jotted down in his field diary a rather cursory, seemingly condemning, opinion of the Fraser and Thompson River canyons as possible rail corridors. Held by the B.C. Archives records, the diary reveals Smith's staccato-like hand:

> Started at 3 p.m. in Barnard's [express] stage. [D]rove through the Canon. [M]iles to Boston Bar very rough and wild and unfavourable for a railway ... up the [F]raser still very rough road. [A]t summit Jack ass mountain said to be 1200 feet above water and nearly perpendicular. [On Thompson River] the banks being gravel, sand or loam and subject to slides — very unfavourable for a railway — more so even than the rocky Canon of the Fraser.

Curiously, these negative references were not subsequently included in a transcribed diary for public consumption. One can only assume that such remarks would have infuriated certain Mainland interests — particularly those of New Westminster and Yale — so discretion was perhaps advisable.

At the end of 1873, there were seven projected routes, all still at the exploratory stage. Yet of these seven, only two were given real attention by an anxiously awaiting public: Burrard Inlet No. 2 and Bute Inlet No. 6.

Both had formidable problems — but the problems associated with Bute Inlet were known and calculated (unlike the Fraser Route), as it had been surveyed instrumentally. As such, Bute Inlet No. 6 presented the only favourable course in 1873. The extension of this route to Vancouver Island, however, was much more formidable, an island-hopping thirty-mile-long fixed link calling for seven clear-span bridges over water channels in Johnstone Strait.

Sanford Fleming believed that the magnitude of such construction was "not only formidable, but without precedent." Nevertheless, on this basis,

Prime Minister Macdonald confirmed Esquimalt as the western terminus by order-in-council.

Contrary to public opinion, railway suspension bridge technology was well established by 1873. This is not to discount the obvious engineering difficulty of such a massive project, but to affirm that the preeminent factor raised against bridging the straits was cost, not technical feasibility. Indeed, the reason CPR surveys were extended beyond 1871 to areas such as Bute Inlet was the enormous cost of rail construction in the Fraser Canyon route.

Along with officially naming Esquimalt as the western terminus, the Dominion government requested the appropriation of a railway belt along the east coast of Vancouver Island all the way to Seymour Narrows — what is today the vast Esquimalt & Nanaimo Railway land grant, which still holds the subsurface rights of all private property landowners.

The Macdonald policy quite clearly committed itself to Bute Inlet, the Island railway to Esquimalt and ultimately the Seymour Narrows bridging scheme. But with the "Pacific Scandal," Macdonald's government was thrown from office and Liberal leader Alexander Mackenzie came to power — a bad omen for supporters of the Bute Inlet route. Mackenzie's minister of justice, Edward Blake, would soon refer to B.C. in the Canadian Parliament as "an inhospitable country, a sea of sterile mountains."

In a Privy Council report of March 13, 1876, the Liberal government enunciated succinctly the prior Conservative Party position:

> By this policy, had it remained unreserved, the [Liberal] Government would have been obliged to provide construction of over 160 miles of railway on Vancouver Island, at a probable cost of over seven million five hundred dollars; besides the building of a railway from the head of Bute Inlet and the bridging of the Narrows, a work supposed to be the most gigantic of its kind ever suggested, and estimated to cost over twenty-seven million and a half dollars.

Unquestionably, Macdonald's promises amounted to politics: balancing the sectional interests of the Island and the Lower Mainland. Yet an overly cynical view is not necessarily in order.

Others, like newspaper editor turned politician Amor De Cosmos, perhaps predictably, believed the transcontinental line should have been treated as an imperial concern with, presumably, imperial financing to allow for the much larger work. As federal member for Victoria City "he took it that this Government would make a very great mistake indeed if, for the paltry consideration of a few millions of dollars to-day, it should select the wrong route."

Work continued on these competing lines, as did the "Battle of the Routes" — the competing regional interests remaining ever vigilant. In June 1874, Marcus Smith embarked upon a pleasure trip to Seymour Narrows and adjacent islands in the company of James Douglas Jr. (the former governor's son) and other notables such as Chief Justice Matthew Begbie. As far as the resident engineer was concerned, on the basis of "what we saw yesterday I have no expectation that a line any better than that of Bute Inlet can be had."

James Douglas Jr., later a member of the legislative assembly (MLA) — and intimately connected to the interests of Victoria — obviously agreed. He judged the Fraser River route to be a "tortuous" and "narrow rocky defile." After having perused Fleming's report for 1874, the former governor's son remarked, "We may consider this opinion as sealing not only the fate of the [southern] routes, but the doom of New Westminster and Burrard Inlet as the Pacific terminus."

By 1876, the trial location survey was finished: the entire distance from Yellow Head Pass to Waddington Harbour. Route No. 6 — not the Fraser River line — became the first fully staked-out course for a railway in British Columbia and elevated the Bute Inlet route above all other routes in British Columbia, which were still at the exploratory or instrumental stage.

By then, five years had passed since union with Canada, with still no signs of actual railway construction. The new province was increasingly irritated by Canada's slow progress in fulfilling Article 11 of the Terms of Union. Secessionist pressure demanded that a decision be made soon.

Consequently, further exploration and surveys were halted in favour of evaluating completed surveys. Eleven individual lines were now assessed for their unique engineering features and the commercial traffic they would have to sustain if chosen.

Sufficient data was available for only one route — that of Bute Inlet No. 6 — so that in most instances this line served as the only real basis for comparison to all other routes. Perhaps this illustrated the faith that many administrators had in the Bute Inlet line!

Times were changing politically. Chief Engineer Fleming ultimately overruled his second in command, Marcus Smith, and without any comparable data for other competing routes confidently asserted that "there can scarcely be a doubt as to Route No. 2, terminating at Burrard Inlet, being the best."

Odd, considering little comparable evidence had been established for the Fraser River corridor.

Why was this?

It's a mystery compounded by a proclamation — still lost to this day — that officially named Bute Inlet the chosen route!

Canada's subsequent application to the Admiralty for particular information on B.C.'s coastal waters is evidence the Bute Inlet scheme had fallen into disfavour.

The principal naval officers who had some familiarity with the province's harbours were invited to comment on the suitability of nine different terminal points selected on the Mainland.

Esquimalt, on Vancouver Island — though it had been selected by Prime Minister Macdonald in 1873 as the western terminus — was noticeably excluded from this survey, much to the chagrin of Island supporters. Of essential importance was that the terminus be as close as possible to Asian trade. The distances from Yokohama, Japan, to each individual port-site in B.C. were compared. Waddington Harbour (Bute Inlet), being centrally located from either Queen Charlotte or Juan de Fuca Straits, placed last.

The real strategy behind the Bute Inlet route, of course, was the ultimate plan of bridging the Valdez Group of islands so that Esquimalt could be made the terminus. Esquimalt, since it was located on the Strait of Juan de Fuca, was obviously positioned more favourably than Burrard Inlet for the reception of Asian trade.

Establishing a terminus on Juan de Fuca was not about Victoria's desire to compete with New Westminster but, rather, the need for the Canadian transcontinental line to successfully challenge the commercial supremacy of its American counterpart.

This goal was fully delineated as early as 1872 by the Honourable Hector L. Langevin, member of the Conservative government in Ottawa. In a reply to a question posed about future railway lands by Amor De Cosmos in the Canadian Parliament, the federal minister acknowledged

> that the Northern Pacific Railway ended at Puget Sound,
> and the competition which that line will make with the

Canadian Pacific Railway renders it desirable to select a terminus that will put us in the best possible position for competition with American railways. If it should be decided that we can cross Seymour Narrows or Johnstone's Straits with a railway train, there can be no doubt that the interests of British Columbia and the Dominion as a whole will be better served by adopting that route.

American business interests had also contemplated a possible rail extension to the Strait of Juan de Fuca at either Port Angeles or Holmes Harbour, on the eastern shore of Whidbey Island. For Vancouver Island interests, it was the possible threat posed by the guns the American government had placed on the recently ceded San Juan Islands to control maritime traffic entering the strait. The well-known Hudson's Bay Company authority, Dr. William Fraser Tolmie, had been quick to point out this possibility in a number of published works.

If the United States were eventually to extend their rail system to Juan de Fuca, Canada would have to follow suit. This option, of course, necessitated the adoption of Bute Inlet No. 6 — the only route that could possibly allow for a future Island-Mainland rail connection.

Of the five opinions received from the Admiralty with respect to harbours, four favoured Burrard Inlet; only one declared for Waddington Harbour. Commander Daniel Pender was quite direct in his support for Burrard Inlet and discounted the head of Bute Inlet as an "indifferent anchorage."

Admiral Farquhar qualified his support. Bute Inlet, he believed, was "more difficult of access" than Burrard or Howe Sound, yet he concluded, "if it were practicable to bridge Seymour Narrows, the railway might be continued to a point on the south or west side of Vancouver [Island]." No Vancouver Island harbours were offered as options.

Admiral George Henry Richards was almost quizzical in his support for Burrard Inlet when he replied that "a practicable route, with an inferior water terminus might be preferable to an almost impracticable route attended with enormous expense and a good terminus, such as Burrard Inlet." Furthermore, others believed that Fraser River No. 2 was simply too close to the United States in the event of hostilities.

The fate of Bute Inlet No. 6 was inextricably tied to Canada's commitment to an Island railway extension. The fact that Canadian authorities were still hesitant in 1877 to name Bute No. 6 as the final route was additional proof that valid considerations were taken into account before the Island extension was finally dismissed. Sanford Fleming admitted as much in his most complete report of that year: "If it be important to carry an unbroken line of railway to one or more of the harbours on the western coast of Vancouver Island, and there is a likelihood that this project will, regardless of cost, hereafter be seriously entertained, then Route No. 6 becomes the only one open for selection."

This point of view was further bolstered by the formidable reputation of Rear Admiral Algernon de Horsey, commander-in-chief of the Pacific Station of Her Majesty's fleet in Esquimalt. De Horsey was against the selection of Burrard Inlet. He believed that a southern line would be open to possible overland attack from the United States and therefore, presented a security risk.

Why the commander-in-chief was not consulted earlier as part of Fleming's original enquiries to the Admiralty is, indeed, rather curious — one would have thought his opinion the most important of all.

In a confidential letter of the same year, Dr. John S. Helmcken wrote that "the Canadian Government for some reason or other, mean to ignore it, and to allow as little as possible of its advantages to be made public — preferring to be governed by their own political or other bias in favour of the Fraser River route ... rather than be guided by the results of scientific explorations of scientific men — the results which lead to the conclusion that Bute Inlet is by far the most advantageous point to touch salt water."

The "scientific men" Helmcken referred to were those such as Marcus Smith, the resident engineer, and Rear Admiral de Horsey, who supported the Bute Inlet route. As officials in the most senior positions of authority — in addition to being resident in the new province — they were well suited to form an opinion on the best route.

Mind you, de Horsey was also against any immediate bridging of Seymour Narrows and favoured instead the extension of Route No. 6 around the north side of Bute Inlet to Frederick Arm, and then a ferry to Vancouver Island. This apparent compromise to the expensive nature of bridging the Valdez Group was later dismissed by Fleming, and in a lengthy summation of the "Battle of the Routes" he offered his somewhat contradictory, but nevertheless, final word:

Burrard Inlet is not so eligible a terminal point as Esquimalt. It cannot be approached from the ocean, except by
navigation more or less intricate. Nor can it be reached
by large sea-going ships without passing at no great distance from a group of islands [the San Juans, recently
ceded to the U.S.] in the possession of a foreign power,
which at any time may assume a hostile attitude ...
Upon carefully reviewing the engineering features of each
route, and weighing every commercial consideration, I
am forced to the conclusion that ... the line to Vancouver
Island should, for the present, be rejected, and that the
Government should select the route by the Rivers Thompson and Fraser to Burrard Inlet.

The obvious question is what caused Fleming to dismiss the Island
link altogether. Previously, he had suggested there was "a likelihood that
this project will, regardless of cost, hereafter be seriously entertained."
This was the period in which British Columbia threatened to secede from
Canada on no less than three separate occasions, due to the Canadian
government's contravention of the Terms of Union.

In the early days of the secession debate, both Island and Mainland
acted in concert to demand proper fulfillment of Article 11 (railway clause).
But once the debate devolved into a contest between sectional interests,
the united call for separation as a bargaining tool was effectively split.

Consequently, the Lower Mainland was ready to give up the cause of
separation once it was assured Burrard Inlet would become the western
terminus of the national dream. Conversely, most of the Island and the
Cariboo District continued the secessionist threat, but it no longer had the
same degree of influence without the other half of the province in league.

John Robson of New Westminster (MLA and, later, premier) suggested
a surreptitious strategy in a letter dated September 27, 1876 (held by the
National Archives of Canada) to the Liberal prime minister Alexander
Mackenzie, an effective tactic to quell the separatists of Vancouver Island
and the Cariboo.

Should this turbulent spirit continue in Victoria, I think
a quiet intimation that the Island might be permitted to
drop out and resume the position of a Crown Colony, the

Mainland of course, remaining to the Confederacy, would
operate as a cure. On the mainland a very decided opinion
against Victoria bluster about separation is growing up . . .
I have reason to believe that a proposition to let the Island
out and establish the seat of Government on the Mainland, from where it should never have been removed,
would be regarded very favourably in that section.

The Honourable Robert Beaven (MLA and later, premier) referred to
Canada's reappraisal of the B.C. political climate in a *British Colonist* article, September 20, 1876, saying they had "discovered the weak points" of
support in British Columbia and had worked on these "regional jealousies"
to the new province's disadvantage.

As a result, when Victoria and the Cariboo next cried secession on
behalf of a divided province, the visiting federal representative, Governor
General Lord Dufferin, simply employed Robson's advice that had obviously been communicated through Prime Minister Mackenzie. This is
not what Victoria and the Cariboo had wanted to hear, but Canada had
no intention of losing the Mainland portion of the province — or more
critically, access to the Pacific Ocean. On the other hand, if the Island
persisted in its temerarious ways . . . it was expendable.

In short, Vancouver Island risked being reduced to the status of a military colony, not unlike Malta or Gibraltar.

After confirming Bute Inlet as the route — while at the same time
suggesting the Island portion of the railway would be postponed indefi-
nitely — Lord Dufferin alluded to the Canadian government's strategy
for killing the secessionist threat to Canada, and gave a veiled warning
while in Victoria:

Should hasty counsels and the exhibition of an impracticable spirit throw these arrangements into confusion,
interrupt or change our present railway programme, and
necessitate any re-arrangement of your political relations,
I fear Victoria would be the chief sufferer . . . A certain
number of your fellow-citizens, gentlemen . . . have sought
to impress me with the belief that if the Legislature of
Canada is not compelled by some means or other, which,
however, they do not specify, to make forthwith these

seventy miles of [Island] railway, they will be strong enough ... to take British Columbia out of Confederation. Well, they certainly won't be able to do that ... When once the main line of the Pacific Railway is under way, the whole population of the Mainland would be perfectly contented with the present situation of affairs, and will never dream of detaching their fortunes from those of Her Majesty's great Dominion.

Nay, I don't believe that these gentlemen would be able to persuade their fellow citizens of the Island of Vancouver to so violent a course; but granting for the moment that their influence should prevail — what would be the result? British Columbia would still be part and parcel of Canada. The great work of Confederation would not be perceptibly affected, but the proposed line of the Pacific Railway might possibly be deflected to the south. New Westminster would certainly become the capital of the Province ... as well as the chief social centre on the Pacific coast. Burrard Inlet would become a great commercial port ... Nanaimo would become the principal town on the Island, and Victoria would lapse for many a long year into the condition of a village.

Bute Inlet No. 6 was the superior scheme, and the Canadian government was prepared to decide in its favour, but the "Battle of the Routes" contest had become so fever-pitched as to threaten Confederation itself — and the loss of access to the Pacific. Canada was prepared to fashion a new political alliance with the Lower Mainland if Island secessionist sentiment continued to grow — and grow it did!

Upon winning the third general election in 1878, Premier George Anthony Walkem (who represented the Cariboo and was the only premier in B.C. history to return to power from earlier defeat) immediately passed the famous secessionist petition to Queen Victoria, which again threatened to pull British Columbia out of Canada. The truly bizarre aspect of this political strategy was the fact that the governor general's original instructions were to publicly proclaim the Canadian government's support for the Bute Inlet route.

Donald Smith driving the "Last Spike" to complete the Canadian Pacific Railway, 7 November 1885.

David W. Higgins, a future Speaker of the B.C. legislature, recalled the political events of the day for historian R.E. Gosnell.

> When Lord Dufferin left Ottawa for Victoria it was semi-officially announced in the papers that he was the bearer of a proclamation that would decide the contest in favour of Bute Inlet and Esquimalt. This dispatch, according to Lieutenant Governor [Joseph] Trutch, was sent from Government House to the Provincial Secretary's office by an official messenger and was handed, so the messenger reported, to the Provincial Secretary. From that day to this the dispatch has not been seen. It never reached the public eye. Who destroyed it if it were destroyed, who secreted it if it were secreted, who lost it if it were lost, will never be known. The parties are all dead. Lord Dufferin always denied all knowledge of its fate, although it was admitted that His Excellency handed the dispatch to the Lieutenant Governor. The

Lieutenant Governor said he personally delivered it to the messenger. The Provincial Secretary and the Premier were equally emphatic in asserting that it never came into their hands. Nine years ago Sir Joseph Trutch told the writer that the proclamation adopting the Bute Inlet route was carefully read by him and that he gave it to the messenger himself. He added that the disappearance was as profound a mystery to him as it was to Lord Dufferin.

If Higgins's story is true, then the governor general must have been instructed to gauge the strength of the separationist movement and act accordingly.

Canada's ultimate strategy called for a railway policy that divided the province, and in so doing, conquered the factional interests and secessionist sentiment of the so-called spoilt child of Confederation. So to my mind, the renewed call of separation by the Walkem government caused the railway to be deflected to the south. The Fraser Canyon route was the expedient means to keep Canada whole from sea to sea. Vancouver Island was not needed as a western entrepôt, nor was the Island essential to the larger Canadian national dream.

Now, just what happened to the proclamation delivered by Lord Dufferin to the B.C. government and apparently read by Lieutenant General Joseph Trutch?

While Higgins wrote that the answer to this mystery "will never be known," perhaps one day some further historical sleuthing may yet provide the answer!

Apparently, sometime in the 1960s, Inez O'Reilly of Point Ellice House (the former home of Judge Peter O'Reilly in Victoria, and today a well-known heritage site) was rearranging the antique furniture of the museum.

One such item was the writing desk of Sir Joseph Trutch that had come into the family's possession. During this move, a hidden compartment was found in the desk. Here was correspondence apparently from Prime Minister Macdonald, which was subsequently transferred to the B.C. Archives in Victoria.

When I first heard this story I began to make enquiries — who would not want to know the contents of the correspondence that compelled Trutch to hide it? But unfortunately, while it is somewhere in the province's archival collections, no one knows exactly where, or in what collection, it has been placed!

This raises some questions: Is it possible Trutch didn't send the Bute Inlet proclamation? Was it also hidden in the secret compartment of his old writing desk? It's well known the private interests of Joseph and his brother John Trutch were intimately tied to the Fraser Canyon route; had Bute Inlet been confirmed it would have spelled the end of their lucrative holdings along the Fraser and Thompson rivers.

Had this great untold story gone differently, it would have produced a human geography and settlement pattern in this province unrecognizable today.

"Hey, Gramps, aren't you glad they blew up Ripple Rock?"

B.C.'S FIRST
RURAL/URBAN SPLIT

The issue that dominated B.C.'s early provincial politics has mostly been forgotten but aroused loud passions and deep divides.

TRADE WARS AND THE THREAT of tariffs command headlines today, but they're nothing new.

My own family were farmers who first settled in 1860 at Swan Lake, below Christmas Hill in Saanich, on Vancouver Island. Since the days of the 1858 Fraser gold rush, there had always been the threat of cheap California produce flooding the B.C. market. So the old B.C. colonial tariff structure encouraged by Governor James Douglas sought to protect local agricultural interests — like those of my family.

All this changed dramatically once B.C. joined Confederation in 1871. From there, a period of harmonization with Canada's federal policies began, including the introduction of the Canadian tariff structure to the newly admitted province.

This is perhaps one of the most significant, yet neglected, topics in B.C. history.

Extensive political debate before, during and after Confederation talks on the fundamental question of tariff protectionism divided legislators and the public into separate camps throughout the first three sessions of the B.C. legislative assembly.

My grandfather on the old family farm at Swan Lake, below Christmas Hill in Saanich, Vancouver Island.

The introduction of the tariff instilled particular misgivings among B.C.'s agricultural and certain commercial interests, which then, as now, fell along established political fault lines: rural interests represented by Premier Amor De Cosmos in Victoria District versus the commercially oriented interests of Victoria City represented by Premier John McCreight.

Amor De Cosmos

Concern over the possible impact of the eastern trade scheme on the fledgling B.C. economy was exemplified in the minutes of the "Debate on the Subject of Confederation With Canada." Dr. John S. Helmcken — who used to ride his horse-drawn buggy out to our old farm — was recorded in the debate:

I feel perfectly sure, Sir, that if Confederation should come, bringing with it the Tariff of Canada, not only will the farmers be ruined, but our independence will be taken away; it will deprive our local industries of the protection now afforded them, and will inflict other burdens upon them; it will not free trade and commerce from the shackles which now bind them, and will deprive

the Government of the power of regulating and encour-
aging those interests upon which the Colony depends.

There can be no permanent or lasting union with
Canada, unless terms be made to promote and foster the
material and pecuniary interests of this Colony ... I am
opposed to Confederation, because it will not serve to
promote the industrial interests of this Colony, but on
the contrary, it will serve to ruin many, and thus be det-
rimental to the interest and progress of the country.

I say that Confederation will be injurious to the Farmers,
because protection is necessary to enable them to compete with farmers of the United States. The [Canadian]
Tariff and Excise Laws do not supply that.

Amor De Cosmos believed that protection for the agricultural interests of the colony were "the very keystone of Confederation" and of more
consequence than responsible government. His newspaper, the *Victoria
Daily Standard*, was a consistent advocate of a modified Canadian tariff
that extended protection to farmers.

In negotiations with the Dominion government, the colony's representatives made compromises that really did nothing to solve the problem. Article 7 of the Terms of Union stated that the old B.C. tariff should
"continue in force in British Columbia until the railway from the Pacific
coast and the system of railways in Canada are connected unless the Legislature of British Columbia should sooner decide to accept the Tariff and
Excise Laws of Canada."

Effectively Article 7 postponed any decision on modified tariffs but
awarded B.C. the right to accept the Canadian tariff in advance of a completed rail connection with the east. B.C.'s entry was secured, and difficult
decisions like tariffs were delayed so as not to break the Terms of Union Treaty.

Future provincial legislators were henceforth given the opportunity to
campaign for the immediate introduction of the Canadian tariff and the
further possibility of electing a legislative body more favourably inclined
to free trade principles.

Article 7 provided the roots of polarization, with a central role in setting
the tone of the first provincial electoral contest between those politicians

seeking an immediate reduction in commodity and other prices and those who favoured adequate protection for fledgling agricultural and industrial pursuits.

In the first provincial election of 1871, the early-acceptance proviso of Article 7 led to quick action by those politicians who adopted a pro-Canadian tariff position most often as the main plank in their platform.

De Cosmos hoped for a majority return of MLAs who supported a modified tariff. But the pro-Canadian tariff forces appeared to have won the day — or at least, the election. From a total of twenty-five MLAs, the cabinet of John Foster McCreight was cemented not so much by shared birthplace, political ideology or other mutual affiliations, but by their shared commitment to the immediate introduction of the Canadian tariff.

The battle lines were quickly drawn. The first issue of consequence in the new legislature was not the founding of responsible government, railway construction or any other capital works of imperial concern, but tariffs.

Motions met with procedural wrangles by opposition forces, who were once again defeated. When the dust settled, members voted fourteen to nine in favour of the Canadian tariff. De Cosmos's newspaper "regretted that all other interests in the province had become subservient to commerce" and ventured to predict that Canadian tariff proponents would "see their mistake by-and-bye, when too late to apply a remedy ... there will be no drawing back, no help for it, however much we hereafter may have occasion to regret the suicidal policy we have pursued."

On March 14, 1872, the bill received its third and final reading, leaving only Royal Assent before the Canadian tariff system had full force. Prime Minister John A. Macdonald, anticipating a *fait accompli*, instructed, "The moment that your act passes adopting the Canadian Tariff, you should send a copy duly certified."

Yet the official consolidation of B.C. into the Canadian tariff structure did not end opposition debate.

The tariff issue helped give McCreight the premier's post, but it also led to a rather tenuous hold on power and ultimately to defeat. On December 19, 1872, his government fell on an amendment to the throne speech, which said the administration of public affairs had "not been satisfactory to the people in general."

The new premier-designate, Amor De Cosmos, now had the opportunity of building a more secure coalition — and the tariff issue remained in play. The new premier had to work with the same group of MLAs who had already largely committed to the Canadian tariff.

Arthur Bunster

One of the first members to publicly switch sides was George Anthony Walkem (a future premier), who retained a cabinet portfolio in the De Cosmos government. As the new attorney general, he advocated a "broader view" of the question than previously, one that afforded "a fair protection for farm produce" as economic conditions for the farmer had worsened. Arthur Bunster, MLA and brewery owner, confirmed this view:

> The Canadian tariff had proved a curse to the country, inasmuch as its tendency was to drive people out of it. The general verdict after a year's trial of the Canadian Tariff was, that they [the farmers] would gladly sell at cost and leave the Province ... Was it not a shame and a disgrace to see Chicago bacon sent away into our mines and under selling Provincial bacon? Was it not a shame to see California flour sold less in this market than Provincial flour was sold?

Evidently, many felt it was a disgrace that home production was being severely undercut. In a committee of the whole on January 27, 1873, MLAs resolved by a majority of one vote (twelve to eleven) to pursue the preparation of a petition that outlined specific changes to federal customs duties. This report represented a complete change in philosophy and direction for the House. Yet before they could applaud their victory, committee chairman Joseph Hunter added his vote against the report, thus effecting a tie (twelve-twelve). With full membership in attendance, the legislature was now more evenly divided than on any previous issue.

Parliamentary procedure required that the legislative impasse be broken in the House; the Speaker, James Trimble of Victoria City, voted against the report. In casting his deciding vote, Trimble attempted to end any future doubt that the province lacked legal jurisdiction on tariffs.

By this time, De Cosmos had left for Ottawa, resigned to working within the federal realm for changes to the Canadian tariff. Back home, MLA Arthur Bunster continued to promote a made-in-B.C. scheme. Under

Bunster's instigation, the B.C. House was again prepared to re-examine the question in committee of the whole, but no report was forthcoming during the remainder of the De Cosmos government's time in office.

With the collapse of the Conservative government in Ottawa over the "Pacific Scandal," the tariff debate soon entered the field of federal politics. In January 1874 at public meetings in Saanich, all contenders for the federal riding of Vancouver [Island] District pledged their support for a modified tariff. In provincial by-elections held at the same time in Victoria District (created by the departure of Arthur Bunster and Amor De Cosmos, who both sought federal office), farmers convened at the Prairie Inn and unanimously endorsed a pledge that demanded each candidate's support for modified tariffs, which the candidates endorsed.

The declaration read, "I sincerely declare that I will not support or accept office from the present or any government until they shall have first introduced some policy or measure calculated to insure such a modification of the Tariff as will afford real and substantial protection to farmers."

Provincially, the Canadian tariff was still the main issue of contention in 1874. Federally, new MP Arthur Bunster also continued the fight. In response to Liberal MP Edward Blake's insensitive, indeed acid, assertion that British Columbia was "an inhospitable country, a sea of sterile mountains," Bunster, before assembled MPs in the House of Commons, hauled a sack of homegrown, prize-winning Saanich wheat from under his Commons desk, "took a handful out of it and indignantly tossed it toward the member for South Bruce [Blake] as the best answer to his statement."

Bunster's efforts were in vain. Having warned the province and the Dominion for so many years that inadequate protection would drive people out of B.C., in 1883 Bunster ultimately vacated to Oakland, California, where he continued to brew ales as he had done in Victoria.

In hindsight it seems so obvious. We know that tariffs were important in any discussion of post-Confederation Canada. Large portions of early B.C. society were clearly dissatisfied, and this feeling manifested itself in the legislative assembly. So why has the introduction of the Canadian tariff in British Columbia and its harmful effects received so little attention from historians?

While historians have focused mainly on Canada's promised railway during the formative years of the province, politics was a war over the introduction of the Canadian trade scheme. The fight over Canada's default on building the transcontinental railway would soon follow!

AN INDEPENDENT
BRITISH COLUMBIA?

How the Carnarvon Club almost removed B.C. from Confederation before the ink was dry.

MANY YEARS AGO IN MONTREAL, during the height of the Quebec separation debate, I announced to some new Quebecois acquaintances that British Columbia had also threatened to secede from Canada.

"Really!?" was the excited and enthusiastic reply.

"Yes," I said, "as far as we are concerned, if anyone should leave Canada, it should be Ontario!"

Incredulity was quickly replaced with laughter, and these proud French Canadian nationalists and I became immediate friends — and they kindly ordered the next round of drinks, too!

In 1871, British Columbia's long-held dream of a transportation link to eastern North America seemed assured when a promised transcontinental railway became enshrined in the Terms of Union Treaty by which B.C. joined Canada.

Indeed, for some, without the Pacific Railway there could be no Confederation.

If it were to compete with the United States, Canada desperately needed access to the Pacific Slope and so further promised and enshrined in the Terms of Union that railway construction would begin within two years of the date of Confederation — and be completed in ten.

This key promise was the dealmaker. In short order, it almost became the dealbreaker.

British Columbia's enthusiasm was not shared by successive federal governments. Their obligation to start construction within two years was carried out only in symbolic form, just one day before the expiry date of July 20, 1873.

In keeping with his order-in-council, which established Esquimalt as the terminus, Sir John A. Macdonald ordered a survey party to run a

location line for a portion of the proposed Island railway. The government in Victoria, aspiring to become the Pacific terminus for a transcontinental nation, argued in favour of a rail line that followed the present-day E&N Railway, but would extend to Campbell River, then cross the islands in the Valdez Group to Bute Inlet and, ultimately, enter the Chilcotin Plateau to the Cariboo and beyond.

Sir John A. Macdonald

Though Macdonald seemingly favoured this course, the federal government — having kept its promise, if only minimally — returned to inaction. The absence of railway construction became apparent once more, especially with the election of Alexander Mackenzie's Liberal government, in 1873.

Mackenzie had previously infuriated the Pacific province, saying the Terms of Union were "a bargain made to be broken," and he quickly rescinded Macdonald's 1873 order-in-council naming Esquimalt the terminus.

The provincial and federal governments argued over the question of relaxing the ten-year timeline — and constructed nothing but deadlock.

This impasse remained until both parties agreed to an impartial mediator: Lord Carnarvon, colonial secretary of the imperial government, who insisted that his decision "whatever it may be, shall be accepted without any question or demur."

Carnarvon's decision would guarantee the building of the E&N Railway. As long as the Bute Inlet route was still seen as viable (which it was), Victoria's hopes of being part of the main nationwide railway would prevail.

Yet, even after Carnarvon made his decision, the Mackenzie government procrastinated and the rallying cry of "Carnarvon Terms or Separation" could be heard in B.C.

Writing to Sir John A. Macdonald, Lieutenant Governor Joseph Trutch described the political mood: "The temper of our community is greatly excited and set against Canada and the Canadians by the nonfulfillment of the Railway Clause of the Terms of Union and especially by the tone and manner regarding it taken by those who have expressed a desire for some readjustment of the obligations of Canada."

Talk of secession was becoming so frequent, it was decided a viceregal visit by Lord Dufferin, Canada's governor general, might help to mend relations. At a large meeting held at Philharmonic Hall in Victoria, an address was prepared and approved for presentation to the governor general: "The action of the Dominion Government in ignoring the Carnarvon settlement, has produced a wide feeling of dissatisfaction towards Confederation ... if the Government fails to take practical steps to carry into effect the terms solemnly accepted by them, we must respectfully inform your Excellency that, in the opinion of a large number of people of this Province, the withdrawal of this Province from Confederation will be the inevitable result."

Upon his arrival in Victoria, Lord Dufferin was made aware of the presentation, but he declined the address prepared for him and instead spoke privately with the meeting's deputation, informing them that the Island railway would be abandoned.

To quell the secessionist threat, Dufferin further warned that "the Crown would allow the Island to go; but ... the Mainland will be held to the Dominion by inducements of self interest which the building of the main line will furnish."

In other words, if the threat of separation continued, Bute Inlet as a railway route would be overturned and "the proposed line of the Pacific Railway might possibly be deflected south" to New Westminster.

This was the political climate the governor general's visit was supposed to alleviate, but Dufferin's consistent refusal to recognize B.C.'s legitimate constitutional complaints intensified emotions instead. As a direct result, on September 9, 1876, the Carnarvon Club was formally established, the main objective being "to organize a society for the purpose of using all constitutional means to compel Canada to carry out her railway obligations with this Province; failing which, to secure the withdrawal of British Columbia from Confederation."

The club, pre-dating the introduction of the "old" line Canadian parties, played an important and influential role in the politics of the province.

Political opposition took the form of a two-pronged attack. The Mainland, and New Westminster in particular, believed that the Island railway would secure the Bute Inlet route over their preferred Fraser River route.

Premier A.C. Elliot's provincial government caused considerable consternation among Victorians, and especially Carnarvon Club members, when he became an ally of Mackenzie's Liberal government and, therefore, of Liberals themselves working in concert against the Carnarvon settlement.

Most of Vancouver Island worked not only against the federal government but also against the proponents of the Fraser River alternative which, as the *British Colonist* described, was "destined to keep the sections asunder and preclude the possibility of united action."

After the Carnarvon Club's inception, three mass public meetings were held at Philharmonic Hall for the purpose of deciding on "Carnarvon Terms or Separation."

The first meeting, September 19, 1876, recorded not only an attendance of "Seven Hundred Citizens in Council," but also a "unanimous vote in favour of separation!"

Supporters of Elliot's government sounded the alarm. Former MLA W.A. Robertson cautioned, "I deemed it in the interest of the public, and the people particularly of Victoria, to let it be known that there is in our midst a political Star Chamber (wrongly called the Carnarvon Club) which, while professing to be working in the interest of the province, is, in reality, wholly and solely run in the interests of a political faction — a faction which is nothing more nor less than the rump of the late (Walkem) Government."

George Anthony Walkem

The warning didn't work.

On election day, May 23, 1878, Walkem was returned to power. Voters in Victoria elected all four opposition candidates and even deprived Premier Elliot of his own seat. Overall, ten out of twelve opposition members were returned for Vancouver Island. The results led the *Victoria Daily Standard* to predict that "any opposition ... to the new (Walkem) Gov't on any of the great questions of the day will be unimportant and inconsiderable."

Indeed, Walkem was determined to act on the great question of "Carnarvon Terms or Separation" and immediately passed the famous secession petition to Queen Victoria, threatening to pull British Columbia out of the Canadian Confederation.

As a pressure group, the Carnarvon Club was the most successful the province has ever seen, bringing down the incumbent government in a landslide victory. In its role as a political party incognito, however, the Carnarvon Club was perhaps even more effective, being the only group in the history of British Columbia to succeed in returning a premier to power after their political defeat — all before the age of political parties.

What was the Canadian government's response? Even though the United States had taken possession of the San Juan Islands and threatened to establish gun fortifications to control the Strait of Juan De Fuca — a serious security risk for future Canadian shipping interests — Canada quickly acted on its threat and confirmed the Fraser River route for the transcontinental railway.

It secured both the loyalty of the B.C. Mainland and access to the Pacific Ocean; Victoria and the Island were deemed nonessential to the Canadian national dream.

Had events been otherwise, the settlement patterns of this province would be entirely different with Victoria a metropolis the size of Vancouver — just imagine that.

SIX:
CURIOUS ARTIFACTS AND CONFOUNDING TALES

THE CURIOUS STORY OF YALE'S GARRY OAK GROVE

Up on the Fraser, there exists a stand of trees that don't belong. How did they get there?

I HAD THE GREAT PLEASURE to mount a short rafting expedition on the Fraser River into an isolated grove of Garry oaks just above the town of Yale.

For years I wanted to visit this curious Garry oak preserve so far removed from the remaining stands in places like Victoria's Beacon Hill Park or the larger preserve of the Cowichan Valley on southern Vancouver Island.

Named after Nicholas Garry (deputy governor of the Hudson's Bay Company, 1822–35), the Garry oak (*Quercus garryana*) is the only native oak tree in western Canada. The oak is part of a unique ecosystem associated with the Mediterranean-like climate found in the rainshadow lands of southeastern Vancouver Island. Below the forty-ninth parallel, these trees are called Oregon white oaks.

Yet, the mysterious Garry oaks north of Yale are far removed from their more southern neighbours — about 160 kilometres — making the Yale location outside the general Savannah-like grasslands they normally favour. Quite an anomaly!

As such, we were determined to explore this hidden site accessible only by water.

The mysterious Garry oak preserve north of Yale, B.C., accessible only by water.

Our base of operations was the historic Teague House in Yale, the original gold commissioner's house dating from the 1860s.

We clambered down the steep embankment below the old house to rendezvous with a Zodiac sent to collect us. There is no better way to see the country of the Fraser Canyon than on the river itself, the amazing highway into the British Columbia Interior that was used before the Cariboo Wagon Road and not one but two transcontinental railways were built.

Once suited up with lifejackets we quickly sailed past Yale, New York Bar, Lady Franklin Rock and Deadman's Eddy towards our destination.

As we briskly sped along on a gorgeous sunny day, I recalled that when Simon Fraser travelled down this river in 1808, he was the first European to record the name Cowichan in the pages of his journal. Warned by upriver Indigenous Nations that the "Ka-way-chin" were to be feared, his own men resisted going any farther, but Fraser prevailed and descended to the river's mouth by taking the north arm of the river, hoping to evade the Cowichan.

But they were nevertheless greeted with open hostility by the Musqueam people. Fraser wrote, "Having spent one hour looking about this place we went to embark, [and] we found the tide had ebbed, and left our canoe on dry land. We had, therefore, to drag it out to the water some distance.

Our guide coming to meet us in a Zoadic on the banks of the Fraser River.

The natives no doubt seeing our difficulty, assumed courage and began to make their appearance from every direction, in their coats of mail, howling like so many wolves, and brandishing their war clubs."

Fraser and party managed to escape and live to tell of the determined proprietorial claims of the Coast Salish peoples to what ironically would later be called Fraser's River.

In a half-hour we reached our destination, swinging the Zodiac into the soft sand dunes of a convenient creek opening among the rock cliffs adjacent to the Garry oak preserve. How exciting!

Clambering up the hillside, we immediately spotted the first of these amazing trees clinging to the rock cliffs. As one who grew up among the Garry oak meadows of Vancouver Island, how strange was it to see these familiar trees thriving in a climate so removed and unlike the coast! Just how did this curious grove come to be here?

By the 1820s, the Hudson's Bay Company (HBC) had made two separate expeditions to the Fraser River in preparation for the establishment of Fort Langley. During this time, HBC officer John Work noted the overwhelming presence of the Cowichan (the name coined by the English; today the people prefer Quw'utsun, their traditional name), commenting on the many "Cowitchin" villages he saw. Perhaps more significantly, Work called the Fraser River the "Coweechin" River. In these first European land-based expeditions to the mouth of the Fraser River, Quw'utsun peoples were recognized as having a large presence.

At first, the HBC hoped that the Fraser River might replace the Columbia as a convenient transportation corridor to the east. In advance of thorough field reconnaissance, the company established Fort Langley on the shores of the Fraser River in 1827, only to discover the following year that the river was largely unnavigable.

Nevertheless, HBC operations continued at this site, and in journals kept by HBC employees there, the significant presence of the Quw'utsun on the Fraser River was further recorded.

Large numbers of Quw'utsun peoples migrated from Vancouver Island to the lower Fraser every year, as they had always done, to take advantage of the huge salmon runs. In 1824, when James McMillan headed a Hudson's Bay Company expedition from Fort Vancouver up the Fraser, he learned the Indigenous name for the river was Cowitchen.

When McMillan returned to Fort Langley again, three years later, he and his party travelled by three separate Quw'utsun villages situated on the south arm of the river, mid-point between New Westminster and the river's end. These three sites consisted of many large plank houses with a combined population estimated by McMillan to be no less than fifteen hundred people. The village names were recorded as Saumni, Pinellahutz and Quomitzen, corresponding to the names of their Island counterparts (known today by their traditional names S'amunu, Penelakut and Kwa'mutsun, respectively).

As a conservative estimate, upwards of five thousand Indigenous people assembled near Fort Langley each summer to fish and trade. In the year 1827 alone, five hundred separate and fully loaded Quw'utsun canoes were counted passing by the fort on their way back to Vancouver Island. Their route is still followed by B.C. Ferries: from the Fraser River across the Strait of Georgia, through Active Pass to Satellite Channel, then passing by Cherry Point to the mouth of the Cowichan River on Vancouver Island.

The attraction of the Fraser River was the incredible salmon resource. Elders tell us that the Quw'utsun were attracted to the vicinity of the canyon above Yale where dip-nets could be easily employed and the enormous catches air-dried by the constant wind-tunnel effect produced by the dramatic geography of this place. But this location was also a trade emporium for First Nations, the Quw'utsun taking large quantities of dried clams and blue camas lily bulbs to exchange for such things as wool from the bighorn sheep of the B.C. and Washington State interiors.

But what of the mysterious Garry oaks? Is it possible that during these yearly forays from Vancouver Island to their fish grounds above Yale, Quw'utsun traders may have planted Cowichan Valley acorns at this site?

The camas bulb, once a staple of the Indigenous diet, has a great affinity with the Garry oak. To ensure the propagation of this once great trade item, Indigenous peoples frequently set grasslands ablaze to encourage the growth of camas. But in the narrow confines of the Fraser Canyon, perhaps the Quw'utsun peoples sought to recreate the Garry oak biosphere of their Island winter home.

Apparently, there is evidence of past fire on the Yale site. To my mind, this is quite possibly the best explanation for the existence of this curious and isolated stand of trees.

The Return of Chief Tsulpi'multw's Ceremonial Blanket

Or, from Long House to Buck House.

I celebrated National Indigenous Day in 2019 with many hundreds of members of the Cowichan Tribes (Quw'utsun Nation) who came to witness the official return of a remarkable artifact: the ceremonial blanket worn by Chief (Charlie) Tsulpi'multw in London, England, 113 years ago during an audience at Buckingham Palace with King Edward VII — Queen Victoria's son and successor.

I was delighted to be in attendance, particularly as I have been researching the life of this amazing Chief for many years.

It was over twenty years ago that I accompanied my good friend and former Cowichan (Quw'utsun) Chief, Wes Modeste (Qwustenahun), to Britain for an extraordinary month-long research trip. We were following in the footsteps of three B.C. Salish Chiefs (two coastal, one interior) who had themselves made the journey in 1906 for a personal audience with the king at Buckingham Palace.

The late Wes Modeste was a remarkable ambassador of the Quw'utsun people. "He was ahead of his time," said fellow Chief Steven Point and former lieutenant governor of B.C. "One of our great leaders, upon whose shoulders we stand today."

Chief Wesley Modeste

Wes and I had been talking for some years about mounting an expedition to seek further historical information on these Chiefs in the British archives, such as the Public Record Office at Kew Gardens and the Rhodes House Library in Oxford.

"When should we go track this history down?" I asked. Wes promptly replied, "You white guys got the watches, but we have the time!" We had a good laugh and in that moment decided to make the necessary preparations.

Wes was the great grandson of Chief Suhiltun, who played a central role in the Indian Rights Association movement of the early 1900s. Suhiltun was not only a hereditary Chief but also head Chief of the Cowichan Tribes during these years. In the Modeste family's oral history, it is remembered that their famous ancestor originally intended to make the pilgrimage to Britain, but an accident prevented him from doing so. As such, Suhiltun ultimately appointed Chief Tsulpi'multw to represent the Cowichan people.

During our month-long stay in Britain we were astounded to find so much information on the epic journey made by these Salish Chiefs to the imperial capital. Certainly Wes, in continuing the "fight for Native rights" family tradition, would have made his great-grandfather, Chief Suhiltun, proud.

We discovered how Tsulpi'multw's long life spanned generations. As a young man he met Governor James Douglas, who visited Cowichan Bay aboard the HMS *Hecate* when the colonial government promised to make payment for lands acquired for non-Indigenous settlement. This unfulfilled promise became the motivation in Tsulpi'multw's fight for Indigenous rights in B.C. during the late nineteenth and early twentieth centuries.

In 1906, along with Chiefs Kayapálanexw (Capilano) of Squamish Nation and Basil David of Bonaparte Nation (in Secwepemc, near Ashcroft), Tsulpi'multw set off to meet King Edward VII. This delegation of three Chiefs and their interpreter, Simon Pierre, a Katzie man from the Stó:lō Nation, made the great journey on behalf of all B.C. First Nations after having appealed in vain to the B.C. and Canadian governments for proper redress.

B.C. Chiefs post-1906: Chief Tsulpi'multw (middle front row) to the right of Kayapálanexw.

Before their departure, a large parade of Indigenous leaders and non-Indigenous allies was held in Vancouver, and a large Indigenous brass band played as the delegation embarked on a steam train that whistled them across the continent. From Quebec City, they boarded a ship for a long sea voyage to Britain.

While waiting some two weeks in London to present their grievances to the king (apparently away on a hunting trip), the Chiefs could be seen walking the streets of London — Tsulpi'multw often wearing his ceremonial blanket as they toured Westminster Abbey, the Tower of London and even Madame Tussaud's Wax Museum!

With the king's delay, imperial authorities privately hoped that the Chiefs would simply return to Canada — but Chief Kayapálanexw informed them that they were not going anywhere and had sufficient resources to wait it out at least two years.

As B.C. colonial representatives had always conducted their business in the name of Queen Victoria — the "Great White Mother" — it was deemed appropriate to go over the heads of the B.C. and Canadian governments and appeal directly to the monarch. London's *Daily Telegraph* reported on August 14, 1906, the crucial moment: "Fortune has crowned the mission of the Red Indian chiefs now visiting London ... and the Indians forthwith prepared themselves for presentation to the 'Great White Chief.'"

Chief Kayapálanexw recorded years later that Tsulpi'multw was captivated by their entrance down the red-carpeted rooms of Buckingham

Chief Suhiltun at the McKenna-McBride Commission's first meeting with the Cowichan Nation, 1913.

Palace, and was particularly entranced by the mirror-lined ceiling in the great room where they met the king and queen.

The 1906 trip brought much attention to the outstanding issue of Indigenous title and the plight of B.C.'s First Nations — it was a public relations success and this initiative was soon followed by the game-changing "Cowichan Petition of 1909," the first legal document prepared by B.C. First Nations that made reference to the Royal Proclamation of 1763 and the assertion that Indigenous title had yet to be extinguished through treaty-making.

The Cowichan Petition subsequently led the British Colonial Office to put political pressure on both the B.C. and Canadian governments to address the outstanding question of the rights of B.C.'s Indigenous people. A Royal Commission on Indian Affairs (known as the McKenna-McBride Commission, 1913–16) was subsequently struck. It eventually toured the entire province but made its very first inquiries with the Cowichan Nation who had taken such a leading role.

After the death of Kayapálanexw, Chief Tsulpi'multw continued the fight for Indigenous rights well into old age with subsequent trips to Ottawa, where he met with Prime Minister Wilfrid Laurier, and to London (in company with Kayapálanexw's son Matthias). The Old Obelisk at Mount Tzouhalem in the Cowichan Valley, marking the final resting place of this great Chief, was originally erected to commemorate his 1906 trip to London and the subsequent and tireless work undertaken by Tsulpi'multw to defend and advance the rights of the Indigenous people of B.C. He apparently lived to be 110 years old.

The National Indigenous Day celebrations were particularly special in 2019 not only for the remembrance of this indefatigable leader, but also because many of his descendants were in attendance. His great-grandson Perry George paid tribute to his ancestor by wearing the returned blanket that had been safely kept by UBC's Museum of Anthropology these last many years.

The return of the ceremonial blanket to the Cowichan peoples is a compelling reminder to current generations, both Indigenous and non-Indigenous, that the work undertaken by Chief Tsulpi'multw is unfinished. Governor Douglas's promise remains unfulfilled 157 years later — and that sure seems like a long time to wait.

THE MYSTERIOUS TALE OF A LOST "HAIDA" TREASURE

The curious story of how an Indigenous artifact "devastated" those who possessed it.

ANCIENT ARTIFACTS HAVE ALWAYS held my fascination, especially those accompanied by curious stories seemingly lost to time. Ever since the Spanish first explored the Northwest Coast, Indigenous artifacts were either gifted or traded with Europeans — and in far too many instances simply stolen. These antiquities, in particular the centuries-old argillite carvings by Haida sculptors of Haida Gwaii (formerly the Queen Charlottes), such as the legendary artist Charles Edenshaw (1839–1920), can be found in museum collections both locally and around the world.

The Haida people were among the forefront of maritime fur traders in the late eighteenth and early nineteenth centuries, trading with Europeans in seal otter pelts so coveted in the Asian markets of the day. But less well known is that Haida Gwaii experienced a brief gold rush in the early 1850s (predating the Fraser and Cariboo rushes) that attracted many American ships to the coastline. In all instances, the fiercely protective Haida beat these early intrusions back and in at least one case ransomed an entire crew of gold seekers, after burning and destroying their ship.

Skidegate Village, Haida Gwaii, B.C., George Dawson, c. 1878.

In the decades that followed, there would be many more excursions by foreign traders and miners who sailed into the waters of the archipelago. But while many sought peaceful trade, others took their chance to loot Indigenous treasures.

Here is a curious story of one such expedition and of one singular artifact — possessed by at least a half-dozen individuals — before it was donated to a prominent California museum in the late nineteenth century.

The *San Francisco Call* reported on April 7, 1897, "the record of this ruin-tracked relic," and "where it has gone disaster and desolation have been rife." The news item of a seafarer who robbed an unspecified Haida village of a mysterious carving, among other antiquities, reads almost like stories of the curse of King Tutankhamun (though Howard Carter did not open Tut's tomb until 1922):

> To one Hans Anderson, an unscrupulous and sacrilegious follower of the sea, is attributed much woe of the past thirty years. This Hans Anderson was a trader who plied the Pacific Coast three decades ago. One evil moment he directed his vessel toward Queen Charlotte Island on the British Columbia coast ... Anderson invaded one of the villages, ostensibly to do some small trading with the

Indians, but with the real heart of a pirate. Awaiting a favorable opportunity he and his men on a dark night raided one of the native temples, if such they could be called, and carried away everything of value and everything that even looked valuable. Then came the retreat to the ship and a hasty setting of sail.

Among the articles taken that night, reported the newspaper, "was a hideous carving" or "idol" (as viewed through the European lens of the time). The theft enraged the Haida people. So, while watching Anderson's ship sail toward the horizon, they called upon their shamans to perform "a series of weird incantations" such that a "terrible curse and the worst luck" would follow all those who would possess it.

What happened next? Apparently Anderson sailed south to Vancouver Island where he died in "horrible agony from convulsions." Soon after, as he had owed a debt to the captain of a sealing schooner called the *O.F. Fowler*, Anderson's assets were liquidated — including the mysterious artifact. The *San Francisco Morning Call* reported, "The O.F. Fowler was as staunch a craft as ever sailed the main, but she could not sail with that 'hoodoo' aboard. The very first voyage she attempted with it as a passenger ended in disaster. She was crushed on the rocks and the captain and several of the crew were lost."

Following the shipwreck, the "Hoodoo" (a parapsychological power, or the cause of harm which befalls the targeted victim) somehow floated ashore with the wreckage, where it was retrieved by a fisherman. A week later, he too was dead, apparently due to a "brain fever."

The *San Francisco Morning Call* story states the mysterious object then made its way farther down the coast in the possession of some whalers who sold the "cursed" artifact to a wealthy and prosperous San Franciscan by the name of Robert Llewelyn.

"Bob," as he was familiarly known along the waterfront, never suspected the evil spell that possessed the curiosity, even when year after year, all sorts of financial reverses beset him and he saw his fortune dwindling away.

He finally found himself poor, and opened a little saloon with the hope of at least keeping the wolf from the door, and through all these years he never parted with the Indian idol. The climax came less than a year ago when poor Llewelyn fell down a flight of stairs and sustained injuries which caused his death.

Four owners and four deaths later, the artifact was purchased by John Coyne, "a tinsmith and plumber" known for his collection of curios. "During the period of his possession ... he had all kinds of bad luck."

"Why, do you know," said Coyne, "while I had that confounded thing in my possession, my business went to absolute rack and ruin. Believe me, I could not get a thing to do, I couldn't sell anything and I began to think seriously of closing my shop for good. That idol sat up on a shelf and seemed to grin all the broader the worse my luck grew. Finally I took it down and stowed it away in a little closet under the stairs, where I changed my clothes. And do you know, I went in there one day, and bless me if I didn't see a wild-eyed Indian chief standing right beside that idol. But I am thanking my lucky stars that I got rid of it at last. I am satisfied that it is to blame for all of my bad luck."

Coyne subsequently sold the Haida artifact to John L. Bardwell, a well-known collector of curios and antiquarian items. "I tell you it is a good thing for him that he got it off his hands right away," Coyne said. Bardwell, "the most magnificent of benefactors," had travelled to California in 1852, and his antiquarian collections were considered the finest on the Pacific coast. Most were donated to the Golden Gate Park Museum, including, it seems, the mysterious Haida artifact. The story continues:

John Coyne

It is an old Indian idol that was recently discovered and purchased by John L. Bardwell — that indefatigable searcher for antiquities — and given by him to the Park Commissioners. A glance at the distorted and horror-inspiring carving is enough to convince anybody that even if the thing did not possess the power to wreck lives and homes, it ought to. Just what it is, or what it was ever intended to represent, not even the museum curators are able to divine.

The story did not end with the museum's acquisition of the Haida object. Apparently, a whole series of mishaps followed. First, according to the *Morning Call* article, a costly Oriental vase, "which had for months rested snugly and peacefully in one of the Park Museum niches," fell off its stand and shattered on the museum's marble floor, consigning it to the dustbin. "Scarcely an hour later another crash was heard" when an ornamental spire on the roof of the museum's "Egyptian structure" smashed itself to pieces. "And the next day something else fell off its perch and again the day after that" — such that, the museum staff "began to grow extremely alarmed."

Dr. John Hays McLaren (1846–1943) — a close friend of the naturalist John Muir — served as superintendent of Golden Gate Park for fifty-three years. The laying out and supervising of the park earned him a worldwide reputation as a landscape gardener. The newspaper solicited his opinion on the strange series of mishaps:

> "There's a hoodoo around this place somewhere, and nobody can convince me that there is not," said Superintendent McLaren in a worried sort of way, when he was told of the mishaps, and had essayed to solve the mystery. "We will have to locate the thing and get it out of here, that's all," he added with a determined shake of his head.
>
> Then was inaugurated the search for the evil-possessed object that was threatening to totally destroy the park's collection of antiquities. It was not until yesterday, however, that the "hoodoo" was cornered, and now it is dollars to marbles that the thing, if allowed to stay in the park at all, will be relegated to some isolated spot out on the hills, where it will have little opportunity to exert its evil influence.

The *San Francisco Call* warned its readers, "People who visit the park from now on need not be surprised if their buttons pop off their clothes, if they stub their toes, slide on banana peels, or get knocked over by bicycles. It will be the work of that idol."

What are we to make of this fascinating story? And what happened to the "hoodoo"?

I began sleuthing archival records for the old Golden Gate Park Museum. Apparently, curators of the time had dedicated a room, among their many exhibits, to John L. Bardwell, their largest donor at the time. "Bardwell's Old Curiosity Shop" contained hundreds of curios; the "hoodoo" was likely among them.

My endless search for the missing Haida artifact produced no immediate results. I began to wonder whether this rather fanciful story by a nineteenth century paper was true, or whether spooked museum officials had truly consigned the carving to the hills. Nevertheless, there were Haida objects in the museum, so I continued in my attempts to locate the provenance for Bardwell's collections — until, suddenly, I hit the motherlode!

The "Hoodoo" That Is Causing Consternation at the Park.

Sketch of the mysterious artifact, or "The 'Hoodoo' That is Causing Consternation at the Park."

Today, listed as a "Feast Bowl" (Accession Number: 5751) by the Fine Arts Museums of San Francisco, the catalogue entry confirms the previous ownership outlined in the 1897 news story. The listing for provenance records not only that it was gifted by Bardwell that year, but that the previous possessors were indeed "Hans Anderson, sea Captain and trader, the Captain of the sealing schooner O.F. Fowler, Robert Llewelyn, San Francisco, [and] John Coyne, tinsmith and plumber, San Francisco."

Eureka!

Did the San Francisco newspaper embellish this strange tale to drive attendance at the Golden Gate Park Museum? Perhaps, though the main elements of this puzzling story appear largely true — that is, but for one further perplexing riddle.

Contemporary Californian museum officials catalogued the supposed "Hoodoo" not as a Haida artwork, but as "Kwakiutl," an Indigenous nation to the south of Haida Gwaii that has re-established their traditional name of Kwakwaka'wakw — no wonder it took so long to locate! And while museums have been known to make mistakes, I will leave further investigations to other interested parties who may want to follow the trail.

LOST IN THE MOUNTAINS ON CHRISTMAS DAY

The untold story of the fearsome winter of 1858.

WHEN I WAS YOUNG it seemed that our winters in British Columbia were colder. I remember skating on frozen farm fields in Saanich with delightful names such as Panama Flats or Quick's Bottom! My father tells me that when he was a young lad, he used to ice skate on Portage Inlet just outside the capital city.

Good story. But surely the best family story of cold times on Vancouver Island came from my grandfather, who was born at Christmas Hill, in Saanich. I vividly remember each time he told the story that his eyes would light up along with his old meerschaum pipe — which I still have.

In 1916, Victoria was inundated with such a tremendous fall of snow (drifting to over six feet in height) that the city came to a standstill — Victoria is the only Canadian city west of the Great Lakes to hold the record for so much snow in so little time. Local military forces deployed 150 soldiers to assist the city.

My grandfather, aged twelve at the time, recalled the snow drifts were so deep that many nearly covered the tops of telephone poles. My great-grandfather, having experienced colder winters in nineteenth century B.C., was nonplussed and simply got out the horse and sleigh.

This got me thinking about what it must have been like in earlier cold snaps. How would you survive? One story generally untold today is about when the Fraser River froze up in the winter of 1858. Many gold miners were stranded, the steamboats they were on were largely unable to break through the ice and many a foreign-born miner was forced to tramp through thick snows and, occasionally, not-so-thick ice.

Captain Thomas "Bully" Wright

It is reported that more than a few prospectors plunged through the ice into the river with their heavy packs and perhaps some weighty gold in a desperate attempt to reach far-distant Fort Langley on foot. Indeed there are accounts of miners found destitute and near the point of death, snow blinded and exhausted, clutching their Fraser River gold while warning away at gunpoint anyone who came close for fear of losing their treasure. Only "Bully" Wright, a riverboat captain who pioneered travel on the Columbia River, made the determined decision to rescue as many gold seekers as he could. He rammed the steamboat through the ice, breaking it up, full steam ahead — apparently with tears streaming down his cheeks at the thought of so many lost in winter's hard embrace.

As Wright steamed up the river, lost gold seekers were alerted to his approach by the continual blast of the ship's steam whistle — you can imagine just how grateful those human souls were that help was on the way.

One of the great storytellers of the British Columbia and California gold-seeking era is Halifax-born newspaperman David W. Higgins, who joined the Fraser River gold rush from San Francisco during the height of the rush north.

During the furious winter of 1858, Higgins decided to stay put in Yale and await the return of both miners and the mining season in spring of 1859. Considering what happened to others, that was probably the smartest move. Higgins remained hunkered down — except for one particular occasion, venturing out in the mountains above Yale.

I found myself drawn to his tale of how harsh and unpredictable nature can be, the kind of pluck and zest for adventure many had — and how fortunate we are today for all the creature comforts of modern living.

It was the day before Christmas. Provisions were low, as the frozen river prevented the arrival of steamboats like Captain Wright's.

> The holiday season of 1858 found the people of the Fraser River town of Yale ill-prepared to face the rigors of a severe winter. Cold weather, which had set in unusually early, found many of the inhabitants still living in tents, and few occupied dwellings that were comfortable or storm and frost-defying. The lower river was closed by a sharp frost on the first day of December, and communication with the outer world, except to those who chose to risk their lives by walking over the ice, was suspended.

> Supplies were scarce and high, and long before Christmas Day arrived people began to talk dismally of the prospects of a famine in the prime necessaries.

The prospect of famine was always a concern in this first year of the gold rush, so dependent were gold seekers on early steamboat technology to avert disaster. For gold seekers like Higgins, one simply boarded such a ship from the docks of San Francisco to Victoria, then took another steamer from Victoria all the way to Yale — it was just that easy. But if the steamers stopped, not only was the flow of miners impeded but also food, booze and other essentials of life.

> When the day before Christmas dawned, the absence of the wherewithal for a seasonable dinner was seriously discussed. There was no poultry in town, but at Hedges' wayside house, some four miles up the Little Canyon, it was known that there were a small flock of hens and two geese that had been specially fattened for the festive occasion.

> It was more in a spirit of adventure than anything else that four of us young fellows, Lambert, Talbot, Nixon and myself, proposed to tramp over the mountain trail to Hedges', and purchase half-a-dozen of his birds for our tables.

We started about two o'clock on the day before Christmas. The snow, which was about two feet deep on the town-site, gradually increased in depth as we ascended the trail, until we reached the summit, where the snow was three feet, rendering locomotion exceedingly difficult. It took us till six o'clock to reach Hedges', a trip that was usually made in one and one-half hours. We were completely exhausted when we came in sight of the smoke from the rude chimney, and saw the welcome glare of a light in the window as a beacon for belated travellers.

Higgins and his confreres had made their destination and were greeted with "a few drops of oh! be-joyful," and "a bountiful repast of pork and beans" while the wind continued to pile snow in great drifts against the roadhouse.

The storm continued throughout Christmas Eve as they sat by a welcoming fire and speculated on the chances of returning to Yale in time for Christmas Day.

The landlord declared that it would be a physical impossibility for any person to pass up or down the river until the storm had abated, but we Yaleites did not agree with him. We told him that we had promised to return to Yale by noon on Christmas Day with some of his fowls … for I had a suspicion that Hedges, in discouraging our leaving, was anxious to retain us as guests until he had milked us of our last coin.

With morning's arrival the storm had not abated in the slightest and the temperature remained intensely cold, with the roadhouse now buried in snow "and enormous drifts everywhere." Nevertheless "we four foolish young men proposed to start for home with the birds after an early breakfast."

Several old miners who had returned from farther up the Fraser and had experienced huge challenges in making it to the roadhouse thought them utterly mad.

One grey-haired prospector likened us to a lot of silly geese, and another said we ought to be sent to an asylum for idiots to have our heads examined. Another produced a tapeline, and with a solemn expression on his grim face proceeded to measure us. "What for?" asked one of our party. "I'm a carpenter out of a job," he said, "and I shall begin to make four coffins the moment you pass out of sight, so that, when you are brought back stiff and stark, there will be nice, comfortable shells to put you in. Bill here (pointing to his mate) will proceed to dig four graves as soon as the storm is over."

We all laughed heartily, but chaff and entreaties were futile. We discarded all advice, shouldered the poultry, and proceeded to pick our way up the mountain side, intending to follow a zig-zag trail. The snow was indeed deep, and as we advanced it grew deeper. We broke our way through several heaps fully six feet high. The wind howled dismally through the trees and underbrush, scooping up as it swept by great armfuls of snow, and piling it in fantastic shapes and drifts on all sides.

Once out of sight of the roadhouse, the path completely vanished with no discernible landmarks visible to guide them. Higgins recalled looking at his watch:

We had started at eight o'clock, and it was now eleven. We had not made, according to my calculation, a mile; besides, we had no compass, and, being off the trail, it was impossible to tell whether we were going north or south.

We floundered on through the snow, which grew deeper and deeper as we ascended the mountain. Sometimes one of the party would step into a hole and disappear for a few moments. We would all stop, and, having hauled him out, would press on again in the hope of again recovering the lost trail. The cold grew sharper and the wind fiercer. We were fairly well wrapped in woollens. There was one fur coat in the party, and the wearer of it, young Talbot, who was not at all robust, seemed to feel the cold more keenly than the other three. Several times he paused as if unable to go on, but we rallied him and chafed him and coaxed him, until he was glad to proceed.

Another hour passed in the senseless effort to overcome the relentless forces of nature, and by that time we were four as completely used up and penitent men as ever tried to scale a mountain in the midst of a howling snow-storm, with the thermometer standing at zero. Talbot at last sank in a drift, panting for breath and weeping from exhaustion. We dug him out with our hands, and he tried to rise, but his strength was spent.

"Boys," he moaned, as he sank down again, "I am done. I can go no further. Leave me here. My furs may keep me warm until you can get help; but, at any rate, save yourselves if you can. I am not afraid to die, but I would rather not die on Christmas Day with my boots on."

"Fiddlesticks!" cried I. "What nonsense to talk of dying. We are all right. Only make another effort and we'll be at the summit. After that it will be all downhill and dead easy."

Talbot shook his head sadly, and continued, "Promise me you won't let me die with my boots on." Tears sprang from his eyes, and froze on his cheeks. He lay helpless and inanimate in the snow. Lambert and Nixon were strong and sturdy young men and as brave as lions; but they were greatly disheartened at the condition of our wretched companion. Besides, like me, they suffered severely from the cold, which had grown more intense as we proceeded.

All wished that we had listened to the expostulations of the people at the inn; but it was too late now for regrets — there was only room for action. Something must be done quickly or all would perish.

We divested ourselves of our packs, casting the fowls from us as if we hoped never to see another goose or chicken so long as we might live. The fowls sank in the new-fallen snow, and we saw them no more, and with them disappeared the wherewithal for a grand Christmas dinner which we were taking to our friends at Yale.

While we deliberated as to the best course to pursue, for it was as difficult to retrace our steps as it was to proceed, the snow having obliterated our footsteps, a sudden cry from Lambert attracted my attention. Pointing to Talbot, he exclaimed: "He has fallen asleep! Wake him up, in God's name, or he'll freeze to death!"

We seized Talbot and stood him on his feet. He was limp and helpless, and fell over again; his eyes were half-closed, and his breathing was so faint that when I put my face against his lips I could scarcely detect the slightest evidence that life still abode in that tired body. We rubbed his face, hands and ears with snow. Lambert and Nixon called him by name and begged him to speak. We pounded him on the back and stood him up again; but although he began to show faint signs of awakening, he was so far gone that he could not raise foot or finger to help himself.

Higgins quickly gathered a few pine limbs and with a knife hurriedly made kindling to start a small fire to sit Talbot by — all the while rubbing and pounding the young lad — and plying him with "a few drops of a cordial commonly known as H. B. Company rum."

Talbot was revived but weak "and kept calling on his mother, who was thousands of miles away." The foursome now decided to wait out the storm by the fire.

"By Jove," said Lambert, "why didn't we think of it before? If we had kept those chickens we might have had a rousing Christmas dinner after all. We might have cooked them at this fire." But it was too late. We searched, but could not find the first feather. So we tightened our belts, consulted our flasks and tobacco pouches, and sat down by the fire. Talbot, having become rested by this time, showed no signs of falling asleep, but he was very weak and despondent.

About two o'clock the snow ceased to fall, and the wind gradually fell from a roaring blast to a gentle zephyr, and then died away altogether. Towards the south, the sky, which for two or three days had presented a hard, steely aspect, seemed to darken. Presently great heavy masses of clouds stole slowly along the eastern horizon, the cold lessened, and the temperature rose rapidly.

Then we knew that a Chinook wind had set in, that the back of the cold weather was broken, and that if we could but regain the lost trail we should be saved!

The problem for Higgins and friends was they could not find the trail — and nightfall was rapidly approaching. Lost in the mountains on Christmas Day, Higgins despaired that they must remain a further night "and tightened my belt another hole" for lack of any provisions. But a sudden welcoming sound pierced the snow-blanketed silence of their makeshift camp "and sent a thrill of joy through my tired and aching frame. 'Is it the ring of a woodman's axe echoing through the canyon?' I asked myself."

Higgins began to listen intently:

My heart almost stood still as I paused to listen. Then there broke full upon my ear the deep bay of a dog! It rolled up from the valley, and reverberated through the rocky depths, disturbing the awful stillness of the forest, and imparting to me hope and confidence at the prospect of a rescue.

I drew my revolver from my belt and fired five charges. I listened to the reports as they echoed through the forest and died away in the distance. Then — oh! thrice welcome sound! Never in all my life did a human voice seem so sweet in my ears as that which I heard utter almost at my feet:

"Coo-ee! — coo-ee!"

I must have "Coo-eed-d" in response, because again I heard clear and full and distinct a man's voice, as he shouted: "Where are ye, boys?"

"Here," I cried, "this way."

In another moment a great mastiff broke through an enormous drift and barked loudly as if to encourage us, my companions having by this time become apprised that help was at hand. Talbot rose to his feet in his excitement and tried to call, but his voice died away, and he could not utter a word. He tried again and again, until his vocal chords at last limbered up, and he managed to burst the bonds of silence that his excitement had imposed upon him, and emitted a long, resonant:

"Coo-ee! — coo-ee!"

We shouted again and again, and soon from the foot of the mountain there came back the answering call of many voices. The mastiff leaped as if with gratification at having found us, and led the way down the mountain side.

We plunged through snow that reached to our armpits, following the dog, and in a short time we came in sight of a large cabin with smoke curling from an ample chimney. As we approached a number of men came out to greet us. I paused to look and rubbed my eyes.

"Is this a dream? Where are we, anyhow?"

Higgins was as astonished as Hedges, the innkeeper of the roadhouse they had left that morning, approached them. "I didn't expect to see you silly boys alive again," he said, "and I ought to have tied you up before I let you go out in the storm. Come in, anyhow, and have something, and then join us in our Christmas dinner, which is just about ready."

Having escaped a narrow brush with death, they were elated to sit down "to a roast of fowl and goose, and spent a jolly evening." Apparently the only one disappointed in their safe return was the "carpenter out of a job" who, rather grim-faced, muttered, "Well, I'll be durned. It's just my luck. I'm out fifty dollars on your coffins." Higgins recorded, "Everyone laughed at this, but few besides ourselves understood how nearly our obstinacy and self-conceit had brought us to the 'narrow home.'"

Steamboat *William Irving* at Yale B.C., c. 1866–70.

Back in Yale, everyone had given them up for lost. But two days on Higgins and company straggled into town thankful to have returned and subsequently rather annoyed that Hedges, the innkeeper, gossiped to the Yale townsfolk that "in all our wanderings and flounderings we had never been more than an eighth of a mile from the inn, having walked around in a circle after we lost the trail!"

Victoria pioneer Edgar Fawcett, in *Some Reminiscences of Old Victoria* (1912), wrote of the colder winters of the past, which he considered in later years "sadly lacking," and "our climate has changed very much since then."

His mark of a good winter was such that "Christmas, to be genuine, should be bright and frosty, with a flurry of snow, and this with walking exercise makes the blood flow freely, and makes one feel better able to enjoy the festive occasion."

After his arduous trek during the winter of 1858, one wonders whether David Higgins would have agreed.

THE CONFOUNDING TALE
OF A "PHANTOM CITY"

How a contrived illusion once enchanted the world
— and the Victoria resident who sniffed it out.

As a historian living alongside the great Juan de Fuca Strait in Victoria, this amazing passageway — surely one of the great waterways of the world — has kept my rapt attention for years.

Whether viewing the magnificent Olympic Mountains as I stroll along the foreshore or scale the heights of Beacon Hill, my thoughts of early explorations abound: the Spanish, British and American ships that plied these waters through ancient Indigenous lands and the Juan de Fuca legend itself: a sixteenth-century tale that foretold of a "land ... rich of Gold, Silver, Pearle, and other things like Nova Spania."

Centuries later, gold seekers travelling up the coast from San Francisco in 1858 sailed directly by a large rock spire, today called Fuca Pillar, at the entrance to the strait. This extraordinary landmark, in fact, was spoken of in English merchant Michael Lok's centuries-old account of Greek pilot Juan de Fuca's voyage, and it's right in our own backyard!

So much human history has been compressed into this ocean corridor — a historian's playground of the imagination — but perhaps less known is that this inland sea produces some of the most amazing natural phenomena to this very day. What is that, you ask? It's a spectacular light

Fuca Pillar at the entrance to the Strait of Juan de Fuca.

show, seen every summer when the conditions are just right for periodic mirages that visually shapeshift the natural order of things.

The Straits of Georgia, Juan de Fuca and Puget Sound are the best areas for viewing "superior mirages," in which objects near the surface are expanded or projected upwards and occasionally are even inverted.

I have always wondered why these curiosities don't receive more public attention, especially considering they so enchanted observers in the past! Apparently, Beacon Hill was, and still is, the favoured viewpoint for a "Fata Morgana." An Italian translation of Morgan le Fay from the legend of King Arthur, the term describes a mirage image of spikes and towers that can appear just above the horizon. Newspaper reports of the nineteenth century from Victoria recorded these mirages as "indescribably grand," which "far excelled anything of the kind we had ever before witnessed." Race Rocks Lighthouse, which is located just off the southern tip of Vancouver Island, at times was seemingly "duplicated on different portions of the reef" and on another occasion "a large vessel with all sail set was speeding towards the straits, and high up in the clouds appeared another vessel, a counterpart of the one on the water, upside down!"

Indeed, a June 6, 1868 account from the *Daily Colonist* recorded the "beautiful phenomenon" from atop Beacon Hill:

Fictional version of superior mirages.

The sea was calm and the atmosphere hot, a large vessel was under full sail down the Straits, when suddenly it changed its appearance; a large black object was then seen floating in the air directly over the mast-head, from which gradually descended sails and masts, until they reached the mast-head of the vessel underneath; after floating about for some time faded away, and again reappeared with double refraction. Two ships in the air and one underneath poised exactly one above the other ... The hills of Sooke became inverted over the light-house, and as if thrown across to the opposite shore, at least 100 feet in the air ... thus forming a natural and beautiful bridge from Sooke to the Olympian range ... the whole scene constantly changing and forming phantasies as strange as they are beyond description. It was a wild and weird scene, which would not be often witnessed in a life time.

In the days before radio, television and the internet, such contorted landscapes and illusory "phantom ships" were seen up and down the Pacific Slope. Did we humans simply spend more time recreating outside than we do today?

By the end of the nineteenth century these "castles in the air" took on increasingly more complex mirage forms — that of cities floating in the air. Audiences were captivated, and the emerging tourism industry took note.

Probably the best known mirage story of the late nineteenth and early twentieth centuries was a wonderous tale told by Richard Willoughby

Richard Willoughby, 1858

(1832–1902), a transnational gold seeker who had participated in the California, British Columbia and Alaskan/Yukon rushes and who was referred to as "Professor" by the locals.

Willoughby, an "Indian-fighter" from Missouri and later a "Texas Cowboy" in the punitive raids into Mexico, took the Pacific coast inland routes via the Columbia and Okanagan river systems to British Columbia in 1858. Of his journey from California to British Columbia, Willoughby recalled the military-like precision with which their party proceeded toward the Fraser River, their intrusion (along with thousands of others) leading to the "Indian Wars" of that year in Washington Territory.

Willoughby had been involved in a battle at McLoughlin Canyon, just south of the border, at the same time that the Fraser Canyon War was unfolding north of the forty-ninth parallel. He eventually mined for gold along the Fraser, the Cariboo and elsewhere in British Columbia before making his way up to Alaska, where today a street and island are named after him — along with a creek in B.C.

In about 1885, he promoted the astounding claim to have photographed a "phantom city" above the Muir Glacier in Alaska.

While anthropologist Franz Boas had photographed a number of mirages on his trip to Baffin Island in 1883–84, Willoughby's 1885 claim was of a far greater magnitude — a substantial Fata Morgana, or "the Silent City" found hovering over the icefields in what is today Glacier Bay National Park.

The *Alaskan News*, on July 26, 1888, was just one of many to report Willoughby's incredible discovery.

> Dick Willoughby succeeded in securing two excellent
> negatives of the wonderful city reflected on the glassy sur-
> face of the Pacific glacier. He photographed it from two

different positions, and there obtained one view looking across the main streets and the other looking down them. The city, or mirage, appears just after the change of the moon in June, and just as the sun is setting in the evening behind the Fairweather range and while the moon is climbing the heavens in the east.

Dick first became aware of the appearance of this city of the icebergs through the Indians, and has since for a number of years past with his own eyes seen it appear and disappear ... Each succeeding year he has noted a rapid growth to the city, and one building, which was but a foundation four years ago, is now a massive structure seven stories high. Dick attempted to photograph it last year, but only succeeded in getting a blurred negative; however, this year, the atmosphere being more favourable, his attempt resulted in two clear negatives.

"Various were the conjectures as to the locality from which the shadow was evolved," wrote the *Colonist* on October 17, 1889. Victoria, Seattle, Portland and San Francisco were initially put forth as the basis for the glimmering mirage, and some went farther, suggesting that "the mysterious city was the phantom of Montreal."

Photograph of the Silent City over Muir Glacier attributed to Richard Willoughby.

While news of the Silent City spread throughout North America, Willoughby commenced selling copies of his now famous photograph in addition to guided tours of the glacier. By 1897, even *Popular Science* magazine published a full account.

As early tourists to Alaska started in search of the mysterious apparition (with Willoughby's guidance), soon the scientific community began to question his claims. The *San Francisco Call* alerted its readership on April 28, 1901, that "a party of scientists" would soon leave Vancouver to study the Silent City mirage.

More than a dozen years had transpired since Willoughby had first proclaimed the Silent City, and as the years went by the city's size and detail grew with the many visitors claiming to have seen the remarkable vision. For instance, the *Colonist* recorded on February 7, 1901, that a Mrs. C.S. Longstreet, a "well-known writer and traveler" had visited Alaska in 1899 with the hope of catching a glimpse: "I was with a party crossing Lake Lebarge. We were going slowly, and had plenty of time to look about us. Suddenly something loomed up ahead of us, and there we saw rising from the mountains a misty picture of an ancient city. Each object was perfectly outlined. The sight was too vivid to doubt of its reality."

Increasing numbers of tourists continued to travel to Alaska to see the fabled sight, and apparently cruise ship passengers were still searching for the phantom city as late as 1928.

There seemed to be no stopping the public's fascination with Willoughby's story; that is, until W.G. Stuart, an employee of Wells, Fargo and Company, happened to see a copy of the picture in a Montgomery Street shop in San Francisco.

He recognized the city at once as Bristol, England, where he had formerly been clerk under the United States Consul. And soon, the anomalies of Willoughby's story began to unravel.

Interestingly, the last word on this story is told by T.A. Rickard, "one of the world's foremost mining engineers," who retired to Victoria and eventually became a president of the British Columbia Historical Association (the precursor to today's B.C. Historical Federation).

In Rickard's semiautobiographical work, *Autumn Leaves* (1948), he tells of travelling to Alaska and investigating the Silent City conundrum.

I was shown an alleged photograph of the so-called Silent City said to have been seen above the Muir glacier. Photographic prints of this marvel were sold to tourists by Richard Willoughby, known locally as "the professor". I scented a pseudo scientific fake and took the trouble to expose it. The fraud was done skilfully, and many were fooled by it for many years. Willoughby asserted that he had seen this vision of a modern city with church towers, office buildings, and people on the streets in the air above the glacier. He had photographed it on June 21, 1885. And if it could be photographed, it must have been there, of course. The Professor had a white beard and a resonant voice. He was impressive. The leading citizens of Juneau decided that the story was a drawing-card for tourists, and they encouraged him to place his prints on sale. When I examined one of them, I noted that it showed trees that were leafless, which seemed inconsistent with what one expects in June. The negative was on glass, and it did not fit Willoughby's plate-holder, nor could the photograph have been taken by his lens, which was meant for portraits. These facts I learned from a friend, who was loath to expose the Professor, because the deception harmed nobody and it brought tourists to Juneau.

Rickard revealed that in 1887 "the Professor had happened to be in Victoria, on Vancouver Island" and while here bought a "photographic outfit, which included a box of glass plates." Among them was one "poorly developed picture of the city of Bristol."

"It reminded him probably of a mirage and the optical effects to be seen above a glacier on a warm day," snitched Rickard, and there "arose the idea of a photograph of a silent city vibrating in the tenuous air of Glacier Bay."

To clinch the evidence, Rickard contacted his cousin near Bristol, to confirm that the exact date of Willoughby's glass plate photograph did not correspond to Silent City's discovery date.

"Some people like to be fooled by alleged marvels" declared Rickard. "Perhaps I should not have interfered with their enjoyment." Or as Mark Twain said, "Reality can be beaten with enough imagination."

I can't help seeing Willoughby right now sailing out the strait past Fuca Pillar, camera in hand, travelling north and marvelling over an inspiring mirage cast by a glacier of the Olympic Peninsula. Perhaps B.C.'s tourism industry should take note.

THE STRANGE CASE OF THE ANOMALOUS ARTIFACT THAT FELL FROM THE SKY

A chance discovery in a Sooke parking lot led to some archaeological sleuthing.

ONE DAY, TRAVELLING INTO THE TOWN of Sooke (named after the T'Sou-ke Nation), on the west coast of Vancouver Island) a friend of mine parked his car outside an office, opened his car door and immediately heard an object hit the ground from the sky. Stepping out of the vehicle, he cast his eyes about to discover that a seagull had dropped something from the air — and was about to retrieve it.

At first, my friend thought it was a piece of plastic and liberated the object; perhaps the bird thought it a nut to be cracked or a shellfish to be opened?

To my friend's surprise, it turned out to be some sort of arrowhead.

He asked whether I could assist in identifying the mysterious find.

"This is astounding," I remarked while taking snaps on my phone. The colour of the stone was unlike any I had seen before. I well knew that such Indigenous antiquities along the southeast coast of Vancouver Island could approach the elusive age of between eight thousand to eleven thousand years old. But the red colour made this find strikingly different, if not an anomaly, compared to other artifacts seen over the years.

Dropped from the heavens: Is it an ancient arrowhead?

I subsequently posted pictures for friends in the various history communities I am associated with throughout B.C. and the larger Pacific Slope region.

The response was fantastic.

Hundreds of opinions were offered. "It's an arrowhead," most claimed. "No, it is a knife, or possibly a scraper" others suggested. Throughout the dialogue, most of these history enthusiasts asked that I keep them posted if further information was discovered.

The public demanded to know! This spurred further investigation and who better to contact than my old friend Grant Keddie, who has since retired as curator of archaeology at the Royal B.C. Museum (RBCM).

Keddie was always so good about taking time from his immensely busy schedule to assist in identifying the myriad of artifacts uncovered in B.C.

"So, what have you got for me today?" enthused Keddie.

I presented him with the artifact without telling him it had been dropped from the sky by a seagull. After an initial examination he promptly said, "I guess you found this in the interior of the province?"

I smiled in return. "No, actually it was found in Sooke!"

With that, we took the elevator to his office in the RBCM's large curatorial tower that houses the museum's immense collections not ordinarily on display.

I asked him from what kind of stone the artifact had been made from. "Red chert" was the immediate answer, with no equivocation from a curator with vast experience in these matters. I knew that obsidian arrowheads found on Vancouver Island had been traceable to lava flows in Terrace or as far away as Oregon. But is there an identified source for red chert in the province?

The answer — there is no known source in B.C. It definitely came from south of the border.

"There are many artifacts made from this material found in the mid-Columbia River region," said Keddie, "but even in that location, the source is still not known."

Keddie consulted his old card catalogues, as I had asked him whether other red chert artifacts had been discovered on southern Vancouver Island.

"Not too many at all really, and certainly not as large as the one you have brought in today," he said, further suggesting only a very few had been collected in the Saanich and Sooke regions.

With each of Keddie's revelations, my curiosity grew. "Can we possibly look at those examples that have been found close to Sooke?" I asked.

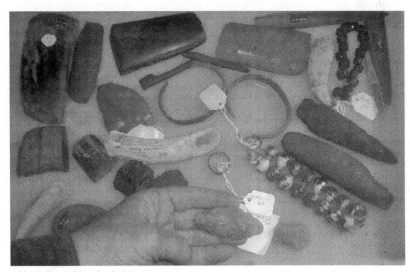

Cabinet of Curiosities, Royal BC Museum.

The renowned archaeologist proceeded to the back room, over-flowing with hundreds of cabinets filled with ancient curiosities. In short order, Keddie opened the Pedder Bay drawer. He plucked out two objects made from red chert that had been collected at Pedder Bay, which is located on Vancouver Island's west coast, south of Sooke, and placed them on a research table. I slid the seagull-dropped object next to them for comparison.

Again, Keddie reiterated that the few red chert–made implements discovered on the Island were rather small next to the one my friend had liberated from the seagull in Sooke.

"If I were a betting man, I'd say that your friend's artifact dates between two thousand to four thousand years old, and perhaps much more," said Keddie, also concluding it was once twice the size it is now. Though possibly an arrowhead, it was more likely an impressive stone knife.

Keddie confirmed that Indigenous archaeological sites existed throughout Sooke Harbour (no surprise, really) and that Spanish explorations had recorded an Indigenous village right below the town of Sooke. The Spanish, of course, had claimed possession of Sooke Harbour, or "Puerto de Revillagigedo," named for the viceroy of New Spain (Mexico) during the first recorded European explorations of this locale by Spanish explorers Quimper and Eliza whose expeditions stayed in this locale in the year 1790, just one year after the Nootka Crisis between Spain and Britain at Yuquot ("Friendly Cove" as Captain Cook called it) on the west coast of Vancouver Island.

This was all very fascinating, of course, but I still wanted to know: How did this extraordinary stone knife make it to Sooke?

Keddie suggested two possibilities: either it was carried during Indigenous warfare from out of the depths of the Puget Sound region or, more likely, it was traded through the extensive Indigenous trade networks that once flourished throughout the Pacific Slope region.

The many more examples of red chert artifacts found in the Okanagan and Kootenay regions certainly suggest the possibility that the Sooke object may have been traded or carried north from below the current international border, from the mid-Columbia Basin (and perhaps even farther south) into the lands of the Interior Salish. From there, it may have been subsequently traded down the Thompson and Fraser River corridors, and then to the Island.

Indigenous Nations on the coast are known to have traded large quantities of dried clams as far away as Spokane, in eastern Washington, and the coastal dentalia shell has been found as far east as the Mississippi River. By the time of the land-based fur trade, the Hudson's Bay Company (HBC) was well aware of these extensive trade networks. My good friend and colleague HBC historian Richard Mackie has stated that the HBC simply grafted company operations onto these pre-existing Indigenous trade networks.

So, there you have it. But the question remains — just where did the seagull get it, and since when do seagulls loot archaeology sites?

The bird obviously failed to crack the "clam" — but I hope I can say that I cracked the case of the anomalous antiquity that fell from the sky.

Thank you, Grant Keddie. Deeply appreciated.

WHAT IS THIS GOLD RUSH CURIOSITY?

A hidden relic from one of mainland B.C.'s oldest remaining houses.

OVER THE YEARS I WAS FORTUNATE to stay at one of the oldest houses still standing along the Lower Fraser River from the gold rush period: the historic Teague House of Yale.

Built in the 1860s, this extraordinarily well-preserved home had a succession of colourful owners, but primarily the family of William Teague. Like thousands of others, Teague had been swept up by the Fraser River excitement of 1858. Teague mined at Cornish (or Murderer's) Bar, south of Hope, and soon held a number of early government appointments, from police officer to gold commissioner to government agent.

Many a night I would sit on the old veranda overlooking not only the mighty Fraser River, but also the original Hope to Yale road that my great-great-great-uncle William rebuilt in the 1870s.

As both Teague and my ancestor were '58ers and from Cornwall, England, it was easy to imagine these two sharing the occasional cup of tea at this very home — a home still filled with Teague's books and other possessions, even his original top hat!

But there is one fascinating curiosity that has gripped my attention for decades: mounted on a nineteenth-century plaque, there hangs a

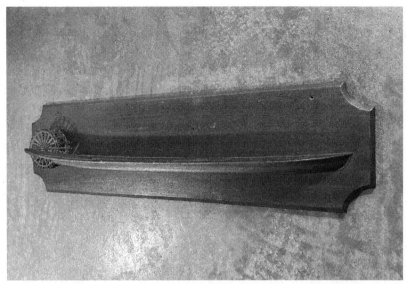

The mysterious artifact hidden in Yale, B.C.

sternwheeler steamship hull, the darkened colour of the wood from which it was fashioned hinting at its significant age.

"What is the story of this amazing piece?" I asked my friends Sue and Darwin Baerg of Fraser River Raft Expeditions, the owners of Teague House at the time.

"Oh that!" they said, their eyes sparkling. "It came with the house and the descendants of the Teague family. They say it has always been here." Beyond that nobody seemed to remember much more about it — but I think now, years later, that I may have uncovered some significant clues!

Yale was the height of steamboat navigation on the Fraser River (steamboats could go no farther than Yale) but even Yale was initially unreachable in the early months of the gold rush. The strong currents and shallow portions of this immense stream prevented most of the first ships from reaching the epicentre of the third greatest rush of gold seekers in recorded history.

The original steamers, coming quickly from Oregon and the Columbia River (and later San Francisco), could only make it as far as Fort Hope. To get beyond Hope, early gold seekers relied heavily on the expertise of Indigenous peoples who offered canoe transport of both miners and goods to Fort Yale.

The boom town of neighbouring Whatcom, on Bellingham Bay in Washington Territory, threatened to supplant Victoria as the major control point of the new El Dorado, in large measure due to an American initiative to blaze a trail across the forty-ninth parallel to the adjacent goldfields.

In short order, Coast Salish peoples (particularly the Stó:lō Nation) were employed to cut firewood and act as deckhands. Their vast years of river experience by canoe was invaluable. One in particular, "Captain John," piloted steamboats, and according to his own reminiscences (given in Chinook and translated in 1898), he amassed some two thousand dollars from his labours.

Jason Allard, son of Hudson's Bay Company chief trader Ovid Allard, recalled the first time the Indigenous pilot was taken aboard the American steamer *Surprise*, anchored off Fort Langley in June 1858. "The pilot was an Indian named Speel-Set. He went aboard the Surprise barefooted and wearing only a blanket. When he returned he came as 'Captain' John dressed in a pilot cloth suit, white hat and calf skin boots, the proudest Indian in the country. More over the sum of $160 was paid through Mr. [James] Yale for the pilot's services — eight twenty dollar gold pieces. The boats thereafter ran to Hope more or less regularly."

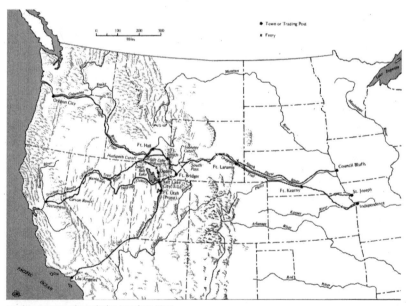

Immigrant routes through the American West.

While the participation of Indigenous peoples was key to the early transportation needs of the gold rush, increasing numbers of gold seekers demanded more efficient and greater lines of supply, and there also was a growing concern to conquer the swift currents and treacherous rapids above Hope with new ships built and fortified for the express purpose of reaching Yale.

Enter William Kelly, a transnational gold seeker who in 1849 had crossed the American Plains to California, then went to Australia in 1852 and subsequently headed to British Columbia in 1858.

Richard Burton

An Irish-born lawyer (I have searched in vain for a photograph of him), Kelly published his account of travels to the California goldfields — a book that subsequently inspired the legendary explorer Sir Richard Burton to follow in Kelly's footsteps. In fact, Burton subsequently nominated Kelly for membership in Britain's prestigious Royal Geographical Society, and he became a fellow member in the early 1860s. Joining this august group would be beneficial to Kelly a few years later.

While in St. Louis, Missouri, Kelly remarked on the allure of gold in California:

> The further west I proceeded, the more intense became the California fever. California met you here at every turn, every corner, every dead wall; every post and pillar was labelled with Californian placards. The shops seemed to contain nothing but articles for California. As you proceeded along the flagways, you required great circumspection, lest your coat-tails should be whisked into some of the multifarious Californian gold-washing machines . . . Californian advertisements, and extracts from Californian letters, filled all the newspapers; and "Are you for California?" was the constantly recurring question of the day; so that one would almost imagine the whole city was on wheels bound for that attractive region.

Kelly also published on his experiences in Australia — he was a regular commentator in the press — and notably argued for Chinese inclusion in the goldfields. The mania described by Kelly is exactly what occurred less than ten years later in the Fraser River rush. When the Fraser River excitement hit, he — like so many others — was once again swept into the mania that quickly transformed what would become British Columbia, a transformative influence that also shape-shifted other economies of the North Pacific Slope: Washington, Oregon and California.

Kelly, already heading to British Columbia before his second book on Australia was published, forecasted from afar the richness of the new El Dorado of the north in *Life in Victoria* (1859):

> I have not the slightest doubt but the discoveries in Brit-
> ish Columbia will offer a temporary check to Australian
> development, because the climate and soil of the new
> colony are more in character with that prevalent in the
> British and European area, from whence the stream of
> emigration was wont to flow towards the antipodes, and
> because the pursuit of gold-getting there is so much
> simpler, speedier, and cheaper. In Victoria [Australia]
> the digger has to penetrate through the obdurate bowels
> of the soil to depths varying from thirty to three hun-
> dred feet, and perhaps, after a vast expenditure of time,
> toil, and money, he may come upon a barren bottom,
> whereas in British Columbia he has only to stand on the
> bar of a river, or throw back the mere alluvial deposit
> along its banks, in order to come at his rich reward.

Arriving in British Columbia in 1858, Kelly established himself in a small shack in Yale, hanging his shingle out as a lawyer. He became good friends with David W. Higgins, later the Speaker of the B.C. legislature, who had also caught the gold bug and decamped from San Francisco in the same year.

Higgins described his first encounter with the argonaut of the Califor-nian and Australian rushes. In his book *The Mystic Spring* (1904) he recorded that he had become homesick for San Francisco, wandering along the foreshore of the town of Yale:

My spirits continued to droop, the melancholy roar of the river as it lapped the huge boulders and the gathering darkness adding to the sombre hue of my mind and deepening my dejection. What might have happened had my thoughts led me further on it is impossible to say, but when a cheery voice in a rich Irish brogue broke the stillness with, "Good evening, sir; I hope you are enjoying your walk" ... My interlocutor was a stout, full-bearded man of about forty-five years. He was very neatly dressed in some black stuff, wore a full brown beard, and was very stout. In his hand he carried a heavy walking-stick. "I Thank you," I replied, "but I am not enjoying my walk a bit. I was just wishing myself well out of the place."

Kelly, veteran of the Californian and Australian rushes, took the young Higgins in hand:

"Tut, tut," replied the man, "you are suffering from nostalgia. Come along with me, my lad, and I'll give you something that'll drive dull care away." Before I could utter a word of remonstrance he had linked an arm in one of mine and led me off towards a little cabin or shack that stood not far from the trail on which I had been pursuing my walk. There, having lighted a candle, he produced a bottle of brandy and a pitcher of water, and insisted on my joining in a glass. He soon became very communicative, and after telling me that his name was William Kelly, a Trinity College man and a barrister, who had passed several years in Australia, and having been attracted to the Fraser River by the reported gold finds on the bars, had decided to try his fortune there. He had also written a book on Australian gold mining adventures, which had been printed in London ... He had a fund of anecdote and could tell a good story, of which I was and still am passionately fond.

The steamship RP *Rithet* in Yale, B.C., c. 1882.

Kelly had quickly perceived that unlike gold rushes in California and Australia, B.C. was hampered by its transportation links to the outside world, and particularly with getting steamers up past Hope. Steamboat technology made the northern goldfields comparatively accessible; a gold seeker in San Francisco could walk down a gangplank, board a ship, travel to Victoria and take another steamer across the Salish Sea (known then as the Strait of Georgia) to enter the mighty Fraser River. Imagine that!

To make that final leg onto the beaches of Yale, one great difficulty had to be surmounted — and Kelly, among others, proposed the solution: specially prepared and powerful shallow-hull steamers that could conquer the rapids and swift currents beyond Hope.

One of the main reasons the Fraser gold rush subsided quickly was the lack of infrastructure: roads, bridges and steamers that could push forward and supply lines of essential goods for an ever-expanding and far-removed field of gold strikes. There is much more to Kelly's story than I have presented here, but on the question of improved steamboat communication, Kelly ultimately left Yale and British Columbia to make his case to the Royal Geographical Society in 1861–62.

Close-up of the sternwheel from Yale, B.C.

Kelly's presentation, entitled "British Columbia and the Proposed Route from Pembina to Yale" is found in the *Proceedings of the Royal Geographical Society* (Session 1861–62). In some ways it is a promotional piece that encouraged emigration while noting B.C.'s disadvantaged position compared to Australia and the United States. Of more particular interest, on May 12, 1862, Kelly exhibited "A Model of a stern-wheel Steamboat, adapted for the navigation of the Fraser River."

Was this the curious model that hangs in the Teague House — or perhaps a copy of the same such model?

Apparently, the art of making half-hulls is as old as shipbuilding itself and the shipbuilders' half-hull model was in common use. Half-hull models were originally made as a design tool but also as a marketing and investment display. Often several models were made before the completion of a full-size ship. To my mind, Kelly presented one such copy of a shallow-hulled model at the Royal Geographical Society, and I have a hunch that the curious Teague House antique may well be the other half of Kelly's exhibit.

What happened to William Kelly after his presentation to the society's members? Oddly, after having published widely on his expedition to

California and his experiences in Australia, Kelly abruptly disappeared. Apparently he had been writing yet another volume of travels — this time to the Fraser River goldfields and British Columbia. This work was neither completed nor published.

Again, what happened to this transnational gold seeker?

If we once again turn to the recollections of his friend David Higgins, a persuasive answer is found:

> On reaching Europe, Kelly, still bent on "Seeing the Elephant," took up his residence at Paris, and there became enamored of a beautiful blonde with a wonderful head of long yellow hair that reached to her heels, and with no morals worth speaking of. In his infatuation he proposed matrimony to the woman and, after settling a round sum in cash upon her, he was accepted and they were married. As the couple were entering a carriage at the door of the church to drive to their rooms a process-server tapped the bridegroom on the shoulder and handed him a court paper, and he was placed under arrest for debt — his wife's debts, contracted before marriage! Of course, he was furious, but he was taken to the debtors' prison and incarcerated, his bride driving away in the carriage her husband had hired to take them to the nuptial chamber. They never met again ... The artful woman had apparently arranged to have her husband arrested immediately after the marriage, so that she might make off with another of her admirers, and the money Kelly had given her. I never heard what became of Kelly. I fear he died in prison.

Higgins himself never found out what became of his companion, but I discovered that apparently Kelly died some ten years after being conned, on March 4, 1872, in Boulogne-sur-Mer, France.

As one of the principal characters in his book *The Mystic Spring*, Higgins never forgot the well-travelled Irish lawyer. When Higgins returned to Yale many decades later, he was still thinking about him:

> As I moved along the road I came to a huge boulder upon which Kelly, the Australian barrister, and I, in the

long ago were wont to recline and smoke our pipes, exchanging stories of our earlier life and speculating as to the future. I took a seat on the rock and my mind was soon busy with the past. As I mused it almost seemed as if my old-time acquaintance sat by my side once more …I recalled that one pleasant evening in July, 1859, we two boon companions sat on this identical boulder and indulged in day-dreams.

Having scoured the Yale waterfront for the last many decades, I believe I know where this giant rock is. I have comfortably perched atop it myself on many occasions where my own daydreams and historical speculations — the kind that have led to this story — were encouraged, perhaps particularly so, because it was the main docking point for all those steamboats to Yale that Kelly had dreamed of; to this day, a great substantial iron ring remains embedded in the rock, where shallow-hulled sternwheelers like Kelly envisaged once securely tied.

How is it that stories like his are forgotten? How is it that we know so little of such a prominent transnational gold seeker and know so little about our foundational experience of a gold rush that, for a moment in time, so caught the attention of the world it was about to potentially eclipse the California experience?

Kelly's story and the sternwheeler model of Yale are clues to this extraordinary past. But perhaps it is no surprise that British Columbia has lost so much of its early memory. After all, gold rushes have produced some of the most transient populations to have ever wandered the globe — the largely unknown William Kelly among them.

SEVEN:
THREE
EXTRAORDINARY
WOMEN

THE MYSTERIOUS
TRAVELLER

The remarkable story of "Harry" Collins, the gold rush and the man who reconnected the Collins family.

PRIOR TO CONFEDERATION with Canada in 1871, British Columbia was part of a natural north-south world west of the Rocky Mountains. I have always been fascinated by this pre-provincial period, and particularly the many historic connections between B.C. and California and the gold rush populations that once freely travelled up and down the Pacific coast.

One of the great storytellers of the British Columbia and California gold-seeking era was newspaperman David W. Higgins, who joined the Fraser River gold rush of 1858 from San Francisco during the height of the rush north.

Born in Halifax, David moved with his family to New York where he was educated and subsequently apprenticed as a journeyman printer. By 1856 the lure of California gold saw his relocation to the Golden State, where Higgins became the joint proprietor and editor of the *San Francisco Morning Call*, the newspaper that later employed Mark Twain as the paper's Nevada correspondent.

Before Twain started reporting for the *Morning Call*, Higgins had already departed for the new El Dorado of the north, established a store in Yale, B.C., the epicentre of the 1858 gold rush, and opened an agency for Billy Ballou's Express Company. He remained there for a little under two years before relocating to Victoria, where he became the editor of the *British Colonist* newspaper and pursued a career in early provincial politics that included nine years as Speaker of the legislature.

"During the half century that I was in active life," wrote Higgins, "I made copious notes of events as they transpired. I carefully studied the peculiarities of speech, the habits and mode of life, and the frailties as well as the virtues of the early gold-seekers on the Pacific Coast." Higgins subsequently authored two volumes of reminiscences, *The Mystic Spring and Other Tales of Western Life* (1904) and *The Passing of a Race and More Tales of Western Life* (1905), concerned primarily with the transnational gold-seeking populations of the Pacific Slope. The books were well received, with one influential journal declaring that "Mr. Higgins has done for Victoria and British Columbia what Bret Harte did for the Western United States mining districts."

Bret Harte was an American short-story writer who featured miners, gamblers and other roman-tic figures of the California gold rush. Without a doubt, Harte (who was seen camping at Point Roberts during the 1858 rush) and Twain popu-larized stories of the California mining frontier. British Columbia has its own equivalent story-teller: David W. Higgins. He sought to capture the life of gold rush communities "who peopled the Pacific Coast" and the "peculiarities that have engrafted themselves upon society of the pres-ent day, and may ever remain prominent features of life ... in California and the British Pacific."

David W. Higgins

Here is one of Higgins's intriguing stories from his time in Yale, enti-tled "A Child that Found Its Father." It's the curious story of Harry Collins, whom Higgins met, befriended and employed subsequently in his Yale store.

Higgins called it "one of the strangest experiences in my life."

To the thousands of gold seekers, gamblers and card sharks roaming the banks of the Fraser in 1858, Harry Collins — a recent arrival from San Francisco — was a slightly built, pleasant young man. He was looking for his older brother, George, who had a mining claim somewhere on one of the many sand and gravel bars along the Fraser River.

Higgins recalled how he had travelled by steamer from Victoria to Yale along with the young Collins lad, who was in a seemingly destitute state:

> We reached Yale before dark and landed at once. I am sorry to say that I forgot all about Collins ... and I went to my own quarters back of the express office ... The next morning, while writing at my desk, I heard a footstep, and looking up saw my fellow passenger of the day before. He looked wan and ill, and black half circles under his eyes gave evidence of great weariness, if not want of sleep.
>
> "Are there any letters for Harry Collins?" he asked, timidly. "None," replied Vann [Higgins' assistant]. "Any for George Collins?" The same answer was returned, and he was walking slowly away when I arose and asked him where he was staying in town? "Nowhere," he replied.
>
> "Nowhere!" I exclaimed. "Do you mean to say — where did you stay last night?"
>
> "I didn't stay anywhere. I just walked back and forth between here and the Indian village."
>
> "Good gracious, man," I cried, "why did you not knock me up? I'd given you a place to sleep."

Higgins subsequently took the young Collins under his wing, providing him food, lodgings and employment on his mining claim at Fort Yale Bar. During one of Higgins's inspections of his claim on the foreshore of Yale, he quickly saw the young man was not particularly suited to the hard rigours of mining life.

> There I saw Collins standing on top of a long range of sluice boxes, armed with a sluice fork, engaged in clearing the riffles of large stones and sticks which, unless removed, would obstruct passage of the water and gravel

and prevent capture of the tiny specks of gold by the quicksilver with which the rifles were charged.

On the way I met the foreman. He was in a white rage because I had sent a "counter-jumper," a mere whipper-snapper, down to do a miner's work. He tried him at the shovel and pick, and he was too weak to handle them, and so he had put him at the lightest of job on the sluices. "He won't take off his coat like the other boys, and all the men are threatening to strike because they have to do harder work for the same pay that he's getting. There he stands, with his long duster flapping in the wind. Like a pillow-case on a clothesline," concluded the foreman with a look of disgust on his face.

"Never mind, Bill," said I, "you won't be troubled with him anymore. I have a better job for him."

Young Harry Collins sitting outside the Express Office.

Higgins promptly installed young Collins in his Yale store where he "proved to be an excellent cook, as neat as any housewife, and a fairly good bookkeeper."

Each evening after his duties Collins "would sit on a box in front of the store and listen to the wonderful tales of gold finds as they were narrated by miners and prospectors."

But through it all, recalled Higgins, he continued to be preoccupied with finding his long-lost brother who, it was assumed, must be somewhere in the upper goldfields. "Of every miner who came into the office from above the canyon Collins made anxious inquiries about his brother. Did they know him by name, or had they met anyone who answered to the description which he gave them? The answers were always in the negative, but he never despaired and every failure seemed only to incite him to renewed inquiries."

As Higgins, too, became increasingly preoccupied with finding Harry's brother, he also confessed to having become "strongly and unaccountably drawn towards him [Harry]."

> A strange emotion stirred in my heart and a wave of tenderness such as I had never before experienced swept through every fibre of my being. What ails me? I asked myself ... Why should I be attracted towards him more than to any other young man? Why was I always happy when he was near and depressed when he was absent? Why did I lie awake at night trying to work out some plan to send word to his brother? Why did the sound of his voice or his footstep send the hot young blood bounding through my veins? What was he to me that every sense should thrill, and my heart beat wildly at his approach?

The mystery of Harry Collins would soon be answered for David Higgins. One day four months into Collins's stay at the Yale Express Office, Harry was taken ill and Dr. Fifer — the local medical physician — was called to attend. After inspecting the patient, Fifer emerged from a back room in the office to report his findings to an anxious Higgins.

"It's my duty to tell you that Harry Collins is no more!"

"Mercy!" I cried, shrinking back. "Not dead? Not dead?"

"Well, no, not dead; but you'll never see him again."

"If he is not dead," I said, greatly agitated, "tell me what has happened or why I shall never see him again. You should not keep me in suspense."

"Well," said the doctor, laughing heartily, "he is not dead. He is very much alive. Harry Collins is gone, but in his place there is a comely young woman who calls herself Harriet Collins, the wife of one George Collins, who is now above the canyon hunting for gold."

"Harry" was really Harriett Collins: a young, pregnant wife from San Francisco searching for her husband in the chaos of the Fraser River gold-fields. Disguised for safety as a man, she looked for her husband, George, amid the rowdy mining town of Yale.

The two were shortly reunited when George returned to Yale. Their baby daughter was subsequently named Caledonia H. Collins, honouring both the location of her birth (British Columbia was previously called New Caledonia) and the "H" standing for Higgins in recognition of her host's kind hospitality. The fact that Harriet felt compelled to masquerade as a male during her trip north and subsequent four-month stay in Yale is suggestive of the chaotic, male-dominated world this young woman was compelled to travel through.

Yale, B.C., where Harry became Harriet.

The reunited couple along with their baby daughter soon left for California never to be seen again but for one last communication from San Francisco:

> Some weeks after Mr. and Mrs. Collins had gone away, engraved cards for the christening at San Francisco of a mite to be named Caledonia H. Collins were received by nearly everyone in Yale. Mine was accompanied by an explanatory note that the "H" stood for my surname, and that I was to be the godfather ... Nine years sped away before I was enabled to visit San Francisco, and diligent enquiries failed to discover any trace of the Collins family. They had moved away from the city, and I never since heard of or from them. Somewhere on the face of this globe there should be a mature female who rejoices in the name of Caledonia H. Collins. If these lines should meet her eye I would be glad to learn her whereabouts, for I would travel many miles to meet the woman who under such extraordinary circumstances became my god-daughter.

Higgins never again met Harriet, George or Caledonia Collins, but perhaps one day a genealogist will discover their whereabouts!

THE FLAPPER AND
THE PREMIER

The scandal that rocked the Dunsmuir Family —
and British Columbia.

OVER THE YEARS I've had more than a few occasions to travel from British Columbia down the I-5 Highway to California, and there is one small town that always captures my interest — just by mere mention of its name.

"Dunsmuir, California, you say?"

My fellow traveller, a British Columbian who had recently moved to San Jose, raced by the historic railway town that clings to a mountainous edge along the upper Sacramento River, with Mount Shasta looming above. I wanted to stop, but admittedly it can be rather tiresome driving with a historian who demands to halt at each and every corner of historical significance!

"We don't have time — we have to reach the B.C. border tonight," he snapped.

I was a bit peeved, though his reaction was understandable, having already detoured through many small-town wonders of California's northern goldfields.

But Dunsmuir! From that point on I was determined to see this intriguingly named town for myself and subsequently had the pleasure of staying twice in future years.

Craigdarroch Castle as it looked in 1910. The mansion came to be as a result of a promise Robert Dunsmuir made to his fiancée Joan that, if she would move to Vancouver Island with him, he would build her a castle for their home.

Who has not heard of the wealthy Dunsmuir family of British Columbia? Surely it is one of the greatest rags-to-riches stories found along the North Pacific Slope. Coal baron Robert Dunsmuir, initially in the employ of the Hudson's Bay Company (HBC), became famous (some say infamous) for the development of the Nanaimo coal mines, for building the historic Esquimalt & Nanaimo Railway and particularly for erecting a promised home for his wife Joan — today's magnificent Craigdarroch Castle in Victoria.

While California had the Bonanza Kings whose fortunes were built on the wealth of Nevada's celebrated Comstock Lode, the Northwest Coast had Robert Dunsmuir the "coal king." In fact, when Dunsmuir visited San Francisco's "Big Four" (wealthy businessmen Leland Stanford, Collis P. Huntington, Mark Hopkins and Charles Crocker) they became the "Big Five," as reported in the press of the time. In short, he accumulated immense wealth from selling high-grade Vancouver Island coal that fuelled the Big Four's extensive railway operations, particularly the Central Pacific Railway.

But why was this Californian town called Dunsmuir? Having taken a room at a cozy, converted railway caboose, I set out the next day for a bit of exploring, wandering the streets and outskirts. The locale was once called Upper Soda Springs. It was a Hudson's Bay Company camp stop on the trail system that once extended from B.C. to HBC's post in Yerba Buena (San Francisco). When the railway was built, the locale became known as Pusher, a name that described the need for additional locomotive force to literally push trains up the steep railbed.

One day Robert Dunsmuir's son Alexander Dunsmuir (1853–1900), came whistling into town, marvelling at the scenic beauty and pristine waters. It was then that he apparently offered to build the town a fountain if the community officially changed its name to Dunsmuir. The fountain he donated was dubbed "Lady of the Fountain."

While British Columbia history tends to focus on Alexander's father, Robert, who had inaugurated harsh labour practices in the coalfields of Nanaimo, or Alexander's older brother, James, the province's fourteenth premier and later lieutenant governor, it was Alexander who was placed in charge of the family's business operations in San Francisco, becoming a well-known bon vivant in the social and cultural circles of the Golden State.

Here again is the California–British Columbia connection that so dominated Pacific Slope communities in past times. As the provincial archivist Willard Ireland once wrote, "A century ago Victoria and San Francisco were close neighbors, so to speak. There was no Vancouver; Seattle and Portland were hardly worth mentioning. British Columbia's first business firms were branches of San Francisco firms. In Victoria were the 'What Cheer House' and 'The San Francisco Baths' and a branch of Wells Fargo" among many others. Victoria, asserted Ireland, "to the horror of those who like to fool tourists, is not, and never was, a bit of old England but a bit of old San Francisco."

While the "Lady of the Fountain" is but one, admittedly obscure, legacy of Alexander Dunsmuir's time in California — including the mountain town's new name — there is also a much greater monument to his fateful life in San Leandro, the city in the San Francisco Bay area where Dunsmuir built a mansion in 1899.

Alexander had been in charge of the family's business operations in San Francisco since 1878. Away from the watchful eye of his mother, Joan Dunsmuir, Alexander started an affair with his favourite bartender's wife, Josephine Wallace. The two subsequently lived together for many years, along with Josephine's two children, William Wallace and Edna Wallace Hopper, who later became a well-known actress.

Alexander Dunsmuir

But the couple did not marry until 1899, delaying the wedding until his father's death, when Alexander and his older brother, James, finally took control of the family business — and therefore were now free of their mother's "disapproving eye and financial control." Alexander and Josephine selected New York for the honeymoon as it coincided with his celebrated stepdaughter's performance on the New York stage. Just like his father before him, Alexander promised his newlywed wife a mansion, and construction was completed during their absence.

Until the marriage, Alexander had not only been "living in sin" but had also become an incurable alcoholic. The secretive life he adopted apparently also encouraged companionship with the whiskey bottle. The immense wealth of the Dunsmuirs could not save him, as "his whiskey habits got the better of him and he died during their honeymoon to New York in January, 1900."

The historic Dunsmuir House, San Leandro, California.

The plan once they returned to California had been that Alexander would cross the marital threshold with his new wife into the Greek-revival mansion — but with his death in New York, Josephine was left to return to the new home on her own.

Just imagine waiting over twenty years to get married, then travelling back across the continent to a grand mansion that had been promised you — only now it was empty.

Josephine's occupation of the California mansion came to a quick end, just a little over a year later in 1901, when she followed her husband to the grave.

Enter the Flapper and the Premier, the B.C. court case that scandalized the public.

Alexander Dunsmuir's famous stepdaughter, Edna Wallace Hopper (1872–1959), was an American actress on stage and in silent films known popularly as the "Eternal Flapper." She inherited the San Leandro home from her deceased mother's estate. In short order, not satisfied with inheriting the family home, Hopper began legal proceedings in both California and British Columbia against Premier James Dunsmuir, who had inherited the majority of his brother's estate.

Accusations were levelled that the premier had used his influence on behalf of the Dunsmuir family with the ailing widow, Josephine, to deny her any rights to the larger Dunsmuir fortune following her husband's untimely death beyond that of the mansion and a payment of twenty-five thousand dollars (possibly an annual annuity) that was ultimately accepted.

Edna Wallace Hopper was of the belief that the premier had used undue influence and had denied the mother her rightful share, especially as she had endured a secretive relationship with

Edna Wallace Hopper

Alexander for over twenty years. The Eternal Flapper had known the hardships of living with an alcoholic stepfather — after all, she had lived with him and her mother during her younger childhood.

James Dunsmuir entered the B.C. legislature in 1898 and in 1900 became the fourteenth premier — though he resigned in 1902, apparently disliking politics. One wonders whether his departure was influenced by the dramatic court cases brought against him during his premiership.

One of the most important and influential families in B.C. history, the Dunsmuirs were not immune to scandal. In the early 1900s, big crowds followed the court cases initiated by Edna Hopper that involved alcohol abuse, inappropriate behaviour and a Broadway star looking for a piece of the Dunsmuir fortune.

Reported in the *San Francisco Morning Call* on January 21, 1902, under the headline "Actress Seeks New Settlement," it was reported that "Edna Wallace Hopper, the actress... is about to enter suit at Vancouver, B.C., against James Dunsmuir, premier of British Columbia and brother of her late stepfather, Alexander Dunsmuir, to set aside her stepfather's will." The report continued:

> If she succeeds in setting aside the will she will get all of her mother's interest in the estate, which under the laws of California amounts to one-half. In this case the estate is variously estimated to be worth from $1,000,000 to $3,000,000. It comprises coalfields of Vancouver Island and a large share of ownership of the Vancouver [Island] Railway. Mrs. Hopper will ask for the setting aside of the will on the ground that James Dunsmuir, the Premier, used undue influence on Alexander Dunsmuir to procure the making of a will unfair to Mrs. Dunsmuir and her heirs, and he unfairly influenced Mrs. Dunsmuir to waive her rights to contest the will... It is alleged that Alexander Dunsmuir was suffering from cerebral meningitis when he signed the will in his brother's favor, and that he died thirty minutes afterwards. Mrs. Hopper also says her mother, Mrs. Dunsmuir, came under the influence of James Dunsmuir at a time when she was hovering between life and death late in 1899, and accepted $25,000 in lieu of her rights to contest.

The case not only titillated British Columbians but increasingly also scandalized the Dunsmuirs as court actions dragged on for four years. Witnesses were called throughout, testifying either for or against the state of Alexander Dunsmuir's mental capacity. The case was considered one of the most complicated and expensive in the annals of British Columbia history. Even Joan Dunsmuir, Alexander's mother, contested Alexander's will!

Former B.C. Premier James Dunsmuir commissioned Hatley Castle in Colwood, B.C., today's Royal Roads University.

Litigation apparently involved five separate actions, appeals and cross actions in the B.C. Courts. At the trial's end in 1906, the Privy Council in London, England — then Canada's highest court of appeal — decided in favour of James Dunsmuir and against both Edna Hopper and Joan Dunsmuir. With the closure of the dramatic trial, the premier, following the example of both his father and younger brother, used the windfall to build his own mansion, Hatley Castle — which still stands, part of Royal Roads University.

Today, Alexander Dunsmuir's "Lady of the Fountain" is located in a remote and somewhat forgotten corner of California, but in the late nineteenth and early twentieth centuries the town attracted many visitors, like Alexander, to the pristine waters and soda springs for their reputed health restoring properties.

Indeed, the Dunsmuir fountain poured "the best waters on earth" (the official city slogan) — a veritable fountain of youth. And so, it is fascinating that his stepdaughter, increasingly known as the Eternal Flapper, would later build on the success of her acting career to lend her name to a range of age-defying cosmetics. Hopper never did reveal her true age,

The Alexander Dunsmuir "Lady of the Fountain," Dunsmuir, California.

always maintaining that her birth record was destroyed in the great San Francisco fire of 1906.

The local historian and journalist James K. Nesbitt wrote, November 19, 1972, that "the darling of Broadway" actually travelled to Victoria twice: first for the court case but once again in the 1920s when "she came here billed as 'the eternal flapper,' and took a bath on the stage of the Royal Victoria Theater, a performance for ladies only, with extraordinary precautions to keep away all Peeping Toms."

While Dunsmuir's fountain was something of a conceit for a man doomed to die at an early age, his stepdaughter, Edna Wallace Hopper — though defeated by the premier — would ride her own fountain of youth to further fame and fortune.

MARGARET A. ORMSBY: A BRITISH COLUMBIA INSTITUTION

A titan of B.C. historians. Gone twenty-three years, her work, influence and reputation are undiminished.

The following originally appeared in *The British Columbia Review*.
All text and images are reprinted courtesy of *The British Columbia Review*.

As a FIFTH-GENERATION British Columbian, I have always been fascinated by the stories of my British (mostly Cornish) ancestors who chased "the golden butterfly" to California in 1849. Then in 1858 — with news of rich gold discoveries on the Fraser River — they scrambled to be among the first arrivals in British Columbia, the new El Dorado of the north.

To our family this was "British California," part of a natural north-south world found west of the Rocky Mountains, with Vancouver Island the Gibraltar-like fortress of the north Pacific. While family stories of the gold rush served to fuel my fascination, it was an early reading of Margaret Ormsby's *British Columbia: A History* (1958) that kindled a sustained interest in the tumultuous origins of the gold colony.

It was my good fortune to meet Professor Ormsby on several occasions before her passing in 1996.

In the early 1990s, as a student at the University of Victoria, I helped form the Graduate History Association, and my colleagues and I were delighted when Dr. Ormsby agreed to be our honorary president. In recognition of her acceptance we decided to hold a formal luncheon at UVic's Faculty Club to honour her many accomplishments.

It was a fabulous gathering and we were fortunate to have many of her past students in attendance, especially professors Pat Roy and Charlotte Girard, former B.C. attorney general Brian R.D. Smith, and the late John Bovey, provincial archivist at the time. These past four students had, in fact, been Margaret's research team in the preparation of *British Columbia: A History*, the release of which coincided with the province's centennial year in 1958.

John Bovey, in his usual flamboyant and intensely anecdotal style, regaled our small gathering with stories of the book's production, and how these research meetings were fuelled by endless cups of tea — which future professors Girard and Roy were charged with preparing!

Margaret Ormsby, 1949

At the conclusion of the ceremony, Professor Ormsby spoke to the assembled audience. She was visibly moved by the recognition received, delighted to be amongst friends, old and new, and expressed her love for British Columbia history and the necessity of taking students beyond the classroom and into the field to see the provincial landscape firsthand. This was an invaluable teaching technique that I have employed in my teaching at the University of Victoria — and which reminds me of the legendary Fraser Canyon field trips of the distinguished historical geographer Cole Harris.

We then presented her with a large sterling silver bowl inscribed with her new honorary title to permanently mark the occasion.

Many of her former students, such as the journalist Don Maroc and the retired head of special collections at UVic, Howard Gerwing, have recounted to me many instances of Ormsby outside of the classroom. Don, then with his long countercultural ponytail, was always expected to wait at the UBC Grad lounge entrance for Dr. Ormsby to escort her officially to her seat.

Gerwing, through Ormsby's encouragement and assistance, gained student employment with the Hudson's Bay Company in London, England, with a brief stint in Paris where he met Henry Miller and received from him a signed copy of the *Tropic of Cancer* (1934), then still banned in Britain. Dr. Ormsby might not have appreciated her role in this Parisian venture.

Many of Ormsby's past students appreciated her mentorship immensely, and now fondly recollect her in warm anecdotes that collectively belie the stern countenance of a "Chairman MAO" as suggested by others.

The next time I saw Dr. Ormsby was in 1992, in the company of my old friend Richard Mackie, who had invited me for a trip to Sugar Lake and to his cousin's home, Lake House, on the shores of Kalamalka Lake two doors down from Professor Ormsby's old family residence.

I remember the day well. We were graciously invited for tea and excellent discussions with regard to her time at UBC, and earlier in Ottawa, where she fondly remembered another graduate of her old alma mater of Bryn Mawr College, Phyllis Ross (1903–88), mother of the Right Honourable Prime Minister John Turner.

When Phyllis Ross (then Turner) returned to Ottawa from college, Ormsby stated, "We felt we must find Phyllis a position in the civil service." And so they did! Phyllis, now married to Frank Mackenzie Ross,

Economist Phyllis Ross, chancellor of UBC, with Frank Mackenzie Ross, c. 1962.

went on to become the first woman chancellor of UBC (1961–66), while Margaret Ormsby was the first woman to hold a permanent position in a Canadian history department (at McMaster University, 1940). Pioneers in the academic world of their time, these powerful women must be celebrated.

Richard Mackie and I were then invited upstairs to peruse her extensive working library — what a shame that it, and her house, were not preserved! — before returning for further refreshments. It was then that I noticed the inscribed silver bowl presented to her previously, which had been given a prominent place on her sideboard for all to see. Again, Ormsby expressed appreciation for being recognized at this later stage of life.

From my own perspective, *British Columbia: A History* was the only substantive book available at the time with regard to the province's early history — and I thought that Dr. Ormsby therefore should have greater recognition beyond receiving the UVic Graduate History Association's silver bowl! Slowly things began to change. In 1993, I, with colleagues such as John Lutz, Kathryn Bridge and others at the University of Victoria, formed the Margaret Ormsby Scholarship Committee to raise both her profile and funds for future students of British Columbia history.

Knowing her associations with Phyllis Turner in Ottawa, I subsequently telephoned former prime minister John Turner, who wholeheartedly agreed to act as the honorary president of our scholarship committee. Himself a

Phyllis Ross's son, future prime minister John Turner, while sports editor at *The Ubyssey*.

Margaret Ormsby with the Order of British Columbia.

UBC grad, Turner always spoke fondly of Dr. Ormsby and demanded to be kept informed of the committee's work and well-being of Ormsby herself.

By the last time I met with Dr. Ormsby, the scholarship committee was in full swing and we worked with the B.C. Studies Conference held in Kelowna of that year to prepare a further tribute to this remarkable academic. I contacted the *Vancouver Sun* columnist Vaughn Palmer and asked whether he would make the keynote address. Palmer, an avid student of British Columbia history himself, was humbled but quickly agreed.

At the address, Ormsby, now in a wheelchair, was rolled into the large gathering of academics from all over the province, and Palmer delivered an incredible tribute that received a large and sustained standing ovation. Ormsby was deeply moved, as were all of us. As I knelt beside her chair for a few final words with her she said quietly, "Thank you so very much for all you have done for me." To which I replied, "No, thank you, Dr. Ormsby, for what you have done for all of us here, and the people of British Columbia!"

EIGHT:
B.C.
THEN AND
NOW

THE LAND AS HISTORY BOOK

Or, stories my grandfather told me.

I REMEMBER TAKING MY GRANDFATHER for a drive around Victoria, travelling the countryside of his youth and reliving stories of the past about Old Victoria.

There was nowhere that we passed by that did not spark memories.

Winding our way down Quadra Street we paused at Saanich Road. Gramps happily puffed away on his meerschaum pipe as he excitedly remembered the site of Victoria's last remaining wolf den, at the intersection of these two roads, and the original family home not far away and still standing.

Toward the funky old community of Fernwood, the pipe stoked once more, he would say things like, "Oh, that's where Dad and Uncle Nick used to hunt pheasants!"

By the time we reached the Inner Harbour these stories only continued to grow. He noted that his father was accustomed to hunt ducks in what was James Bay before it was filled in to make way for the Empress Hotel.

Of course, he marvelled at the extent of business and residential development that had sprawled over the once pristine countryside. Occasionally he would grumble, too, that things had gone downhill once all the eastern Canadians had moved in after World War I — usually mentioned in the presence of my Ontario-born grandmother!

The Swan Lake Family of the Hicks: My grandfather Arthur, the youngest boy, clasping the hand of great-grandfather George.

It reminded me of similar road trips with Indigenous Elders throughout their traditional territories. For them, seeing the landscape firsthand was usually the trigger for remembering stories of the past, especially for Elders whose oral cultures see the land as a history book.

This was also very much the case for my grandfather. As our day together rolled on, and with the assistance of additional tobacco, the stories increased and he shared a great journey he made when he was just nine years old with his father.

My grandfather was born in 1904 on the family farm at Christmas Hill, situated above Swan Lake in what would become Saanich, a location first homesteaded by my great-great-great-uncle William in 1860, just two years after having joined the Fraser River gold rush of 1858.

My great-grandfather, a die-hard member of the Conservative Party, was up early one morning on the farm, busy saddling up one of their horses to a democrat (or buggy) to make the long journey from Swan Lake to the Goldstream Hotel, nearby to Goldstream Provincial Park.

The old man was in a hurry — "tiredness is laziness," he announced — as they would travel to see Premier Richard McBride give a speech in

The Goldstream Hotel, c. 1905.

what the *British Colonist* of July 27, 1913, called "the sixth grand Conservative picnic."

While other members of the public chose to take the E&N Railway to the "red letter day," my great-grandfather chose the old-fashioned method of travel. He had apparently become Saanich's superintendent of roads, so perhaps he was also inspecting the early "highways."

After a long horse-drawn ride, they and hundreds of other picnickers watched fiery speeches from well-known politicians, but "unquestionably, the piece de resistance was the speech made by Sir Richard McBride," enthused the *British Colonist*.

Throughout my grandfather's life, he always referred to McBride — a most popular politician of the times —rather affectionately as "Dickey." Such was Dickey's popularity that years later Dr. Margaret Ormsby (the first woman to hold a permanent position in a Canadian history department) devoted an entire chapter of her 1958 book, *British Columbia: A History*, to McBride entitled, rather innocently, "The People's Dick." After publication, Ormsby's UBC colleagues took the professor aside and suggested, in hushed tones, that she might want to rethink her chapter title. B.C. book collectors and bibliophiles would do well to remember that subsequent editions renamed the McBride chapter "The People's

THE LAND AS HISTORY BOOK

Choice." And now you know the key for identifying first editions.

I was fortunate to have many such expeditions with my grandfather before his death in 1997, and it was during these times that I learned the most. He was my living link to British Columbia's historic past.

Sir Richard McBride

In the natural landscape of the Indigenous world, the mountains, rock spires and boulder-strewn streams record the memories of the ancient past, history embedded into the very geography. From the Indigenous perspective, long before history books were ever created, the natural world was like a book itself, to be read and reread by each successive generation.

In oral cultures, one could walk the landscape and literally watch history unfold before their very eyes. And so, in a similar way, my grandfather — my own elder — travelled the landscape that day and shared the oral history of our family that has spanned the generations as residents of the Colony of Vancouver Island, then of the "United" Colony of British Columbia and finally as a province of Canada.

HIKING THE
"GRAVEYARD
OF THE PACIFIC"

An early tourist on what became Vancouver Island's legendary West Coast Trail.

I REMEMBER WELL THE TIME when my father and I travelled to Bamfield on the west coast of Vancouver Island.

I was about eleven years old, and the purpose of our journey was to deliver my brother and cousin to the top end of the West Coast Trail, which they planned to hike. We joined them for the first leg of the excursion and camped for the night just before the Pachena Point Lighthouse.

What a night it was! The weather had begun to turn, hundreds of seagulls landing on the shoreline below (an indicator of what was to come). My father quickly constructed a lean-to shelter against a high rock cliff that overlooked the wide expanse of the ocean below.

That night, I lay under a makeshift enclosure on a bed of freshly cut bracken ferns while the heavens opened up in a massive deluge of rain. The wind roared the whole of the evening, and my father periodically lit a candle (we had no flashlight) to check the time.

It was an exciting night indeed, and I remember turning my head towards the coastline below, the mighty Pachena Point Lighthouse station blowing its horn and casting its brilliant, circulating beam of light across the wave-crested waters to warn ships of the perilous reefs beneath us.

"Wow, Dad, is that a ship I see below us?"

Indeed it was, hugged to the coast directly below us to escape this sudden and fearful storm.

This was my first experience on the Graveyard of the Pacific.

Through the long night of fitful sleep, my father began to share the stories of his own expedition on the trail many years earlier, long before it became a national park.

British Colonist headline on wreck of the SS Valencia, 25 January 1906.

The Graveyard of the Pacific earned its name from the hundreds of ships that met a watery grave along the coast — stretching from around Tillamook Bay, on the Oregon Coast, all the way up to Cape Scott, on the northern tip of Vancouver Island. On the south and west sides of Vancouver Island alone, there have been close to some five hundred wrecks since the early days of European exploration, but it was one in particular in 1906 — the ocean liner SS *Valencia* — that saw one hundred lives lost and is considered by some to have been the worst maritime disaster in the Graveyard of the Pacific — that was the impetus for building the Dominion Lifesaving Trail the following year.

In 1953 my father, Tom, along with his two chums John Mugford and Fred Vosper (later captain of the legendary tugboat, the *Nitinat Chief*), were dropped off outside the community of Jordan River (about 70 kilometres

My father Thomas Marshall (L) and John Mugford (R), c. 1953.

west of Victoria), where they began their search for the beginning of the old lifesaving trail — it extended that far south in those days. This portion of the 1907 lifesaving trail was later developed as the Juan de Fuca Trail, a separate section not included in the Pacific Rim National Park created in 1973 that encompasses the West Coast Trail.

They had a heck of a time finding the trailhead, toiling around the impenetrable bush of high, dense salal the entire day. By 1953, the trail had become overgrown and infrequently travelled. Reaching Loss Creek (near Sombrio Beach), their first test of endurance was to transport themselves across the canyon using an old cable car strung hundreds of feet in the air, a steel cage with the original floor boards rotted away.

The salal was so thick and overgrown at the approach that they had no idea of the height they were about to cross, but a previous traveller had tacked the remnants of a cigarette package onto the side of the car penned with the reassuring words that a "safe crossing made by a man and his dog" had been accomplished some six months earlier.

It was decided that Mugford, as the smallest of the three, should be the first to try the rusting, dilapidated conveyance. Sitting on the edge of the steel cart, Mugford quickly rolled out into the middle of the canyon — his first view of the incredible height he found himself at led to his

The sandy shores oftentimes presented an easier route than hiking up the dense, overgrown trail.

excited yell, "Get pulling that damn rope quick!" Each held their breath and made a safe crossing.

As they continued their journey, this trio of young adventurers found the terrain tough and challenging, with many of the old-growth trees cast down by winter storms used as impromptu footpaths above the dense underbrush that was reclaiming the original 1907 trail, and oftentimes these friends beat a retreat to the sandy foreshores for an easier transit. Imagine what it must have been like for shipwreck survivors in previous times, this trail being their only means of escape, passing through the traditional territories of the Nuu-chah-nulth peoples (the Pacheedaht, Ditidaht and Huu-ay-aht Nations) who have lived along the coast for thousands of years.

Non-Indigenous use of the trail first started with the building of a telegraph line that ran from Cape Beale all the way to Victoria. Shelters for the use of linesmen and shipwreck survivors were also constructed at eight-kilometre intervals on the trail, each with a telegraph and instructions on using it in a variety of languages, survival provisions, blankets and rations. At one point my father and his friends encountered a linesman who heard them coming in the distance. Thinking it must be a bear approaching, he had his shotgun ready and levelled right at their heads.

Typical linesman's hut on the trail, c. 1953

"What the hell you boys doing out here?" he exclaimed.

This was not the hiking trail of modern times. He was rather shocked to see anyone that far out into the bush. After some conversation he invited them to make full use of the cabin shelters, which they did throughout their two-week journey toward Bamfield. Along the way, they fished and did a little hunting with my father's .22-calibre rifle to augment their limited food supplies.

At one of these huts, my father decided to give the old telegraph system a try, cranking up the telephone to call his mother back in Victoria.

"Where are you, son?" she asked, relieved to hear from him.

"I'm at Camper Bay!"

She had no idea where that was exactly but was glad to know he was alive and well.

The hearty trio continued their journey, Carmanah Point Lighthouse being their next destination. The trail through this section was apparently in better shape, with suspension bridges which they were glad to walk on.

Continuing to make use of the lifesaving shelters found every eight kilometres, the trio eventually wound their way to the Carmanah Point Lighthouse. As before, the lighthouse keeper (possibly G.D. Wellard, 1952–58) was astounded to see these three young lads drift in:

The village of Clo-oose as my father saw it in 1953.

"What are you doing here?" he asked.

Imagine a time when lighthouse keepers were so happy to see another soul, certainly not like today when the trail has become inundated with modern tourist-hikers (reservations are required and limited to about 10,000 people per season). Marshall, Mugford and Vosper were made so welcome that they stayed as guests at the Carmanah Lighthouse for two nights, were fed and provided lodgings and had plenty of time to explore that part of the coast and see evidence of at least three past shipwrecks.

In fact, my father was given the task the first evening of manually cranking up the mechanism that powered the movement of the old light, and using a striker, he lit the kerosene that provided the big-beamed torch that swept the evening sky.

From Carmanah the lads continued their journey. While they had managed to supplement their limited stores with the occasional fish or duck, by the time they reached the Indigenous village of Clo-oose their food supplies were running a bit thin. Hiking into this legendary village along an elevated boardwalk they were made welcome, and they purchased cans of beans and other essentials from the local Indigenous-run store.

Other than the linesman, these were the first people they had seen; nobody was hiking the trail at this time — certainly not young tourists like my father and his friends.

A young Tom Marshall (my father) in Port Renfrew, B.C., 1953.

With their food supplies replenished, they hiked on. At Nitinat Narrows, two Indigenous teenagers obliged them and ferried them across the river in a large canoe in exchange for half a case of .22-calibre shells — the teens were delighted.

The trio eventually wound their way toward Bamfield, stopping in at Pachena Point Lighthouse, where they were also welcomed by the lighthouse keeper there. No tents or upscale camping gear accompanied this trip — so unlike today — but then modern hikers do not have the luxury of stocked cabins strategically placed at defined intervals!

When the threesome finally arrived in Bamfield the employees at the historic Cable Station (the terminus of a seven thousand mile–long cable between Bamfield and Australia) were just as surprised as all the other folks my father and his friends had encountered along the way. Three twenty-year olds had walked the entirety of the original 1907 Dominion Lifesaving Trail, and not for the purpose of being rescued but for recreation. In that way, they were a harbinger of the immense crowds of enthusiastic hikers who would follow in later years.

Perhaps as recognition of their youthful determination and accomplishment, Marshall, Mugford and Vosper were treated to lunch in the big dining hall of the cable station. This was, indeed, Old Vancouver Island.

It's incredible to think just how much has changed even during my own lifetime, let alone my father's. The West Coast Trail today is considered one of the top hiking trails in the world.

"Do you want to hike it again?" I asked my eighty-six-year-old father.

"Yes," came the instantaneous reply. "But while the spirit is willing, the flesh is weak."

"ONE OF GENERAL CURRIE'S BOYS!"

The tragic story of Daniel Marshall's great-uncle in the Battle for Hill 70.

REMEMBRANCE DAY always brings family stories to the fore.

Imagine what life must have been like on southern Vancouver Island in 1893, the year my great-uncle was born. British Columbia had been in existence for only thirty-five years since our family's arrival during the tumultuous days of the Fraser River gold rush, and B.C. had been a part of Canada for only a little over two decades.

The second oldest of five children (my grandfather being one of the youngest), my great-Uncle Ernie was born into the wild rural landscape of Saanich just beyond the capital, then a land of splendour largely untamed and dotted with tranquil farms and expansive hunting grounds.

Ernie knew much about pioneering life: his father had been Judge Peter O'Reilly's "factotum" at Point Ellice House (the home of the judge), where his parents first met. Ernie spent a pretty much carefree youth wandering the lands, fishing and hunting, soon to become a crack shot with the rifle. Vancouver Island was full of this sort of young man who, when war was declared, signed up for overseas duty in "the war to end all wars."

"I forbid you to go!" implored my great-grandmother Mary, also having beseeched Ernie's older brother, my great-uncle Rupert, who also enlisted.

But all her ardent attempts failed; the two young lads — now in their early twenties — had taken up the fervent call to arms. No wonder: the celebrated General Arthur Currie (first Canadian commander of the Canadian Corps, who would later command the troops in France) was a well-known Victorian who actively supported the large-scale recruitment of local men and the formation of the 88th Battalion as part of the Canadian Expeditionary Force to Europe.

General Arthur Currie

It was Currie's military genius (not without controversy) that would put Canada on the map and, in many ways, it was Currie's influence both at home and abroad that ultimately placed my great-uncle into a terror-filled front-line trench in France during the Battle for Hill 70 in the month of August 1917.

My grandfather, Art, reflected years ago that his older brother, swept up with the patriotic fervour of the moment, was indeed "one of General Currie's boys!"

The 88th Battalion leaving Victoria, British Columbia, for overseas, 23 May 1916.

The day Ernie departed from the docks of Victoria's Inner Harbour, May 23, 1916, aboard the SS *Princess Charlotte*, the *Daily Colonist* wrote the immense send off was "one of the most inspiring that has been seen here since the beginning of the war." Ernie had enlisted in the 88th (Victoria Fusiliers) Battalion of over one thousand men.

From Vancouver, these fresh troops were whistled across the continent by rail to Halifax and departed from there on the RMS *Olympic*, an immense luxury liner and sister ship to the infamous *Titanic*, converted into a troop carrier.

For a twenty-three-year-old Island boy like Ernie, this was about as far away as he'd ever been — and yet the overseas expedition had barely begun. His tranquil farmlands would be a memory shortly eclipsed by the horror of war.

Disembarking in England on June 8, 1916, Ernie was first transferred to the 3rd Canadian Pioneer Battalion, then shipped out to France and reassigned to the 7th Battalion (1st British Columbia) of the Canadian Expeditionary Force destined for the frontline trenches of Hill 70 in Lens, France, a coal-mining town that had been occupied by German forces in 1914. The better-known Battle of Vimy Ridge (April 1917) fought so valiantly by Canadian troops had concluded some four months earlier; unlike Vimy, the Battle for Hill 70 was the first time that a Canadian, Victoria's own General Currie, was put fully in command.

There may have been some small comfort knowing one of the Island's own was in charge; once in the trenches the soldiers faced the grim reality of war head-on, with German snipers and heavy artillery just a short distance across a foreboding "no man's land."

While British generals advocated a direct attack on Lens, Currie successfully argued they should first take the high ground of Hill 70 (so named because it was seventy metres above sea level).

My grandfather recalled a poignant story shared with him in later years by his brother. One day during these strategic deliberations, while squatting down in a deep trench at the Western Front, Ernie received a letter from his mother. Inside, my great-grandmother had included some much-needed tea — the very foundation of existence in our family!

These men were not among the American latecomers ("the Rainbow boys" as one Vimy Ridge vet informed me years ago) that were apparently being supplied ice cream and other luxuries. Simple pleasures were far and few.

Ernie and his comrades set to building a campfire in the bottom of the trench — a "billycan" was placed atop the flames to boil water and steep the tea. "What a treat this would be," my grandfather remembered his brother saying. But it was too hot for immediate consumption, and so they foolishly placed the impromptu pot atop the trench to cool ... only to have a German sniper shoot the can to oblivion. So much for tea time! It was a great disappointment, their anticipation of a simple respite gone in a flash.

Finally, the fateful day arrived, August 15, 1917. Currie's surprise plan of attack was finally launched at 4:25 a.m. "under a creeping barrage and smoke screen" in the words of another Canadian soldier from the book *Letters of a Canadian Stretcher Bearer*:

> At 4:20 am you'd have thought the earth had cracked open. My God, it was marvelous! I don't know how many guns we have, some say one to every three men ... With the first roar we manned the trench and began to move ... No power on Earth could keep us from getting on the parapet to have a look. It was too dark to see the men advancing behind the barrage, but the line of fire — ye Gods! Try to imagine a long huge gas main which had been powdered here and there with holes and set fire to. The flame of each shell burst and merged into the flame of the other. It was perfect. It was terrible. The flames were dotted with black specks which were bits of rock and mud ... After some while, the barrage died down. Only the scream of the heavies overhead and the whirr of planes and the heavy crump, crump, crump of Fritzie's shells behind us searching for batteries. He might as well have tried to shove the sea back with a broom.

Unfortunately for Ernie, during the mayhem of the very first day, he was wounded, hit in both legs at the knees with flying shrapnel, which is recorded in his military medical records as "G.S.W." or gun shot wounds.

In our family's oral history, Ernie pleaded with his trenchmates to get the hell out of the trench and head for the backline, but they were all too panicked and frightened to follow. He reluctantly left them behind, never to see them again. In epic fashion, Ernie proceeded to drag himself hand over hand across the battlefield, his legs having become of little to no use, until finally he reached help.

Just imagine the intensity of the smoke and fire, snipers and howitzers ablaze, the bombardment from the air — all experienced by a young farm lad in his early twenties, desperately dragging himself through hell on earth.

If that was not already enough, German gas attacks commenced three days later, on August 18, and Canadian soldiers were exposed to mustard gas which burned the skin and caused blindness. (Both German and Canadian forces used such poison.)

Although Hill 70 was taken successfully, the casualties for the first six days of battle were incredible: fifty-six hundred wounded, killed, or missing.

Ernie was one of the wounded, but lucky for him he was shipped back to England, where the shrapnel was removed from his legs, and he convalesced in a number of hospitals for the next six months. From his "Medical History of an Invalid" dated August 8, 1919, we learn that "once in a while when walking a long distance (8 miles) [Ernie] gets sharp pains in knee joints, painful to bend on knee." Nevertheless, Captain Blackadder, the medical officer in charge, certified that he was "Likely to be raised within six months" for further active duty.

"Return to the family farm," my great-uncles Hal (L) and Ernie (R), Christmas Hill, Saanich, B.C., 1921.

While six Canadians received the Victoria Cross for their actions of valour during the Hill 70 battle, for my great-uncle there remained the stark memory of leaving his companions behind and just barely escaping death. In our family lore, after Ernie had made an almost complete physical recovery from his injuries, he was considered for further frontline duty — until his brother Rupert, who worked as a blacksmith in England for the war effort, convinced military authorities not to send him back.

Can you imagine the prospect of being sent back?

Ernie remained in England for the remainder of the war. Once the cheery and innocent farm lad, Ernie suffered the consequences of war or what we today would recognize as profound post-traumatic stress disorder. It was something he contended with for the rest of his life, and his frequent depression finally got the best of him.

It was 1972, and I remember a fateful Christmas Day, when I was still quite young and we kids were excitedly awaiting our trip to my grandparents' house for our celebratory dinner. That is, until my mother received an urgent telephone call from her father — it was announced then that Christmas was cancelled.

My grandfather had found his brother dead. Ernie took his own life, having turned his own gun upon himself — the remembrance of the so-called Great War undoubtedly haunting him to his grave. How terribly tragic indeed.

Is my ancestor's story unique? Unfortunately not. Look at any number of cenotaphs in British Columbia that mark the memory of a lost generation of young sons (and fathers) who gave their lives in the tragic battles of the First World War.

Unlike Vimy Ridge and Passchendaele, the Battle of Hill 70 was largely forgotten for about one hundred years. But every Remembrance Day our family never forgets Uncle Ernie or the incredible sacrifice he and so many thousands of others like him made in "the war to end all wars."

On Remembrance Day, have a look at one of the many cenotaphs found throughout this province — think of the incredible hardships endured by these brave souls and, more importantly, never forget. Ernie is commemorated on the Municipality of Saanich's WWI Honour Roll. May our ancestors Rest in Peace.

BRITISH COLUMBIA AND THE PANDEMIC OF 1918

Since the last major pandemic, what's changed and what lessons are still applicable today.

IN 1918, A MEDICAL OFFICER in the City of Victoria became one of the great unsung heroes in British Columbia history.

To combat the rising tide of the (misnamed) Spanish influenza epidemic of 1918, he set up immediate prevention programs and closed all public venues in the Capital Regional District.

He had good reason. Some 500 million persons worldwide had apparently contracted the disease, resulting in the deaths of at least 50 million people — vastly more than the total attributed to the First World War.

From 1918 to 1920, three successive waves of this virulent influenza raged, seemingly originating in China. The Canadian military historian Mark Humphries asserts that "newly unearthed records confirm that one of the side stories of the war — the mobilization of 96,000 Chinese labourers to work behind the British and French lines on World War I's Western Front — may have been the source of the pandemic."

There is a connection to Vancouver. Humphries' research "found medical records indicating that more than 3,000 of the 25,000 Chinese Labor Corps workers who were transported across Canada . . . ended up in medical quarantine, many with flu-like symptoms."

Rather than transport the labourers around Africa, "British officials turned to shipping the laborers to Vancouver on the Canadian West Coast and sending them by train to Halifax on the East Coast, from which they could be sent to Europe."

Masked by symptoms most often associated with a common cold bug (chills, fever, headaches, sore throat, respiratory infection and so forth), the misdiagnosed fever quickly swept the continents into a full-fledged pandemic — and physicians and pathologists in British Columbia were caught in a state of unpreparedness.

At the time, Canada had no centralized government health authority to launch a national defence plan. As a consequence, emergency programs fell to provincial and local municipal authorities, who enacted differing responses to the threat.

Enter Victoria's medical health officer, Dr. Arthur G. Price.

By early October 1918 increasing reports from Canadian cities detailed the death toll of those who had succumbed to the virulent disease; this was the likely impetus for Dr. Price to institute immediate prevention programs in Victoria. A little over one hundred years later, official health advisements on curbing the spread of the coronavirus (COVID-19) were fundamentally the same as in 1918: avoid crowds; if you feel ill, self-isolate and get immediate bedrest.

Dr. Arthur G. Price

Human nature being what it is, mandatory measures soon followed — not unlike what occurred in in 2020 and 2021. In a *Victoria Daily Times* article published on October 8, 1918, entitled "Prohibitions of meetings to check spread of germs," the B.C. Provincial Board of Health issued new regulations to support local community efforts to halt the spread of the contagious disease with "the closing of all places of assembly as a preventative measure against the spread of Spanish influenza."

The Honourable J.D. MacLean, B.C.'s minister of health and education (and later premier) used the Public Health Act to empower the city's medical health officer to close public spaces at will, enforced by the police.

Apparently Dr. Price had strongly urged a closure in Victoria while Vancouver remained wide open (according to an article in the *Daily Colonist* on October 8, 1918). Upwards of one hundred cases of the influenza had already been reported in Victoria, and so Dr. Price was quick to implement the closure power he had sought over all public and private gathering places. Shortly thereafter, schools, churches, libraries, theatres, colleges and dance halls were shuttered for a total of thirty-three days, and community gatherings in general were banned.

In addition to closures and a ban on public gatherings, Price repeatedly issued ongoing advice to maintain good health (diet and exercise) and steer clear of potential carriers of the disease that might be transmitted through coughing and sneezing. Furthermore, if one was exhibiting any of the symptoms, they should immediately go to bed and call a doctor; the first twenty-four hours were deemed critical to ward off severe pneumonia and potentially encourage an early recovery.

Along with these measures came an extensive regime of disinfection plans for public institutions. In 1918, Dr. Price catalogued a total of 166 Victoria-wide fumigations of "dwellings, hospitals, schools, churches, hotels, stores, offices, and salesrooms." (Disinfections of this sort were also carried out in the face of other diseases such as smallpox, measles and diphtheria.)

In Victoria, private businesses took measures to reassure a doubting public, in some cases publicizing that regular disinfections were being undertaken every twenty-four hours. Some would go further, recommending that local banks should disinfect paper currency every night, though Price rightly stated, "I am afraid they are too prone to rely upon this means of combating the disease."

As the contagion spread, Victoria's hospitals were soon stretched to the limit. Other facilities were quickly prepared where patients could be isolated, including two fire halls. Closing public spaces and banning community events also impacted the revenues of both the municipal government and commercial enterprises — but apparently the shortfall was in part covered by an increase in liquor sales!

And so, just like today, the sheer necessity of getting people back to work, of buying and selling goods and services — in short, of maintaining a healthy economy — placed increasing pressure on medical authorities like Dr. Price to lift the restrictions placed upon Victoria's business

Corner of Fort and Government Streets, 7 November 1918, following rumours of armistice.

community and public alike. By mid-October, discontent was already rising when Price refused the local clergy's request to hold open-air services.

By month's end, faced with overwhelming public pressure to assemble in large gatherings with the imminent end of the war, Price issued his strongest warning yet: "Wake up! Realize that there is a war on, a war in our very midst, an epidemic of influenza. Do not sneer at the enemy. Do not belittle it by calling it 'Flu.' Give it its full name, be serious and realize that the undertakers are busy."

While Price was adamant the ban on public assembly remain in place, mounting pressure from both the religious and business communities continued to increase. Ultimately, some days after armistice was declared on November 11, 1918, the month-long ban was rescinded. Fortunately, infections decreased during the remainder of 1918 — but then in January 1919, a third wave of infection rose alarmingly for a brief time. And yet, no comparable closures to Price's original war on influenza were enacted beyond local schools.

What can be made of all this? Perhaps this one telling statistic: in the influenza epidemic of 1918, Victoria fared much better than Vancouver, where similar closures were delayed for the greater part of the critical month of October, so much so, that while Victoria experienced a mortality rate of 3.6 percent, in Vancouver it was an astounding 10 percent.

As the Vancouver Coastal Health authority noted in 2018, "An estimated 4,000 people died in B.C. from the 1918–1919 influenza pandemic — about a quarter of those in Vancouver. In today's numbers that would be about 37,000 deaths for B.C. and 9,000 for Vancouver."

In 2020, we saw the same debate over the need to self-isolate, close public gatherings, and possibly even quarantine — yet always balanced alongside the competing need to maintain trade, travel and the health of local, provincial and national economies.

Not much has changed, really.

Health authorities in countries around the world grappled with a tsunami-like virus and the very real dilemma of securing public health that, at times, was seemingly in competition with the health of imperilled economies.

It seems to me we experienced a delicate dance between two competing goals, that of maintaining the health of interdependent economies and of literal public health. This balancing act informed the global medical debate: a reactive wait-and-see stance versus proactive mandatory measures like those considered by Washington State governor Jay Inslee when Seattle was an epicentre of the coronavirus.

Inslee had a historic precedent to follow: Washington State decreed mandatory public closures over one hundred years ago in response to the 1918 Influenza pandemic — about the same time as neighbouring Victoria.

In a *Seattle Star* article of October 7, 1918, it was reported that our neighbours to the south had taken quick, decisive, proactive measures:

> Preparations were under way Monday by Mayor [Ole] Hanson and municipal health authorities to transform Seattle's big public dance halls, and churches if necessary, into emergency hospitals to care for Spanish influenza cases if the epidemic is not checked. This action was decided upon as a preparatory measure, supplementing the order of Saturday that closed schools, theatres, motion picture houses, pool halls, and all indoor assemblage . . . "I have the police to enforce the order, and intend to see

that it is observed. The health department is doing everything possible to prevent the spread of the epidemic."

"Of course we will have kickers," declared Hanson, "but we would rather
have live kickers than have to bury them." The mayor's declaration was swift.
When a Seattle pool hall refused to obey closure orders "police locks were
placed on the doors."

In 1918 Victoria's medical health officer, Dr. Price, also took decisive
measures, placing a ban on public gatherings that lasted for thirty-three
days, with seemingly good results. Vancouver had stubbornly refused to
follow Victoria and Seattle's example.

Price's mandatory measures were subsequently not limited to the
Capital Regional District. By mid-October 1918, some sixteen munici-
palities in B.C. had implemented similar bans on public gatherings.
A general fear began to grow that if Vancouver did not follow suit, the
virus would spread to these closed towns. With increasing public pressure,
Premier John Oliver's provincial government began to push Vancouver to
get in line — and an impatient Victoria went so far as to ask the B.C.
government to institute a quarantine against Vancouver!

Part of the problem stemmed from disagreement between two schools
of medical thought on the way to grapple with the highly contagious
influenza. Many felt that the City of Vancouver was misguided; as the
largest population centre in the province it should ban public assemblies.
The provincial government, at first reluctant to issue stern threats, nevertheless made it abundantly clear that if the pandemic didn't subside soon,
it would intervene with a mandatory closure order. And so it did, moving
swiftly on October 18, 1918, to make Vancouver comply, as reported in a
Victoria Daily Times article entitled "Largest City is proclaimed under
Inhibition Order":

> The Provincial Executive passed an Order-in-Council
> at noon to-day proclaiming the Spanish Influenza Reg-
> ulations in force in Vancouver immediately and to remain
> so until such times as the danger from the epidemic shall
> be deemed past. In other words the Terminal City must
> now bow to the inevitable and follow the lead set by
> Victoria, the adjacent municipalities, and more than a
> dozen other municipalities throughout the province. All

forms of public assembly as defined by the regulation
… are now forthwith prohibited in the largest city of the
Province, after an immunity from restriction extending
for ten days … [and] done without application from the
civic authorities in the Terminal City.

Vancouver had been forced to get in line with Victoria and Seattle. "The chief of police has been given orders. Dances halls were ordered closed last night. No private dances must be held. Persons spitting on sidewalks or in street cars are to be immediately placed under arrest." Police officers served notice to close all theatres, movie houses and other places of public assembly.

Clearly, the institution of closure powers in the transnational triangle of Victoria, Seattle and Vancouver (belated as it was) was more effective when each city, with their historic connections, worked in concert. And in this instance, securing public health was done even at the risk of imperilling these regional economies.

THE BIG ONE (SO FAR)

Are the 2021 B.C. floods the biggest natural disaster in Canadian history — and did the state of emergency receive the biggest response?

THE WEEKS IN NOVEMBER 2021 kept me riveted to the news.

The fury of massive flooding, homes and livelihoods destroyed, roads and bridges gone, supply chains down — and many sleepless nights followed firsthand accounts from friends of the devastating effects of the atmospheric rivers that pummelled southwest British Columbia.

Abbotsford, Chilliwack, Mission and Hope — and plenty of individual folks I know throughout the Fraser Valley — were hit so hard. The scale of the destruction of livestock was immense. And what of the B.C. Interior? Princeton, Tulameen, Merritt — indeed all along the Nicola River to Spences Bridge — savaged by raging torrents. Huge swaths of ranch and Indigenous reserve lands, such as those of the Shackan people, swept away, with voluminous silt spilling into the Thompson River.

Immediate news of these tragedies was slow to make the mainstream press — Spences Bridge residents cut off with the utter destruction of Highway 8 in particular. The community, feeling distant, alone and neglected, was not alone in the sheer expanse of this disaster.

Mike Farnworth, minister for public safety (and also solicitor general and deputy premier), confirmed "we're dealing with an unprecedented

"On Fraser's River looking up from near Mouth Chiloneyuck [Chilliwack] River, British Columbia," watercolour by James Madison Alden, U.S. Boundary Commission, 1858.

time right now in our province's history," and we have just experienced "probably the largest natural disaster in the history of the country."

Actually, flooding of the Lower Fraser River is nothing new. In May 1860, Governor James Douglas experienced it firsthand. Travelling by land from Langley to Sumas, Douglas recorded at "Frasers River Camp" in the "Chilwayhook" [Chilliwack] District how his journey to Hope was halted.

> I proceeded on horseback from Langley with the intention of riding the whole way to Hope; that intention could not however be fully carried into effect as Frasers River had overflowed its banks, and inundated the low plains through which the road has been injudiciously led. After a ride of 13 miles our progress was arrested by a flooded plain, impassable in its present state for horses, and we were therefore compelled to seek the river and to proceed by canoe.

It would seem there have been more than a few injudiciously located roads ever since. Douglas was certainly not the first colonial emissary to the Sumas Prairie region. In fact, he was preceded in 1858 by a com-

View of Lake Sumas from Mount Sumas, 1913.

pany of Royal Engineers charged with locating the international boundary along the forty-ninth parallel.

While American counterparts had established a base camp at Semiahmoo under Chief Commissioner Archibald Campbell (establishing an initial boundary location on Point Roberts), British forces led by Captain John S. Hawkins established a camp near Sumas Prairie, with a second at Cultus Lake.

But then the winter rains set in, and the legendary Sumas Lake mosquito infestations — well known to both Indigenous peoples and gold seekers alike — made their work a "perfect agony," as recorded by one of the men:

> We sit wrapped up in leather with gloves on and bags round our heads & even that cannot keep them off; none of us have had any sleep for the last two nights & we can scarcely eat.
>
> My hands, during the last few days, have been so swollen & stiff that I could hardly bend my joints & have had to wrap them in wet towels to be ready for the next day's work; one's hands are literally covered with them

when writing & even when wearing kid gloves the bites through the needle holes in the seams were sufficient to produce this. Each mule, as it is packed, is obliged to be led into a circle of fires continually kept up, as they are quite intractable when worried by mosquitoes; two of [them] have been blinded & 6 of our horses were so reduced that we had to turn them out on the prairie and let them take their chance of living. I never saw anything like the state of their skins, one mass of sores. Our tents used frequently to be so covered with mosquitoes inside & out, that it was difficult to see the canvas ... We are all of us, as you may imagine, a good deal pulled down by want of sleep & continual irritation.

Nevertheless, these intrepid Royal Engineers laboured through the entire season, marking the line of the forty-ninth parallel from Chilliwack to the crest of the Cascade Mountains. Just as the Chilliwack region was a base in 1858 for the Royal Engineers, perhaps it is no surprise that some eighty-eight years later, in 1946, the federal government established Camp Chilliwack as the permanent home station for the Corps of Royal Canadian Engineers. A further twenty years after that, in 1966, Canadian Forces Base Chilliwack was born.

Sumas Lake in flood, from Vedder Mountain Road, c. 1918–28.

But in 2021, there remains no military base, as CFB Chilliwack was closed in 1997. At the time, there were about sixteen hundred personnel at Chilliwack (one thousand military and six hundred civilians were employed, not including some seven hundred students enrolled in the Canadian Forces School of Military Engineering and the Canadian Forces Officer Candidate School).

Imagine if CFB Chilliwack still existed during "probably the largest natural disaster in the history of the country" — and so close to the failing dikes! Instead, all we got were some five hundred troops shipped out from across the Rockies. When I talk with British Columbians throughout southwestern B.C. (including a retired Canadian Armed Forces brigadier general), the response has been always the same: "It's a drop in the bucket!"

Why was our need for troops on the ground so severely underestimated? I decided to investigate further, beyond the general consensus of the ball simply having been dropped.

In times of natural disaster, provinces may ask the military for help. Operation LENTUS is the Canadian Armed Forces (CAF) response to natural disasters in Canada. The operation follows an established plan of action to support communities in crisis, and the CAF's objectives include "to respond quickly and effectively to the crisis" and "to stabilize the natural disaster situation." Furthermore, "the number of people deployed is based on the scale of the natural disaster," but most interestingly, it is up to provincial authorities to submit a request for emergency assistance, which outlines just how much help is required.

The CAF then establishes how many troops to send into the disaster zone. The Canadian National Defence website states, "in recent years, this has been anywhere from 60 to 2,600 members. The operation could also include ships, vehicles, aircraft, and a variety of equipment."

For comparison, the severe floods of Quebec in 2017 forced that province to seek military help — and help arrived, with a whopping 2,600 CAF members (and reservists) immediately deployed, along with 400 trucks and armoured vehicles, 7 helicopters and a Halifax-class frigate, among other assets.

Clearly, the five hundred army personnel deployed to B.C. was, indeed, a drop in the bucket.

This is not to condemn the CAF; the request for military assistance had to come from the provincial government. Presumably that request would have come from B.C.'s minister of public safety in tandem with the premier's office (as confirmed to me by a former B.C. cabinet minister).

I suspect that the B.C. government severely underestimated our need for military assistance. I wonder if we will ever know the full extent of the B.C. government's request for emergency support?

In the meantime, and as but one example, in remote communities like Spences Bridge on Highway 1 and all along Highway 8 that follows the Nicola River, folks were completely cut off by the scale of this disaster and seemingly forgotten.

"It feels like we are living on a cul-de-sac," lamented one Spences Bridge business owner when Highways 1 and 8 were both closed. And even if they could travel south for supplies and assistance, their nearest neighbour, the town of Lytton, no longer exists due to the forest fire that destroyed the town that summer.

Highway 8 was destroyed, and the only access to their farms, ranches and Indigenous reserve lands was by helicopter. Where was the military? I heard from a reliable source that they finally got a couple of helicopter rides, but it was difficult to communicate with a community that still had no cell-phone service.

The B.C. Emergency Program Act states quite explicitly the powers of the provincial minister during a state of emergency, among them, to "cause the evacuation of persons and the removal of livestock, animals and personal property from any area of British Columbia that is or may be affected by an emergency or a disaster and make arrangements for the adequate care and protection of those persons, livestock, animals and personal property."

Clearly, this did not happen in a timely manner and raises the question: Why did we close CFB Chilliwack?

British Columbia is the third-largest and fastest-growing province, and today we have no remaining regular army force. The government of then premier Mike Harcourt should have strenuously objected to the closure of CFB Chilliwack back in 1997. And in the case of Operation LENTUS, it is up to the provincial government to make the demand. So what was that demand? Someone should be asking.

The B.C. government simply did not act quickly enough. It was all fine and well to declare yet another state of emergency, but we needed significant numbers of boots on the ground from the start.

Apparently, all we had to do was ask.

THE GREAT BRITISH COLUMBIAN DELUGE

2021 was not the first time coastal B.C. was severed from the rest of Canada by road and rail — but there's one important difference between the flood of 2021 and the floods of 1894 and 1948.

THE YEAR 2021 was calamitous for British Columbians.

The "heat dome" brought destruction with the wildfire infernos, followed by the great British Columbia deluge of 2021 — and all this through a pandemic!

We prayed for rain and received it in massive abundance. Much of our transportation infrastructure was destroyed, supply lines were further stressed and the "atmospheric river" that so inundated B.C. was responsible for yet another declaration of emergency.

And while we were severed from the rest of Canada by both road and rail, this was not the first time.

Historically, the single greatest disadvantage of the lower Fraser has been the annual flooding that typically occurs each summer. Early gold seekers soon discovered how high the Fraser River can climb, submerging their early gold claims.

As early as 1860, Governor James Douglas encouraged the expansion of farm settlement in the Lower Fraser Valley, but apparently few were interested due to the unpredictable threat of flooding. Of course, the original attraction of those who came was for gold — not land.

Douglas was well aware that the fertile lands of the Lower Fraser River were "exposed to overflow during the periodical inundations of the Fraser." With his usual foresight, Douglas recorded further observations just as applicable to our current state of emergency — especially with regard to supply chains and food self-sufficiency: "The durable prosperity and substantial wealth of states is ... derived from the soil. Without the farmer's aid British Columbia must remain forever a desert, to be drained of its wealth and dependent on other countries for its daily food."

With the farms of the Sumas Prairie (a region that apparently accounts for about half of the province's production in poultry and eggs, among other foodstuffs) having been inundated in 2021, the words of the first B.C. governor in 1860 still have relevance today.

Small-scale diking was apparently first tried in 1864 by a farmer in Delta. That success led others to dyke their own farms along the Lower Fraser River, including "Honest" John Oliver, later B.C. premier (1918–27). From Douglas's time, the threat of flooding essentially precluded serious large-scale land reclamation for the next thirty or so years, until larger-scale

Flooding of the Canadian Pacific Railway, 1894.

dikes, drainage channels, pumps and gates provided the infrastructure that reclaimed some of the province's most fertile agricultural land.

With the coming of the Canadian Pacific Railway and rapid growth of the new City of Vancouver (1886), local food production was essential. In fact, since the 1858 gold rush, B.C. has always contended with importing California produce to meet shortages. British Columbia is not particularly advantaged when it comes to agriculture. Its mountainous geography encompasses over nine hundred thousand square kilometres, but only a miniscule 3 percent is potentially arable. Vancouver itself is largely hemmed in by steep rocky slopes and great forest lands — not great land for farming. Hence, draining and diking in the Lower Fraser Valley was deemed an obvious and essential solution.

In the history of our province there have been two earlier great floods that wreaked similar damage to what was witnessed in 2021: both events were during the period of greater land reclamation in 1894 and 1948.

In one of the great tragedies of B.C. engineering, the first large-scale dikes were constructed and completed by 1894 — only to be hit hard by a devastating flood.

They had been built two feet higher than the previous record water

Flooding at Chilliwack, c. 1894.

height of 1882, but this was simply not enough; they were soon breached. Devastation was quick. But perhaps more importantly, the level of debt incurred to build, and subsequently rebuild, these early land reclamation works, though substantial (the dikes were again heightened by a further two feet), showed that the funds were not enough to fully counter the unpredictable flooding of the Fraser River.

And so it was in 1948, when the Fraser eclipsed the water level of 1894 and broke the dikes once more, the Lower Fraser Valley flooded again. More than twenty-three hundred homes were destroyed, and the number of evacuees exceeded sixteen thousand people, along with extensive crops and livestock lost, prompting — for the first time — the intervention of the federal government, which offered substantial financial aid to B.C. to invest in better diking and drainage.

I wonder, with climate change, will this be our solution again: to keep building taller dikes?

Like 2021, in 1948 all road and rail transportation to the rest of Canada was halted due to submerged highways and damaged train tracks. But unlike 1894, Vancouver was now a significantly larger port, Canada's western entrepôt on the Pacific. Canada could simply not afford to have their communication with B.C. remain broken.

Alexandra suspension bridge on the Fraser River during the Flood of 1894.

The Royal Canadian Navy was given command of the Lower Fraser River, with the power to requisition boats to rescue those stranded. By March 31, the provincial government announced a state of emergency and the army took charge of all dikes. From that point on, the federal government became involved in all future land reclamation projects in the province. The federal government of Prime Minister Mackenzie King also pledged five million dollars in disaster relief, in addition to agreeing to pay 75 percent of all reconstruction of the dikes and drainage channels that had been destroyed: "Dikes are not the concern of the people living behind them alone, but are also of vital interest to the nation."

Perhaps this time, Canada, in securing its national interest, might go one further. Let's not just secure and improve existing dikes. Canada should reasonably pay for a new one that will effectively impede the rising waters of the Nooksack River (north of Bellingham) in neighbouring Washington State. The spilling of additional waters from across the border has been a major contributing factor in the flooding of Sumas Prairie. A dike along the forty-ninth parallel? Now that would be something!

And there is perhaps greater incentive to do so if the projections of climate change are taken seriously. Because the one main difference between the great floods of 1894 and 1948 and the great deluge of 2021 is this: previously, floods have occurred with the usual spring melt. In our case, the great British Columbian deluge of 2021 occurred in November; winter had just begun, and the immense flooding was squarely attributable to one month's worth of rainfall in just two days, a massive rainfall — an atmospheric river.

To my mind, extraordinary times call for extraordinary measures.

BRITISH COLUMBIA ON FIRE

Daniel Marshall shares his reflections on truth and reconciliation.

WE ARE ON FIRE.

British Columbia is burning literally, a tinderbox ignited not just from insufferably high heat and increasing numbers of lightning strikes, but it is also burning figuratively, as old narratives of the province's historical unfolding are under increasing fire — along with churches burned, statues toppled and even an Indigenous totem torched.

Through it all, the vast majority of our population — both Indigenous and non-Indigenous — watch in rather silent amazement as the passions of popular, and indeed usually uninformed, protesters enflame and divide this province.

Where do we go from here? It is easy to tear down markers of history, but the real question is whether a truly inclusive narrative of this province will continue to be written without the kind of severe backlash that has been seen south of the border.

In 2022, the Malahat Lookout totem pole, on Vancouver Island's Trans-Canada Highway, was set ablaze (and thankfully not consumed). The general determination was that this act of vandalism was in direct response to the Canada Day toppling of the Captain James Cook statue

A rather charred Malahat Lookout totem pole, originally erected in 1966 to commemorate the 100th anniversary of the Union of the Colonies of Vancouver Island and British Columbia.

in Victoria's Inner Harbour. The culprit had spray-painted the caption "One Totem — One Statue" near the charred carving as a seeming statement of retribution.

How terribly ironic. The Malahat Lookout totem pole was originally erected in 1966 (along with two other such poles on the Island) to commemorate the hundredth anniversary of the union of the colonies of Vancouver Island and British Columbia, in 1866. It's more ironic still, considering that the totem pole, carved by former Cowichan (Quw'utsun) Chief Stan Modeste, was a "Project of Native Indians' Participation Centennial Sub-Committee to Commemorate the Centenary" — indeed, a marker of British Columbia's colonial past — as noted on the original bronze plaque that can still be seen to this day. How times have changed!

The Chiefs of southern Vancouver Island rightly condemned these acts of vandalism in an official statement, knowing that these sorts of flagrant attacks will do little to forward the cause of reconciliation.

As the province grapples with the historic claims of Indigenous Nations and their justifiable grievances, especially since joining Canada in 1871 (post-Confederation issues of the federal Indian Act, banning of the potlatch, residential schools and unmarked graves, among many others), the current penchant to destroy monuments has caused many to become increasingly concerned whether this assists in moving us forward.

While in my own way I have worked for the better part of four decades on B.C. history (including on matters of Indigenous rights, title and, indeed, reconciliation), I fear at times that all the good work done toward greater understanding between Indigenous and non-Indigenous communities might potentially unravel.

The chair of Canada's Truth and Reconciliation Commission, former senator Murray Sinclair, forewarned in 2017 that indiscriminate removal of monuments of the past would smack of revenge: "The problem I have with the overall approach to tearing down statues and buildings is that it is counterproductive... because it almost smacks of revenge or smacks of acts of anger, but in reality, what we are trying to do is... create more balance in the relationship."

Senator Murray Sinclair

Sinclair's view seems to have gone largely unnoticed by many members of the public engaged in this kind of hands-on activism; equally disconcerting is the degree to which educated, trained professionals — such as our legal profession — have either fallen silent on the issue or, indeed, have contributed to an increased politicization of history based on poor historical evidence.

Case in point: during a B.C. Law Society's annual general meeting, a proposal was introduced by former B.C. Supreme Court justice, the late Thomas Berger (and seconded by University of Victoria law professor Hamar Foster, one of the foremost specialists in B.C. legal history) to revisit the Law Society's decision to remove their statue of B.C.'s first chief justice, Sir Matthew Baillie Begbie. It warrants mentioning that Berger has been described as "a great champion of Indigenous peoples and rights," by MP Jody Wilson-Raybould.

In truth, those calling for a review were perhaps less concerned with the statue's removal than with the fact that the decision was made without consulting the society's membership or "without independent historical inquiry." More particularly, society members believed that the subsequent characterization of Begbie as "racially-prejudiced and an oppressor of the First Nations people" was not supportable from their extensive knowledge of B.C. history: "We believe that Begbie's life was devoted to the rule of law and its equal application to all, and should no longer remain undefended ... As each generation discovers, no historical figure is without flaws, and this is no doubt true of Chief Justice Begbie. But it would be a mistake for the profession to allow Chief Justice Begbie's life and work to be dismissed in the way this has been allowed to happen."

Matthew Baillie Begbie

While the proposal to revisit the Begbie decision ultimately received a stunning 75% support from its membership, since that day apparently no further action has been taken, the accepted proposal seemingly ignored. Why is that?

Historically, the creation of British Columbia was definitely not the American experience. This province was founded in opposition to our neighbours to the south and on different principles — "Equality under the law for all" was in fact British policy enacted locally by Governor James Douglas and indeed implemented by Chief Justice Begbie through the chaos of the British Columbia gold rush.

It is important to remember the context of those times. In a world that seems increasingly divided by racial tension, it's worth remembering that those who sought asylum here in 1858 were attracted to B.C. expressly for the guarantee of equality under the law for all.

Among those who escaped persecution in California were Black Americans. By 1858, exclusionary policies and legislation passed by the California state legislature increasingly disenfranchised and discriminated against African American people. They were welcomed by Governor Douglas.

In the same way, Douglas also extended similar rights to Chinese people who relocated from California. Victoria's Chinatown wasn't just a colonial outpost — it was a comparative sanctuary for its time.

During Douglas's time in office, Indigenous peoples, too, were guaranteed equality in the colonial courts of law. In his meetings with Indigenous populations in the aftermath of the Fraser Canyon War, Douglas assured those who assembled that "Her Majesty's Government felt deeply interested in their welfare" and that they would be treated the same as all other subjects to the Crown. He stated, "I strove to make them conscious that they were recognized members of the Commonwealth."

So, there is much in the historic record that would cause legal experts such as Berger and Foster to question the B.C. Law Society's decision — or lack thereof — and perhaps more extraordinary, to question legal experts that have contributed so much to the advancement of Indigenous rights and title.

For true reconciliation to work effectively, all sides of this complex issue should be heard.

"We have lost a giant," stated then premier John Horgan with regard to Thomas Berger's death in 2021. He was right. Let's hope that Berger's last stand for truth and justice will not be forgotten and that Chief Justice Begbie may yet have a new trial — this time with a full and complete examination of all the evidence by those remaining legal scholars who have spent the better portion of their lives studying these matters.

For as the B.C. Law Society's own Truth and Reconciliation Committee has confirmed, "without truth, justice is not served, healing cannot happen, and there can be no genuine reconciliation."

APPENDIX

THE USE OF INTERPRETERS IS AN ESSENTIAL POINT TO BE MADE, ESPECIALLY SO AS THIS ISSUE IS CENTRAL TO THE ONGOING DEBATE REGARDING INDIGENOUS UNDERSTANDING OF THE TREATY COUNCILS OF THE PAST.

Fur Trade Interpreters West of the Rocky Mountains

Name	Employment
Annance, Francis Noel	(North West Company [NWC] 1820), Hudson's Bay Company (HBC) clerk and interpreter to Columbia with Governor Simpson's party in 1824; explored Fraser River with James McMillan 1824; Thompson River under McLeod; in charge Okanagan 1825–26; with McDonald at Kamloops 1826–27; helped to establish Fort Langley 1827–28; 1833–34 Mackenzie River (Fort Simpson); to Montreal 1834; returned to his Abenaki village, St. Francis, in 1845.
Charpentier, Francis	(Hudson's Bay Company [HBC] 1817), middleman and interpreter Fort Vancouver 1827–28; Walla Walla (Nez Percés) 1829–32; died in Snake country 1834.
Gingras, Jean	(NWC 1820) HBC middleman, interpreter Kamloops 1827; settled in Willamette Valley 1841; died 1856.

Lafantasie (Lafentasie), Jacques (NWC 1820, HBC 1821), Fort George 1822; interpreter at Kamloops 1827; died at Thompson River in 1827.

Laframboise, Michel (Pacific Fur Company 1810, NWC 1813, HBC 1821), overseer and interpreter at Fort George from 1822; with A.R. McLeod on Clallam Expedition to avenge the murder of the Alexander McKenzie party in January 1828; settled in Willamette Valley about 1841; died 1865.

Leolo (Lolo) Interpreter and guide, New Caledonia and Thompson River; daughter became fourth wife of HBC Chief Trader John Tod.

McKenzie, Patrick Clerk at Colvile, Flathead House, listed as apprentice postmaster 1841–44, postmaster 1844, interpreter 1851–53; at Thompson River 1844–46.

Montignis (Montigny) (Pacific Fur Company 1810, NWC 1813, HBC 1821), Fort George overseer 1822; middleman, interpreter; 1829 Cowlitz region; Fort Nisqually 1836–42; died c. 1849.

Ouvrie, Jean Baptiste (Pacific Fur Company 1810, NWC 1813, HBC 1821), Fort George overseer 1822; middleman, interpreter; 1829 Cowlitz region; Fort Nisqually 1836–42; died c. 1849.

Payette, François (NWC 1814, HBC 1821), interpreter at Spokane House; Snake Country expeditions with John Work 1830–31; Fort Colvile 1833–35, Flathead and Kootenay posts; at Fort Boise (Idaho)1835-44 when he retired to Canada.

Rivet, François (NWC 1813 Astoria), came to Pacific coast with Lewis and Clark 1804; HBC Spokane 1822, interpreter; on Snake River expeditions; interpreter at Fort Colvile 1827–37; retired to Willamette Valley, where he died in 1852.

SELECT BIBLIOGRAPHY

Primary and secondary sources

Adams, John. *Old Square-Toes and His Lady: The Life of James and Amelia Douglas*. 2nd ed. Victoria: Touchwood, 2011.

Bancroft, H.H. *The Works of Hubert Howe Bancroft*. Vol. 32, *History of British Columbia, 1792–1887*. San Francisco: The History Company, 1887.

Birch, Arthur N. "Reminiscences titled 'Victorian Odyssey,' (1863–1873)." British Columbia Archives.

Bowsfield, Hartwell, ed. *Fort Victoria Letters, 1846–1851*. Winnipeg: Hudson's Bay Record Society, 1979.

Cail, Robert Edgar. *Land, Man, and the Law: The Disposal of Crown Lands in British Columbia, 1871–1913*. Vancouver: UBC Press, 1974.

Collins, John Eric. "The Reclamation of Pitt Meadows." Master's thesis, Simon Fraser University, Department of History, 1975.

Cook, James. *Captain Cook's Voyages 1768–1779*. Selected and introduced by Glyndwr Williams. London: Folio Society, 1997.

Cook, Warren L. *Flood Tide of Empire: Spain and the Pacific Northwest, 1543–1819*. New Haven: Yale University Press, 1973.

Douglass, Frederick. *My Bondage and My Freedom*. Miller, Orton and Mulligan, 1855.

Duff, Wilson. "The Fort Victoria Treaties." *BC Studies,* no. 3 (Fall 1969): 3–57.

Dunn, John. *History of the Oregon Territory, and the British North-American Fur Trade; with an Account of the Habits and Customs of the Principal Native Tribes on the Northern Continent*. London: Edwards and Hughes, 1846.

Fawcett, Edgar. *Some Reminiscences of Old Victoria*. Toronto: William Briggs, 1912.

George, Henry. *Progress and Poverty*. Stirling: New York: D. Appleton & Co., 1879.

George, Henry Jr. *The Life of Henry George*. New York: Doubleday and McClure, 1900.

Gibbs, Mifflin Wistar. *Shadow and Light: An Autobiography with Reminiscences of the Last and Present Century*. Washington, D.C., 1902.

Gooch, Capt. T. Sherlock. "Journal Across Vancouver Island." In *Colburn's United Services Magazine and Journal of the Army, Navy, and Auxillary Forces*, 517-18. London: Simpkin, Marshall and Co., 1886.

Hansard's Parliamentary Debates (Hansard), Third Series (1830–91). London: Cornelius Buck, 1858.

Hayman, John, ed. *Robert Brown and the Vancouver Island Exploring Expedition*. Vancouver: UBC Press, 1989.

Heizer, Robert F. *The Destruction of the California Indians*. Lincoln: University of Nebraska Press, 1974.

Hendrickson, James E., ed. *Journals of the Colonial Legislatures of the Colonies of Vancouver Island and British Columbia, 1851–1871*. Vol. 5. Victoria: Provincial Archives of British Columbia, 1980.

Higgins, D.W. *The Mystic Spring and Other Tales of Western Life*. Toronto: William Briggs, 1904.

———. *The Passing of a Race and More Tales of Western Life*. Toronto: William Briggs, 1905.

Hittel, John S. *Resources of California, Comprising the Society, Climate, Salubrity, Scenery, Commerce and Industry of the State*. San Francisco: A. Roman & Co., 1866.

Humphries, Mark Osborne. *The Last Plague: Spanish Influenza and the Politics of Public Health in Canada*. Toronto: University of Toronto Press, 2013.

Ireland, Willard E. "British Columbia's American Heritage." *The Canadian Historical Association Annual Report 27, no. 1* (1948), 67–73.

Jackson, John C. *Children of the Fur Trade: Forgotten Métis of the Pacific Northwest*. Missoula, MT: Mountain Press, 1995.

Johnson, Susan Lee. *Roaring camp: The Social World of the California Gold Rush*. New York: W.W. Norton, 2000.

Kahn, Edgar Myron. "Andrew Smith Hallidie." *California Historical Society Quarterly* 19, no. 2 (1940): 144–56.

Keddie, Grant. *Songhees Pictorial: A History of the Songhees People as Seen by Outsiders, 1790–1912*. Victoria: Royal BC Museum, 2003.

Kelly, William. *An Excursion to California Over the Prairie, Rocky Mountains, and Great Sierra Nevada, With a Stroll Through the Diggings and Ranches of That Country*. London: Chapman and Hall, 1851.

———. *Life in Victoria, or Victoria in 1853, and Victoria in 1858*. 2 vols. London: Chapman and Hall, 1859.

Laforet, Andrea, and Annie York. *Spuzzum: Fraser Canyon Histories, 1808–1939*. Vancouver: UBC Press, 1998.

Lundin Brown, R.C. *British Columbia: An Essay*. New Westminster, B.C.: Royal Engineer Press, 1863.

Mackie, Richard Somerset. *Trading Beyond the Mountains: The British Fur Trade on the Pacific, 1793–1843*. Vancouver: UBC Press, 1997.

Marshall, Daniel. "'An Early Rural Revolt:' The Introduction of the Canadian System of Tariffs to British Columbia, 1871–74." In *Beyond the City Limits: Rural History in British Columbia*, edited by R.W. Sandwell, 47–61. Vancouver: UBC Press, 1999.

———. "Carnarvon Terms or Separation: B.C. 1875–1878." *British Columbia Historical News Quarterly* (Summer 1993): 13–16.

———. *Claiming the Land: British Columbia and the Making of a New El Dorado*. Vancouver: Ronsdale Press, 2018.

———. "Conflict in the New El Dorado: The Fraser River War." In *New Perspectives on the Gold Rush*, edited by Kathryn Bridge, 125–139. Royal BC Museum, 2015.

———. "Grim Legacy." In *The Trail of 1858: British Columbia's Gold Rush Past*, edited by Mark Forsythe and Greg Dickson, 31–33. Vancouver: Harbour Publishing, 2007.

———. "Mapping A New Socio-Political Landscape: British Columbia, 1871–1874." *Social History* 31, no. 61 (May 1998): 127–53.

———. "Mapping the New El Dorado: The Fraser River Gold Rush and the Appropriation of Native Space." In *Interpreting Canada's Past: A Pre-Confederation Reader,* 4th ed., edited by J. M. Bumstead, Len Kuffert, and Michel Ducharme, 406–421. Oxford University Press, 2011.

———. "Mapping the Political World of British Columbia, 1871–1883." Masters thesis, University of Victoria, 1991.

———. "Margaret Ormsby's Milieu." *The Ormsby Review,* no. 296 (October 3, 2018). https://thebcreview.ca/2018/10/03/296-margarets-ormsbys-milieu/.

———. "No Parallel: American Settler-Soldiers at War with the Nlaka'pamux of the Canadian West." In *Parallel Destinies: Canadian-American Relations West of the Rockies,* edited by John M. Findlay and Ken S. Coates, 31–79. Seattle: University of Washington Press, 2002.

———. "Rickard Revisited: Native 'Participation' in the Gold Discoveries of British Columbia." *Native Studies Review* 11, no. 1 (1997): 91–108.

———. "The British Columbia Commonwealth: Gold Seekers and the Rush for Freedom." In *New Perspectives on the Gold Rush,* edited by Kathryn Bridge, 49–61. Victoria: Royal BC Museum, 2015.

———. "The Fraser River War." *Native Studies Review* 11, no. 1 (1997): 139–45.

———. *Those Who Fell from the Sky: A History of the Cowichan Peoples.* Reprint 2007. Duncan, BC: Cowichan Tribes, 1999.

McClain, Charles J. "The Chinese Struggle for Civil Rights in Nineteenth Century America: The First Phase, 1850–1870." *California Law Review* 72, no. 4 (1984): 529–68.

Merivale, Herman. *Lectures on Colonization and Colonies.* London, 1841.

Nugent, John. *Message from the President of the United States communicating the Report of the Special Agent of the United States, Recently sent to Vancouver's Island and British Columbia.* 35th Congress, 2nd Session. Ex. Doc. No. 111. 1859. Reprint, London: Forgotten Books, 2018.

Ormsby, Margaret A. *British Columbia: A History.* Toronto: Macmillan, 1958.

Pemberton, Joseph Despard. *Facts and Figures Relating to Vancouver Island and British Columbia Showing What to Expect and How to Get There with Illustrative Maps.* London: Longman, Green and Roberts, 1860.

Reid, Robie L. "John Nugent: The Impertinent Envoy." *British Columbia Historical Quarterly* 8 (1944): 53–71.

Rich, E.E. *The Fur Trade and the Northwest to 1857*. Toronto: McClelland and Stewart, 1967.

——, ed. *The Letters of John McLoughlin: From Fort Vancouver to the Governor and Committee: First Series, 1825–38*. Vol. 1. Hudson's Bay Company Series 4. Toronto: Publications of the Champlain Society, 1941.

Smith, Carl T. *Chinese Christians: Elites, Middlemen, and the Church in Hong Kong*. Hong Kong University Press, 2005.

Smith, Dorothy Blakey. *The Reminiscences of Doctor John Sebastian Helmcken*. Vancouver: UBC Press, 1975.

Stanley, George F.G., ed. *Mapping the Frontier: Charles Wilson's Diary of the Survey of the Forty-Ninth Parallel, 1858–1862*. Toronto: Macmillan, 1970.

Suttles, Wayne, ed. *Handbook of North American Indians: Northwest Coast*. Vol. 7. Washington: Smithsonian Institution, 1990.

Teit, James. *Traditions of the Thompson River Indians of British Columbia*. Introduction by Franz Boas. Boston: American Folk Lore Society/ Houghton, Mifflin, 1898.

Tolmie, William Fraser. *Physician and Fur Trader*. Vancouver: Mitchell Press, 1963.

Watson, Bruce McIntyre. *Lives Lived West of the Divide: A Biographical Dictionary of Fur Traders Working West of the Rockies, 1793–1858*. 3 vols. Kelowna, B.C.: Centre for Social, Spatial and Economic Justice, UBC Okanagan, 2010.

Watson, Ralph Beverly. *Letters of a Canadian Stretcher Bearer*. Little, Brown, 1918.

Wickwire, Wendy. *At the Bridge: James Teit and an Anthropology of Belonging*. Vancouver: UBC Press, 2019.

Williams, David R. *The Man for a New Country: Sir Matthew Baillie Begbie*. Sidney, B.C.: Gray's Publishing, 1977.

Primary Archival Sources

Bancroft Library, University of California, Berkeley
Beinecke Rare Book and Manuscript Collection, Yale University
Britain, Colonial Despatches, British Columbia Archives
British Columbia Archives
British Columbia Colonial Correspondence, British Columbia Archives
British Library, Newspaper Library, Richmond, U.K.
California Historical Society Archives
Fine Arts Museums of San Francisco
Hudson's Bay Company Archives
Manuscript & Archives Division, University of Washington
National Archives of Canada
Oregon Historical Society Archives
Surveyor-General's Vault, Department of Lands, Victoria, B.C.
Special Collections, University of British Columbia
U.S. Library of Congress
Vancouver City Archives
Washington State Archives

ILLUSTRATION CREDITS

Page 117	Courtesy of UBC
Page 120	Wikimedia Commons
Page 122	Image A-03568 courtesy of BC Archives
Page 124	LOC, LC-DIG-cwpbh-01280
Page 124	Public Domain
Page 129	Public Domain / Wikimedia Commons
Page 130	Courtesy NYPL 1160318
Page 131	San Francisco Public Library
Page 134	Public Domain / Wikimedia Commons
Page 138	Digital image courtesy of Getty's Open Content Program
Page 139	Carole J. Buckwalter / Wikimedia Commons
Page 141	Courtesy of DeGolyer Library, Southern Methodist University
Page 143	LOC, LC-USZ6-910
Page 143	LOC, LC-DIG-pga-03553
Page 145	Public Domain / Wikimedia Commons
Page 147	The Province of British Columbia Centennial Medal, Russell Fairburn, Fairburn Photographic, 2024, Marshall Family Archive
Page 152	Image A-08340 courtesy of BC Archives
Page 156	McCord Stewart Museum 1-67119
Page 160	Image A-02841 courtesy of BC Archives
Page 165	City of Vancouver Archives, AM361-S9-: CVA 78-249, Sherwood Lett, photographer
Page 176	LOC, LC-DIG-npcc-27765
Page 180	Marshall Family Archives
Page 180	Image C-06116 courtesy of BC Archives
Page 183	Image E-09110 courtesy of BC Archives
Page 186	LOC, LC-DIG-cwpbh-00412
Page 188	Item C-03794 courtesy of BC Archives
Page 191	The Great Seal of the Colony of Vancouver Island and Its Dependencies, Victoria Numismatic Society, c. 1966 Russell Fairburn, Fairburn Photographic, 2024, Marshall Family Archive
Page 193	Courtesy Charlotte McDonald
Page 194	Courtesy Charlotte McDonald
Page 198	Courtesy of Daniel Marshall

Page 199   City of Vancouver Archives, AM54-S4-: In P41.1, Major
             James Skitt Matthews, photographer
Page 200   Image H-03660 courtesy of BC Archives
Page 203   Image B-03660 courtesy of BC Archives
Page 205   Internet Archive / *San Francisco Call*, 7 April 1897
Page 207   Internet Archive / *San Francisco Call*, 7 April 1897
Page 210   Public Domain / Wikimedia Commons
Page 218   City of Vancouver Archives, AM1376-: CVA 3-4,
             Frederick Daily, photographer
Page 220   Public Domain / Wikimedia Commons
Page 221   Public Domain / Wikimedia Commons
Page 222   Image B-05235 courtesy of BC Archives
Page 223   Public Domain / Wikimedia Commons
Page 228   Courtesy of Daniel Marshall
Page 229   Courtesy of Daniel Marshall
Page 233   Darwin Baerg, Yale, B.C.
Page 234   Public domain
Page 235   LOC, LC-USZ61-236
Page 238   Image C-03819 courtesy of BC Archives
Page 239   Darwin Baerg, Yale, B.C.
Page 243   Alaska-Yukon Pacific Exposition medal, Seattle,
             Washington, c. 1909, The Greene Collection
             My sincere thanks to Ron Greene of Victoria, B.C.
Page 245   Image E-01366 courtesy of BC Archives
Page 247   Reprinted from D.W. Higgins, *The Mystic Spring, and
             Other Tales of Western Life*
Page 249   City of Vancouver Archives, AM54-S4-1-A-6-: A-6-166,
             George Fowler Hastings, photographer
Page 252   City of Vancouver Archives, AM1376-: CVA 1376-375.33
Page 254   Image B-02273 courtesy of BC Archives
Page 254   David Broussard / Wikimedia Commons
Page 255   LOC, LC-USZ62-79323
Page 257   Courtesy John Newcomb
Page 258   Public Domain / Wikimedia Commons
Page 260   Marshall Family Archives
Page 261   Courtesy of UBC
Page 262   Courtesy of UBC

INDEX

ABOUT THE AUTHOR

A fifth-generation British Columbian, Daniel Marshall is an author, professor, curator, documentarian, and researcher focused on untold stories of B.C.'s rich history. He is a recognized leader and award-winning researcher on historic Indigenous-newcomer relations, and their evolution and implications on Indigenous rights today. His award-winning documentary, *Canyon War: The Untold Story*, aired on PBS, Knowledge Network, and Aboriginal Peoples Television Network. In 2015, he was Chief Curator of the Royal BC Museum's popular Gold Rush! El Dorado in British Columbia exhibit. His previous books include the multi-award-winning *Claiming the Land: British Columbia and the Making of a New El Dorado* (Ronsdale Press) and *Those Who Fell from the Sky: A History of the Cowichan Peoples* (Cowichan Tribes). He lives in Victoria, B.C.